NUMBER 13
CHAPTER ONE

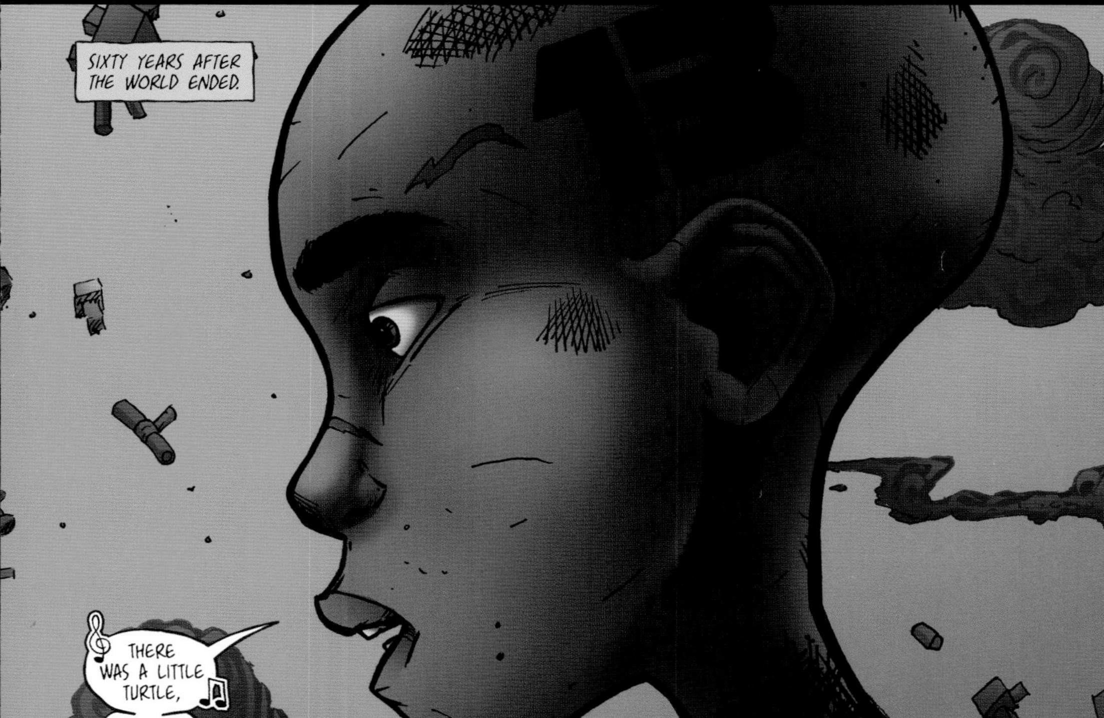
SIXTY YEARS AFTER THE WORLD ENDED.
THERE WAS A LITTLE TURTLE,
HE LIVED IN A BOX.
HE SWAM IN A PUDDLE,
HE CLIMBED UPON THE ROCKS.
ARE YOU MY DAD?
"I AM MYSELF AND MYSELF IS MYSELF. I AM ME. I AM HERE. I AM SOMETHING. I AM SOMEBODY." –CHARLES PERRY

Publisher **MIKE RICHARDSON**   Editor **PHILIP R. SIMON**

Assistant Editor **EVERETT PATTERSON**

Designer **IRINA BEFFA**   Production **JASON HVAM**

Special thanks to **ADAM GRANO** and **ALLYSON HALLER**

Dark Horse Books | A division of Dark Horse Comics, Inc. | 10956 SE Main Street | Milwaukie, OR 97222

DarkHorse.com

Advertising Sales (503) 905-2237
International Licensing (503) 905-2377
Comic Shop Locator Service (888) 266-4226

First edition: August 2013
ISBN 978-1-61655-157-5

1 3 5 7 9 10 8 6 4 2
Printed in China

This volume collects issues #0–#3 of the Dark Horse Comics miniseries *Number 13*. The contents of *Number 13* #0 were originally serialized in *Dark Horse Presents* issues #2–#6.

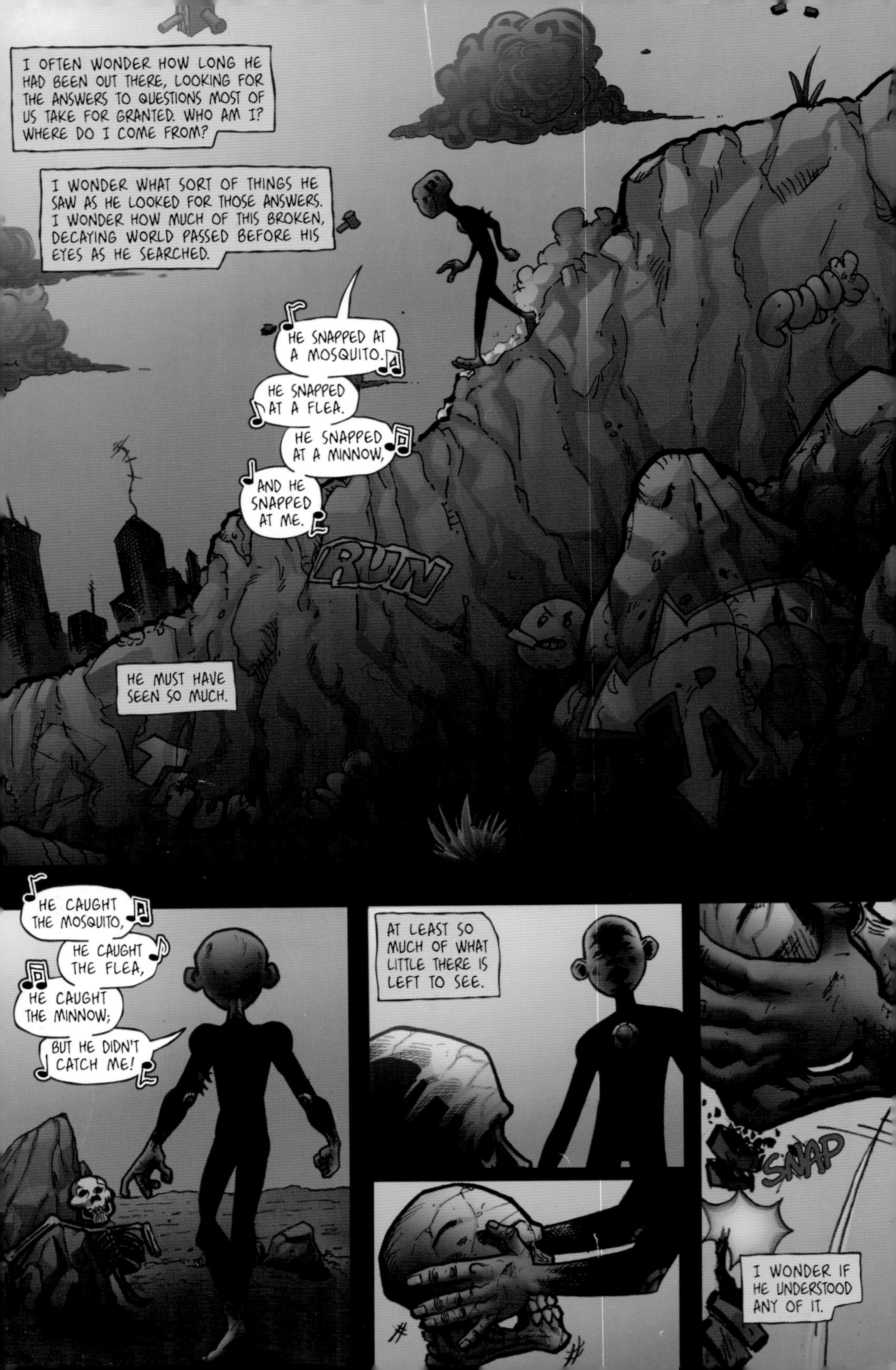
I OFTEN WONDER HOW LONG HE HAD BEEN OUT THERE, LOOKING FOR THE ANSWERS TO QUESTIONS MOST OF US TAKE FOR GRANTED. WHO AM I? WHERE DO I COME FROM?
I WONDER WHAT SORT OF THINGS HE SAW AS HE LOOKED FOR THOSE ANSWERS. I WONDER HOW MUCH OF THIS BROKEN, DECAYING WORLD PASSED BEFORE HIS EYES AS HE SEARCHED.
HE SNAPPED AT A MOSQUITO.
HE SNAPPED AT A FLEA.
HE SNAPPED AT A MINNOW,
AND HE SNAPPED AT ME.
RUN
HE MUST HAVE SEEN SO MUCH.
HE CAUGHT THE MOSQUITO,
HE CAUGHT THE FLEA,
HE CAUGHT THE MINNOW;
BUT HE DIDN'T CATCH ME!
AT LEAST SO MUCH OF WHAT LITTLE THERE IS LEFT TO SEE.
SNAP
I WONDER IF HE UNDERSTOOD ANY OF IT.

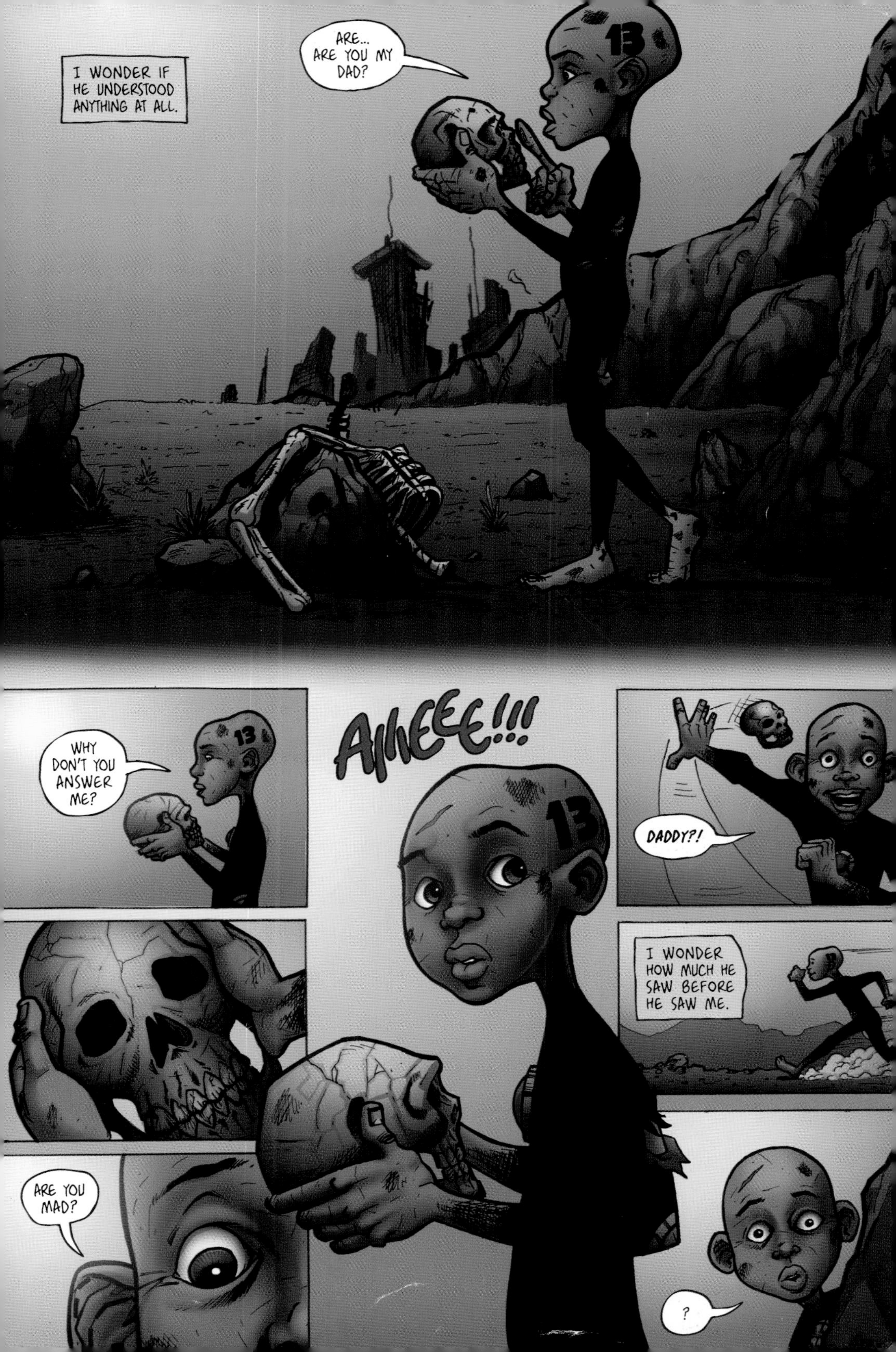
I WONDER IF HE UNDERSTOOD ANYTHING AT ALL.
ARE... ARE YOU MY DAD?
WHY DON'T YOU ANSWER ME?
AIIEEE!!!
DADDY?!
I WONDER HOW MUCH HE SAW BEFORE HE SAW ME.
ARE YOU MAD?
?

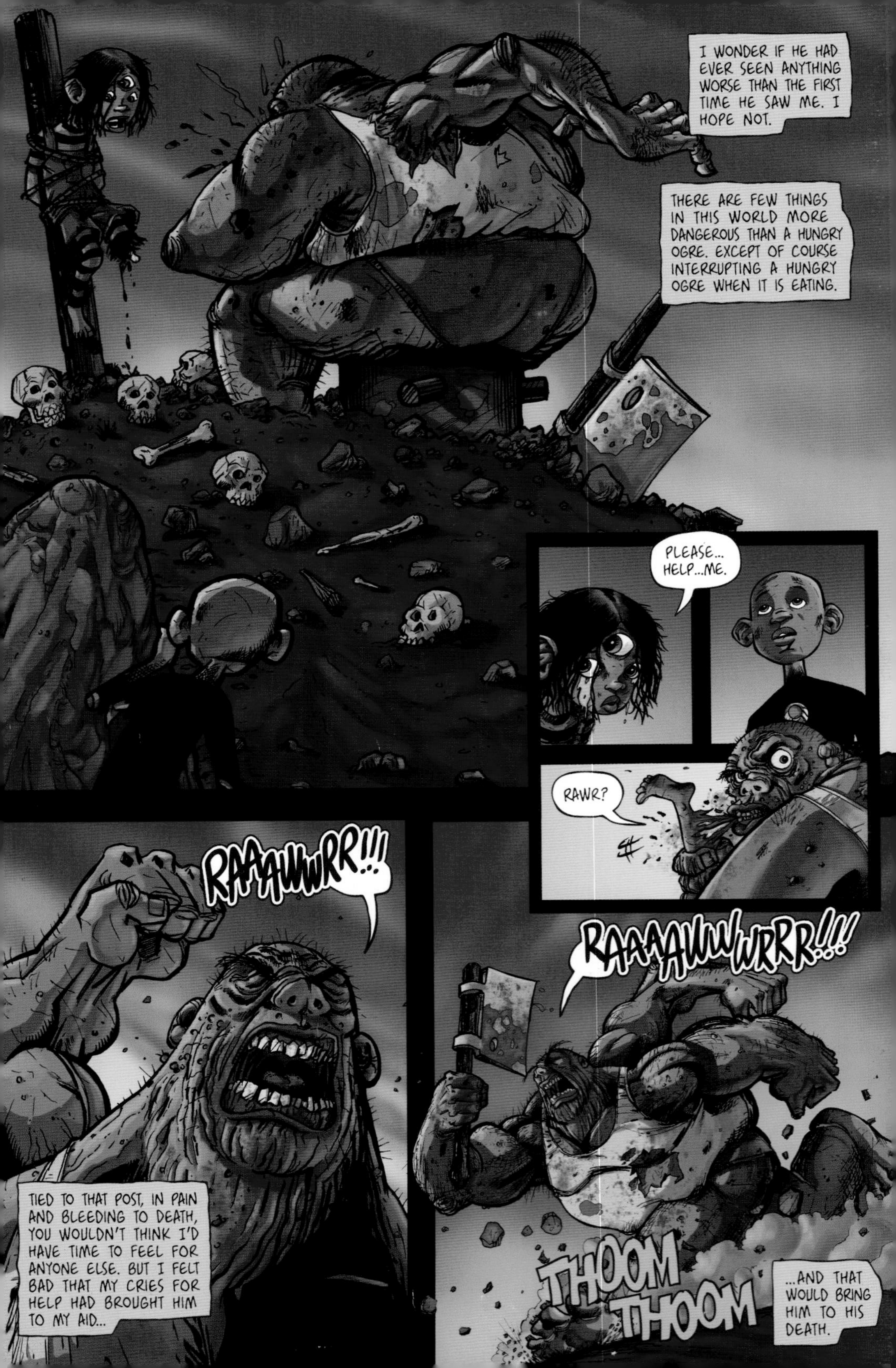
I WONDER IF HE HAD EVER SEEN ANYTHING WORSE THAN THE FIRST TIME HE SAW ME. I HOPE NOT.
THERE ARE FEW THINGS IN THIS WORLD MORE DANGEROUS THAN A HUNGRY OGRE. EXCEPT OF COURSE INTERRUPTING A HUNGRY OGRE WHEN IT IS EATING.
PLEASE... HELP...ME.
RAWR?
RAAAWWRR!!!
TIED TO THAT POST, IN PAIN AND BLEEDING TO DEATH, YOU WOULDN'T THINK I'D HAVE TIME TO FEEL FOR ANYONE ELSE. BUT I FELT BAD THAT MY CRIES FOR HELP HAD BROUGHT HIM TO MY AID...
RAAAAWWWRRR!!!
THOOM THOOM
...AND THAT WOULD BRING HIM TO HIS DEATH.

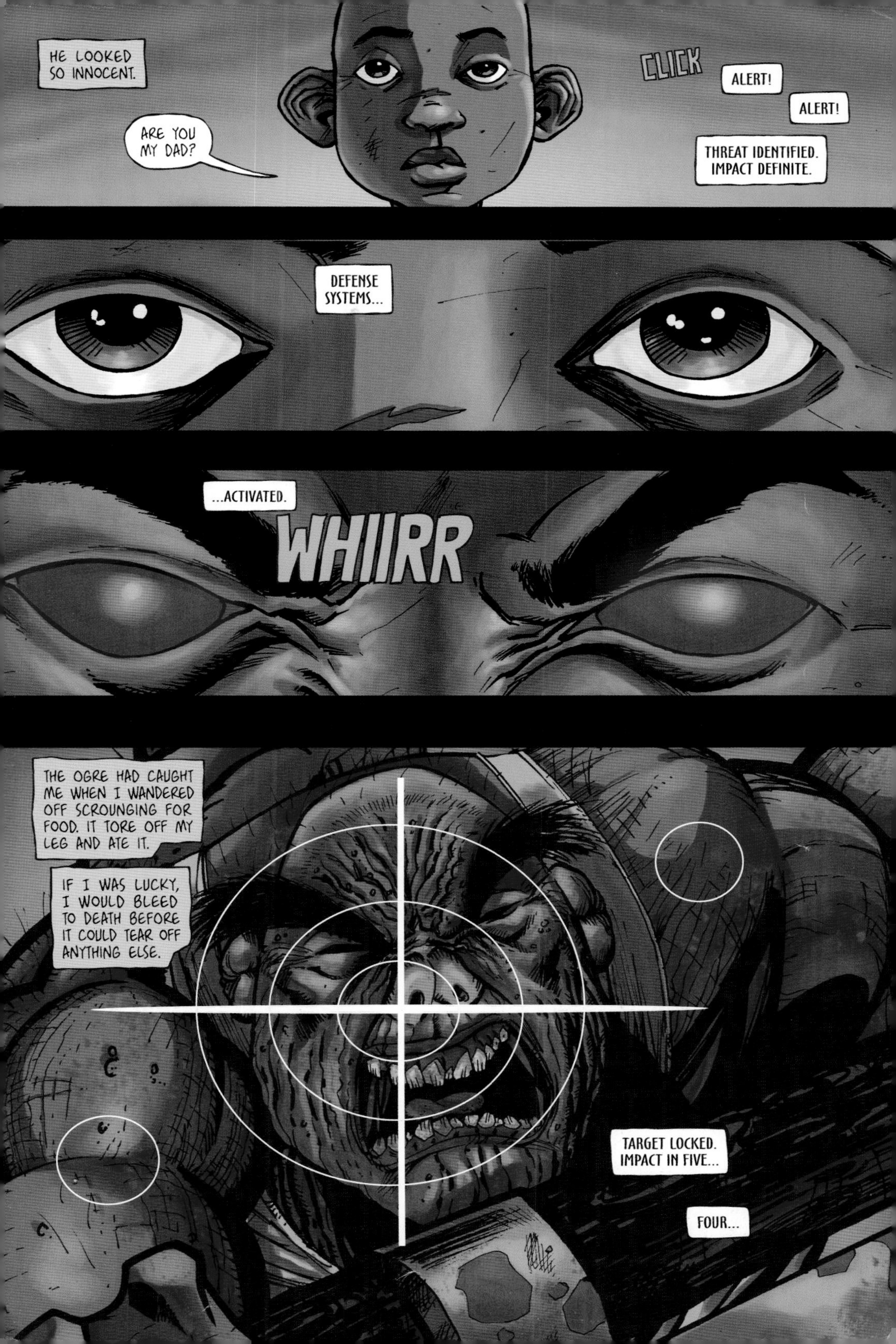
HE LOOKED SO INNOCENT.
ARE YOU MY DAD?
CLICK
ALERT!
ALERT!
THREAT IDENTIFIED. IMPACT DEFINITE.
DEFENSE SYSTEMS...
...ACTIVATED.
WHIIRR
THE OGRE HAD CAUGHT ME WHEN I WANDERED OFF SCROUNGING FOR FOOD. IT TORE OFF MY LEG AND ATE IT.
IF I WAS LUCKY, I WOULD BLEED TO DEATH BEFORE IT COULD TEAR OFF ANYTHING ELSE.
TARGET LOCKED. IMPACT IN FIVE...
FOUR...

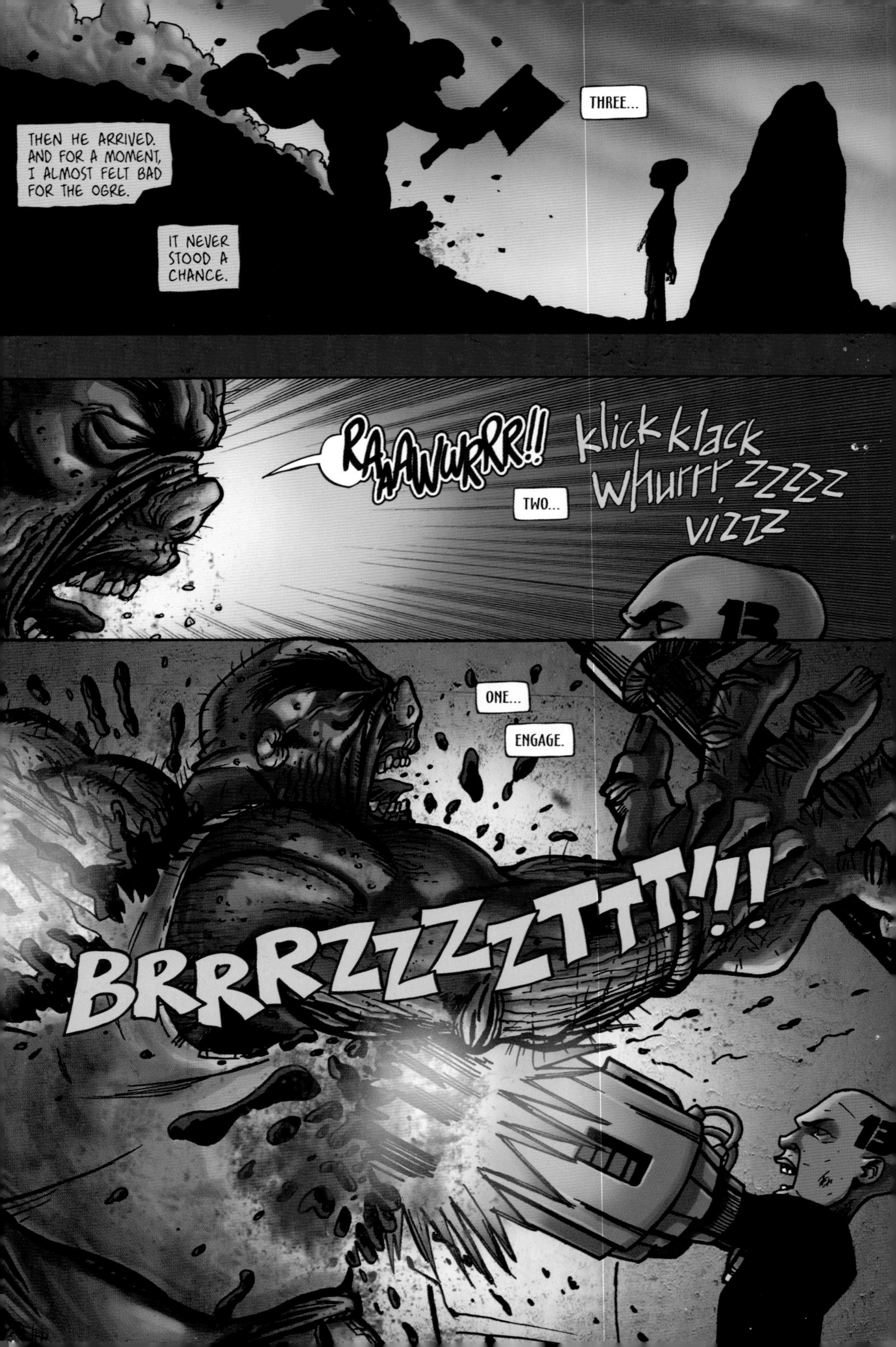
THEN HE ARRIVED. AND FOR A MOMENT, I ALMOST FELT BAD FOR THE OGRE.
IT NEVER STOOD A CHANCE.
THREE...
RAAAWURRR!!
klick klack
whurrr, zzzzz
vizzz
TWO...
ONE...
ENGAGE.
BRRRZZZZTTTT!!!

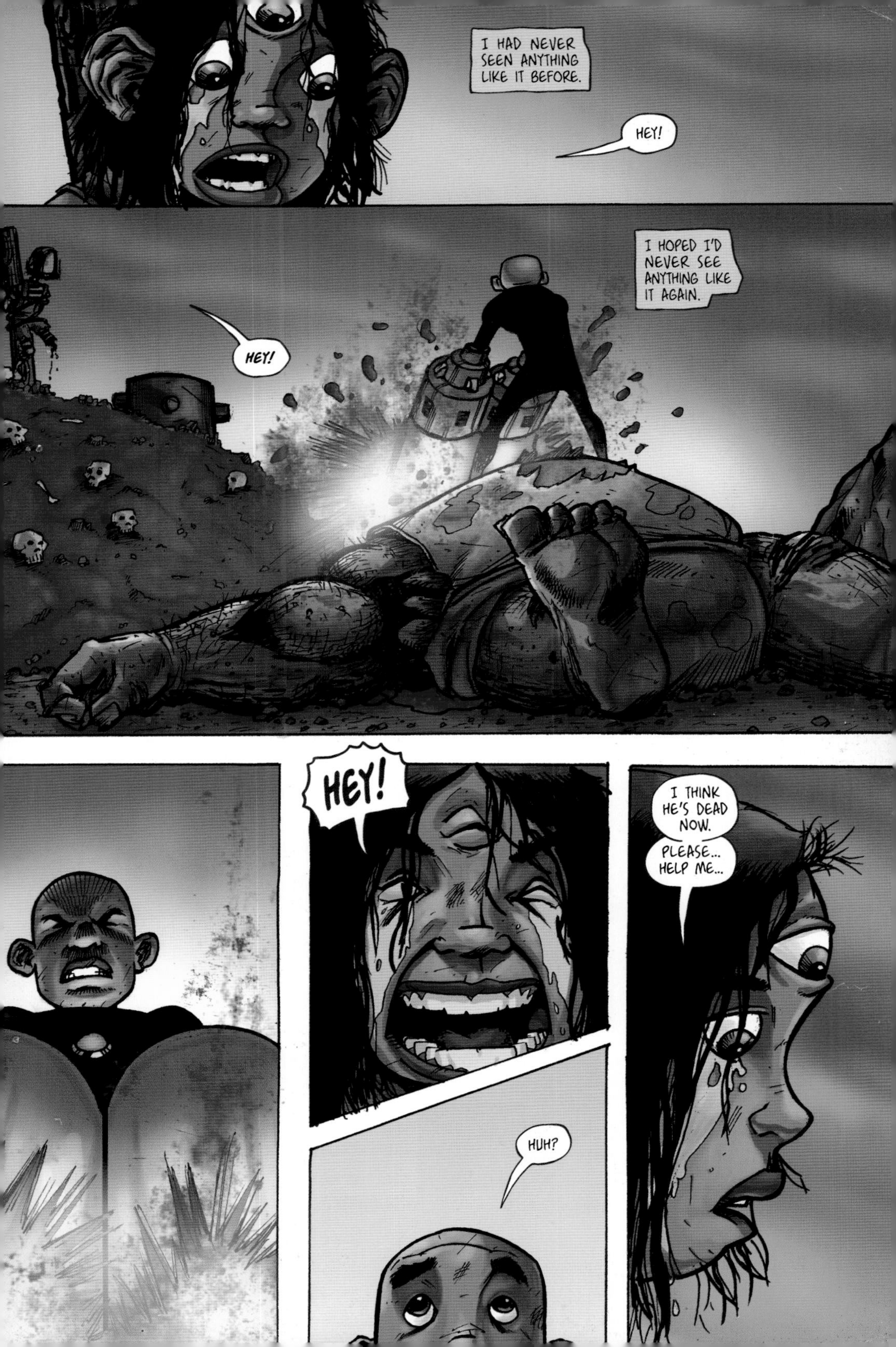
I HAD NEVER SEEN ANYTHING LIKE IT BEFORE.
HEY!
I HOPED I'D NEVER SEE ANYTHING LIKE IT AGAIN.
HEY!
HEY!
HUH?
I THINK HE'S DEAD NOW.
PLEASE... HELP ME...

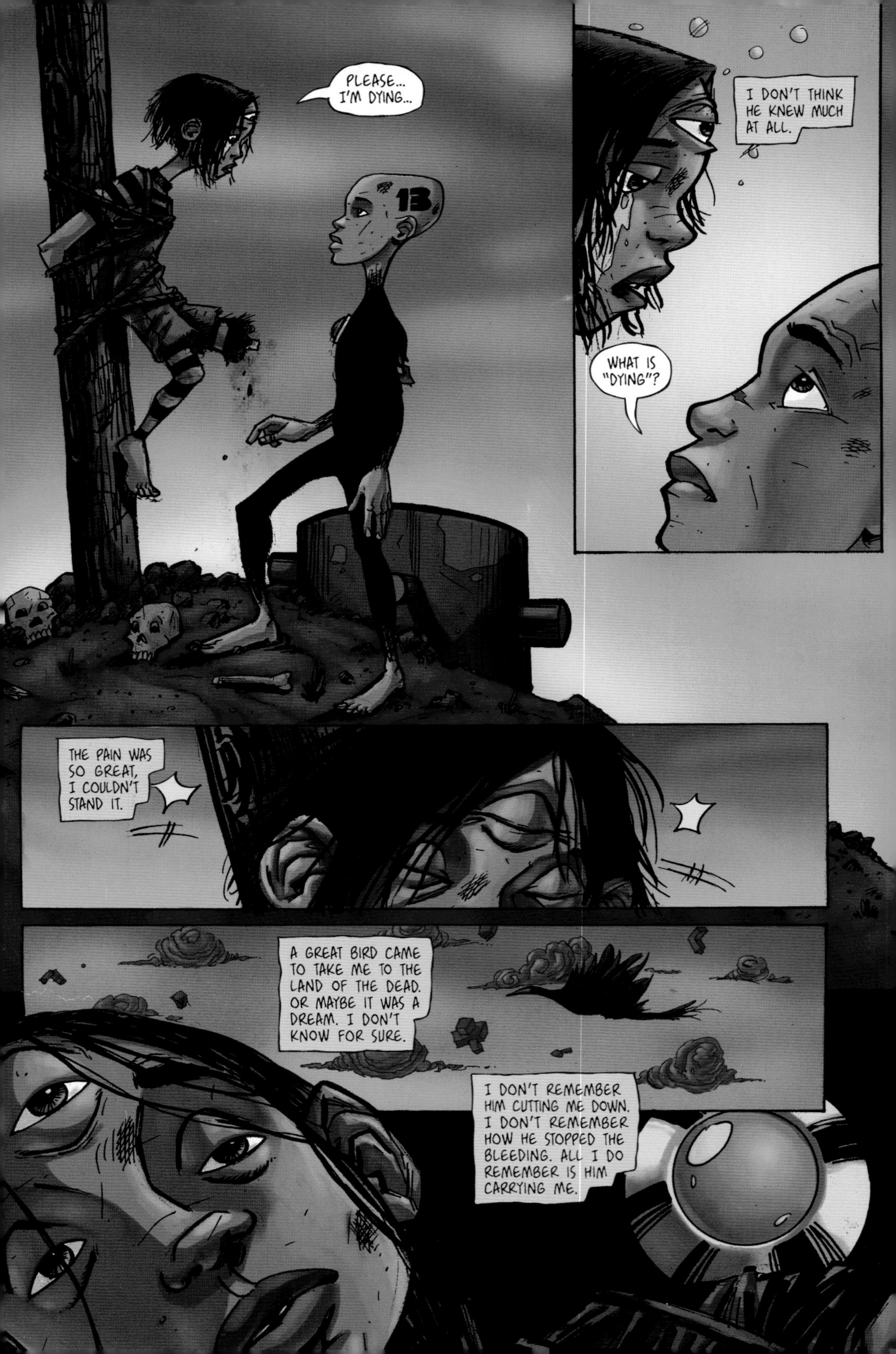
PLEASE... I'M DYING...
I DON'T THINK HE KNEW MUCH AT ALL.
WHAT IS "DYING"?
THE PAIN WAS SO GREAT, I COULDN'T STAND IT.
A GREAT BIRD CAME TO TAKE ME TO THE LAND OF THE DEAD. OR MAYBE IT WAS A DREAM. I DON'T KNOW FOR SURE.
I DON'T REMEMBER HIM CUTTING ME DOWN. I DON'T REMEMBER HOW HE STOPPED THE BLEEDING. ALL I DO REMEMBER IS HIM CARRYING ME.

NUMBER 13
CHAPTER TWO

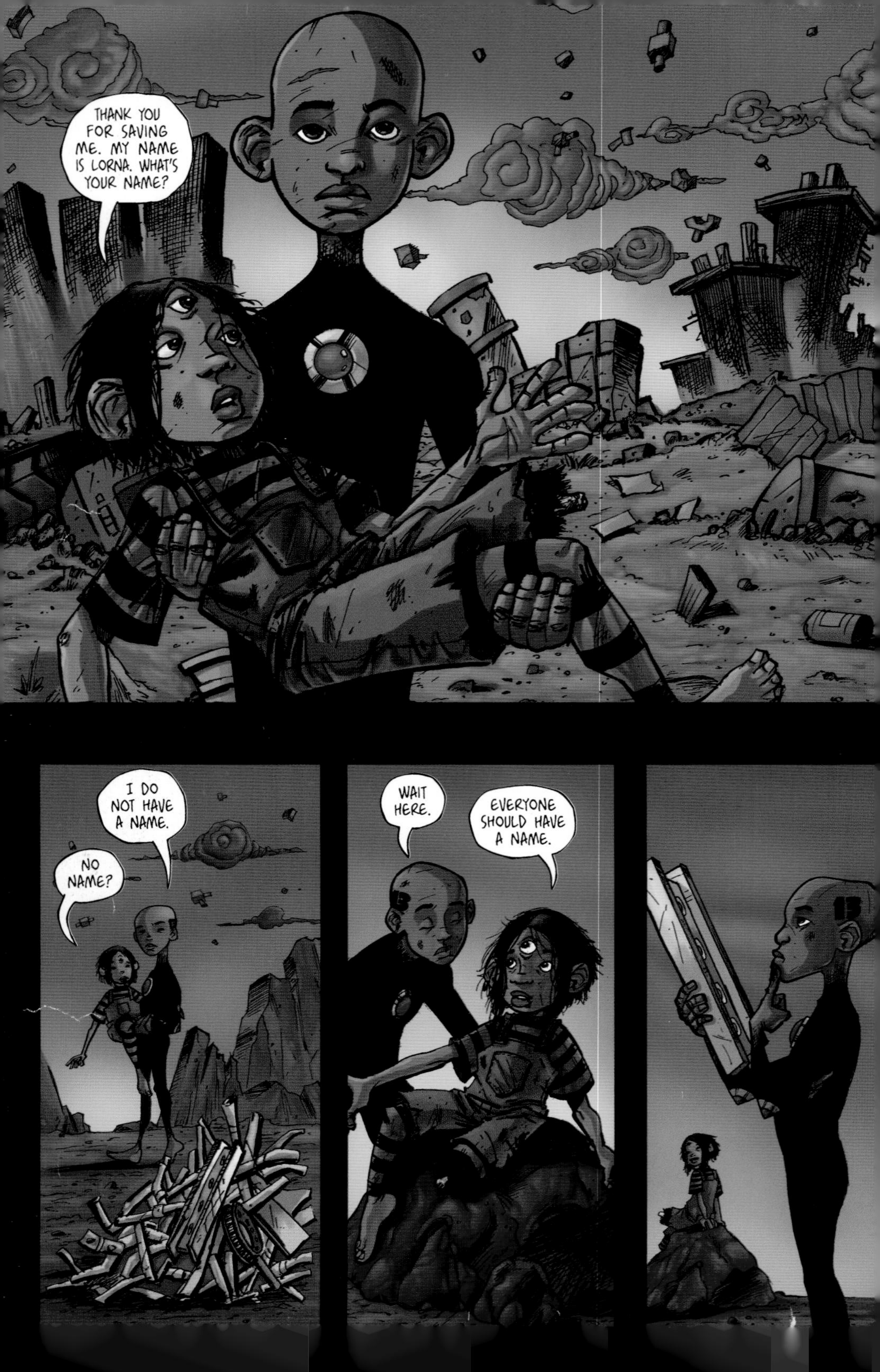
THANK YOU FOR SAVING ME. MY NAME IS LORNA. WHAT'S YOUR NAME?
I DO NOT HAVE A NAME.
NO NAME?
WAIT HERE.
EVERYONE SHOULD HAVE A NAME.

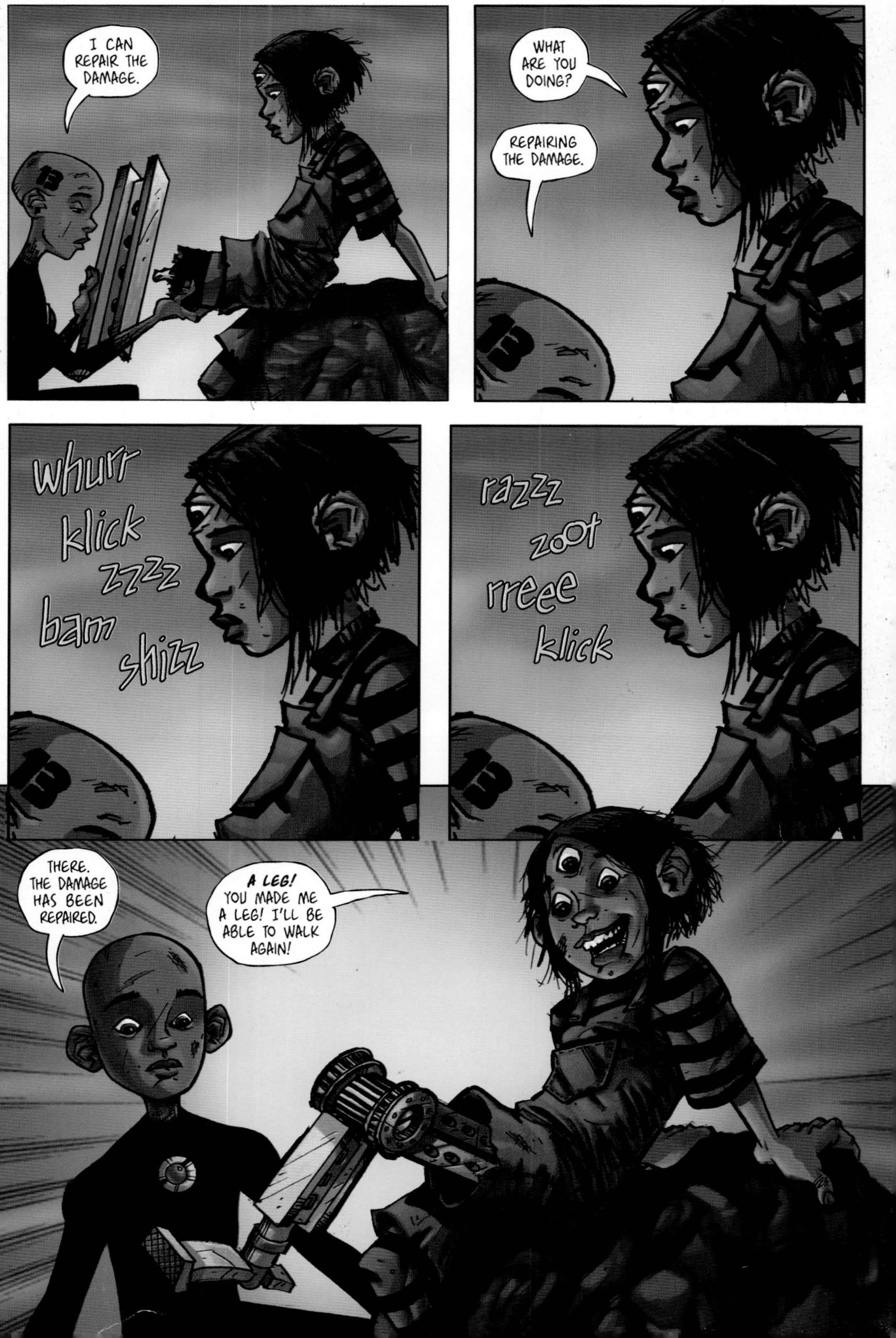
I CAN REPAIR THE DAMAGE.
WHAT ARE YOU DOING?
REPAIRING THE DAMAGE.
whurr
klick
zzzz
bam
shizz
razzz
zoot
rreee
klick
THERE. THE DAMAGE HAS BEEN REPAIRED.
A LEG! YOU MADE ME A LEG! I'LL BE ABLE TO WALK AGAIN!

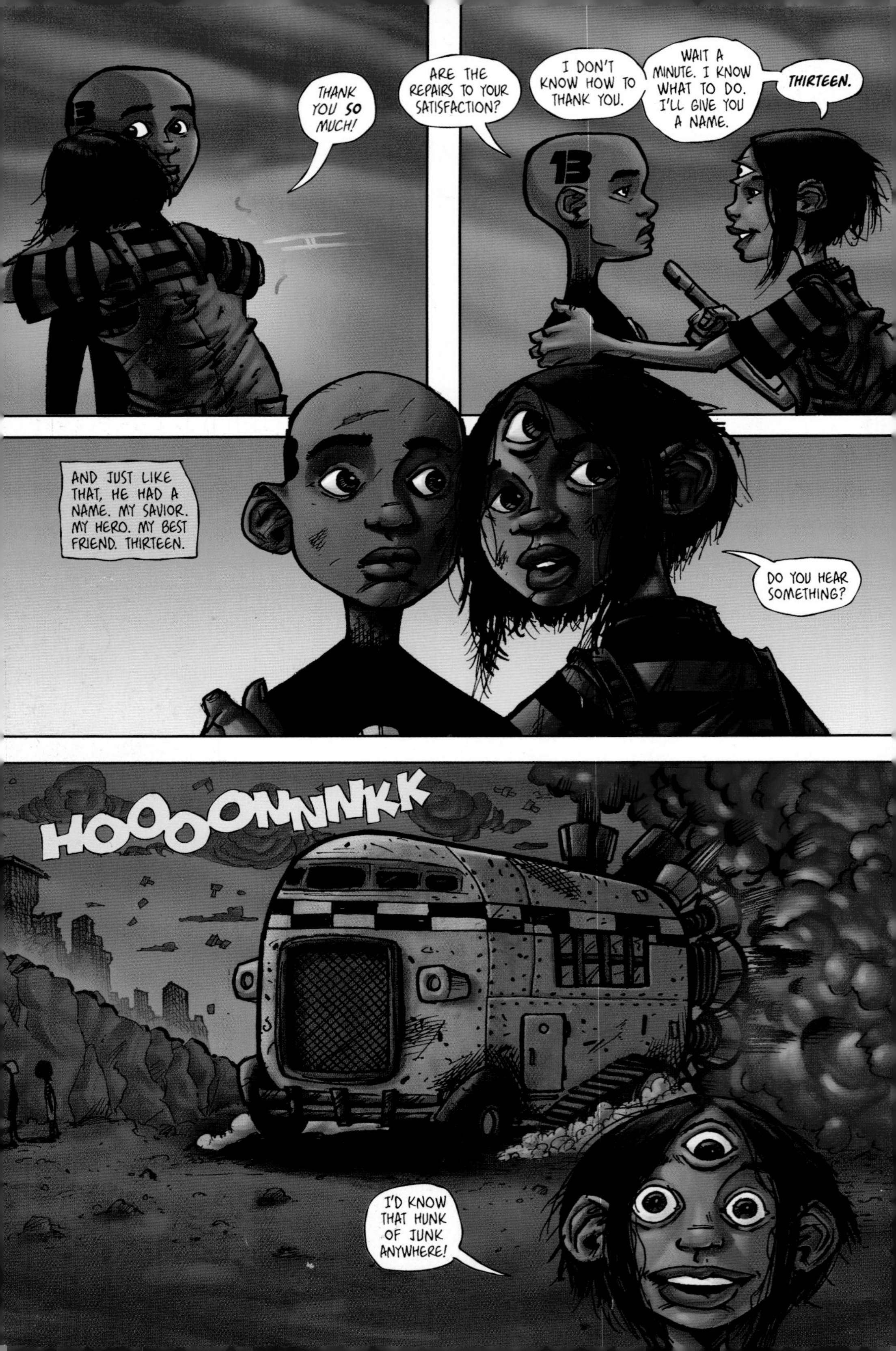
THANK YOU SO MUCH!
ARE THE REPAIRS TO YOUR SATISFACTION?
I DON'T KNOW HOW TO THANK YOU.
WAIT A MINUTE. I KNOW WHAT TO DO. I'LL GIVE YOU A NAME.
THIRTEEN.
AND JUST LIKE THAT, HE HAD A NAME. MY SAVIOR. MY HERO. MY BEST FRIEND. THIRTEEN.
DO YOU HEAR SOMETHING?
HOOOONNNKK
I'D KNOW THAT HUNK OF JUNK ANYWHERE!

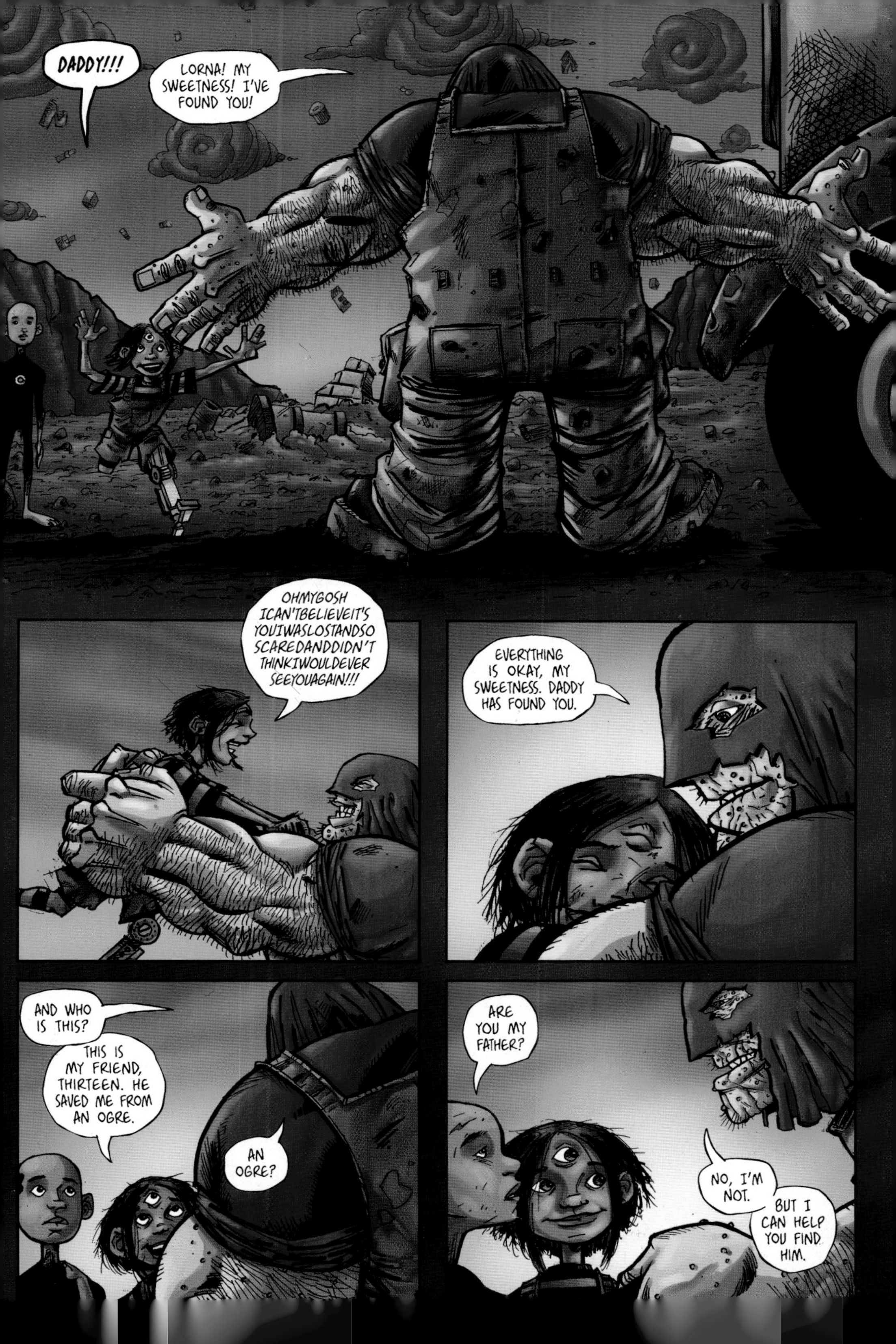
DADDY!!!
LORNA! MY SWEETNESS! I'VE FOUND YOU!
OHMYGOSH ICAN'TBELIEVEIT'S YOUIWASLOSTANDSO SCAREDANDDIDN'T THINKIWOULDEVER SEEYOUAGAIN!!!
EVERYTHING IS OKAY, MY SWEETNESS. DADDY HAS FOUND YOU.
AND WHO IS THIS?
THIS IS MY FRIEND, THIRTEEN. HE SAVED ME FROM AN OGRE.
AN OGRE?
ARE YOU MY FATHER?
NO, I'M NOT.
BUT I CAN HELP YOU FIND HIM.

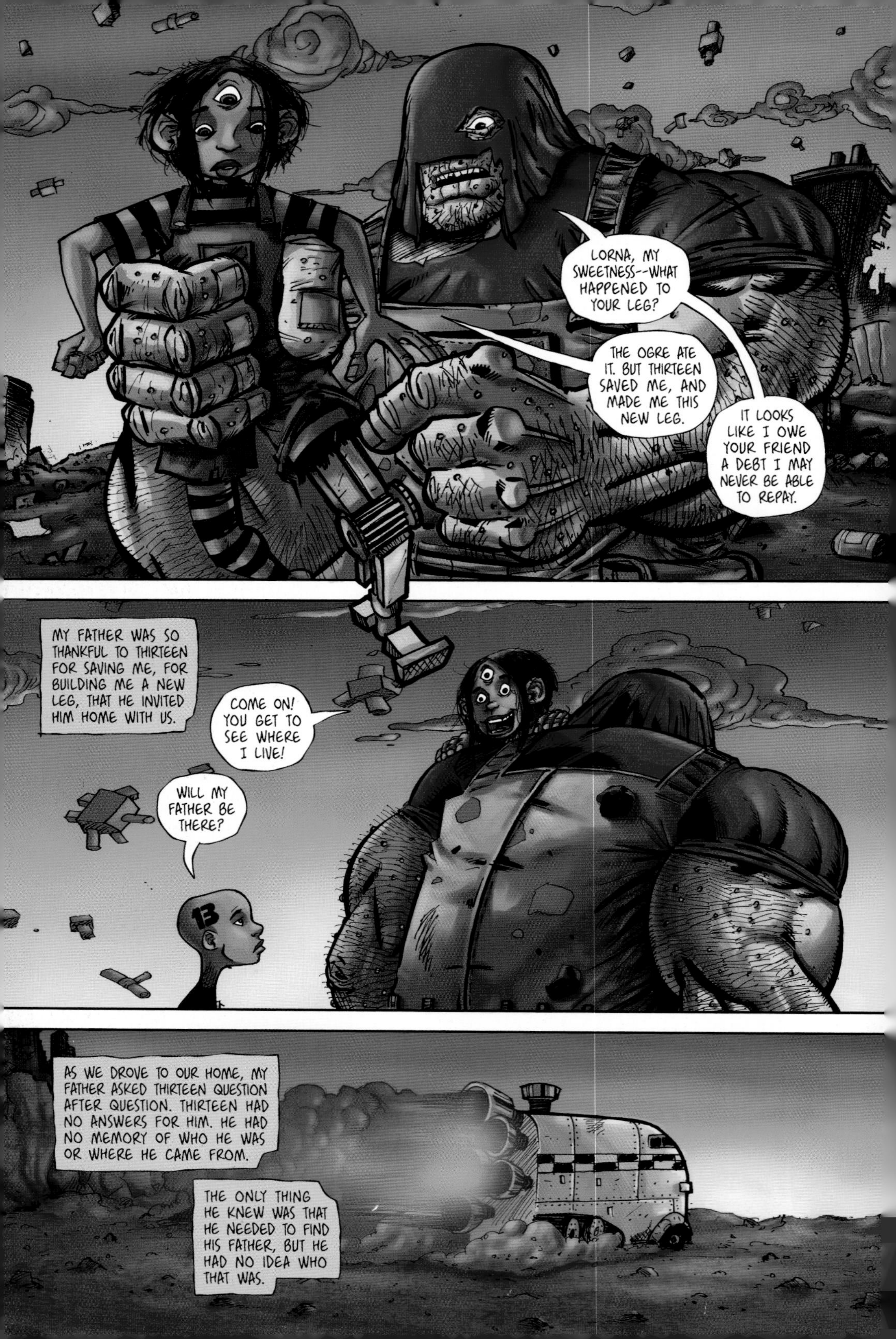
LORNA, MY SWEETNESS--WHAT HAPPENED TO YOUR LEG?
THE OGRE ATE IT. BUT THIRTEEN SAVED ME, AND MADE ME THIS NEW LEG.
IT LOOKS LIKE I OWE YOUR FRIEND A DEBT I MAY NEVER BE ABLE TO REPAY.
MY FATHER WAS SO THANKFUL TO THIRTEEN FOR SAVING ME, FOR BUILDING ME A NEW LEG, THAT HE INVITED HIM HOME WITH US.
COME ON! YOU GET TO SEE WHERE I LIVE!
WILL MY FATHER BE THERE?
13
AS WE DROVE TO OUR HOME, MY FATHER ASKED THIRTEEN QUESTION AFTER QUESTION. THIRTEEN HAD NO ANSWERS FOR HIM. HE HAD NO MEMORY OF WHO HE WAS OR WHERE HE CAME FROM.
THE ONLY THING HE KNEW WAS THAT HE NEEDED TO FIND HIS FATHER, BUT HE HAD NO IDEA WHO THAT WAS.

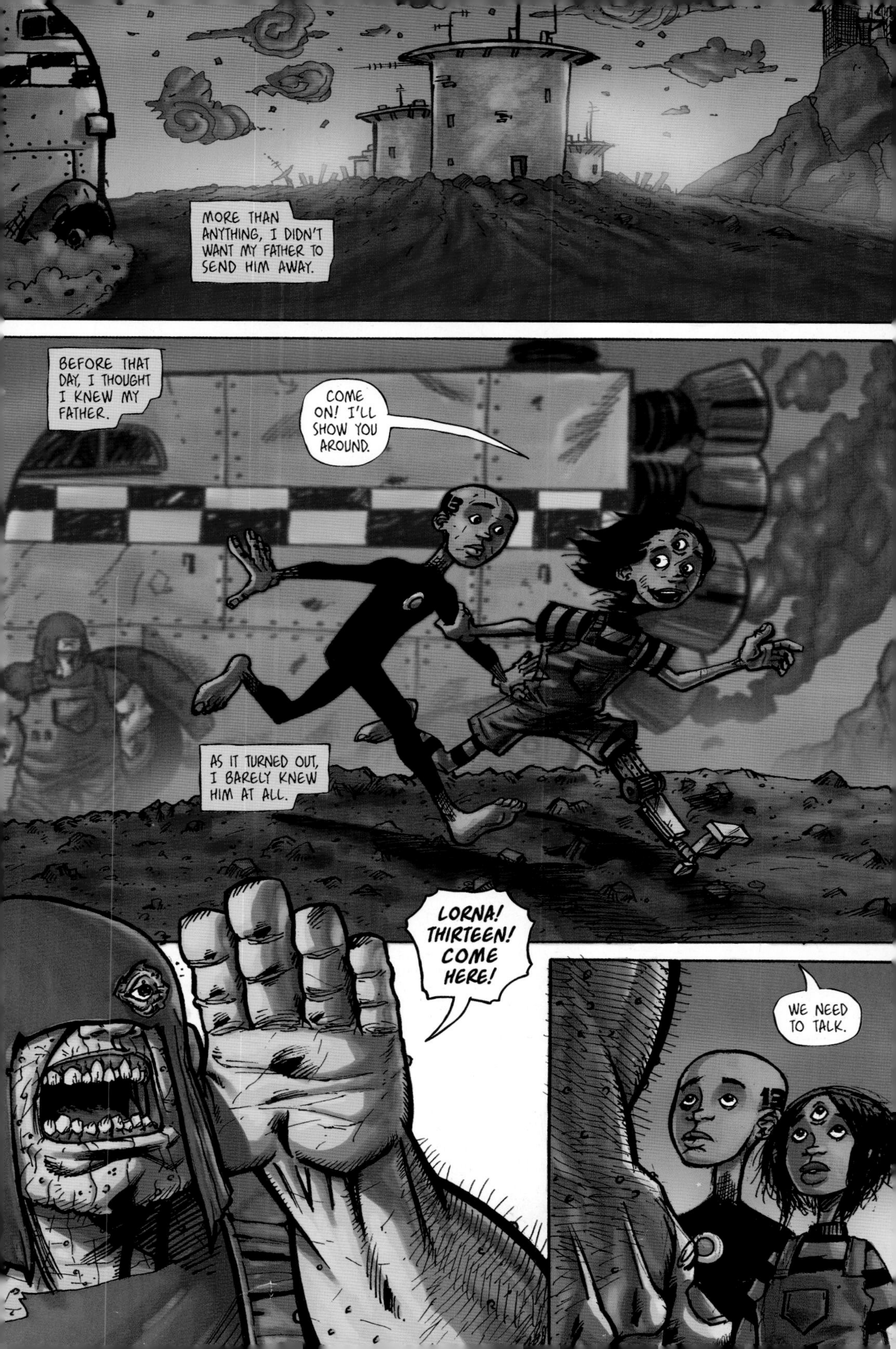
MORE THAN ANYTHING, I DIDN'T WANT MY FATHER TO SEND HIM AWAY.
BEFORE THAT DAY, I THOUGHT I KNEW MY FATHER.
COME ON! I'LL SHOW YOU AROUND.
AS IT TURNED OUT, I BARELY KNEW HIM AT ALL.
LORNA! THIRTEEN! COME HERE!
WE NEED TO TALK.

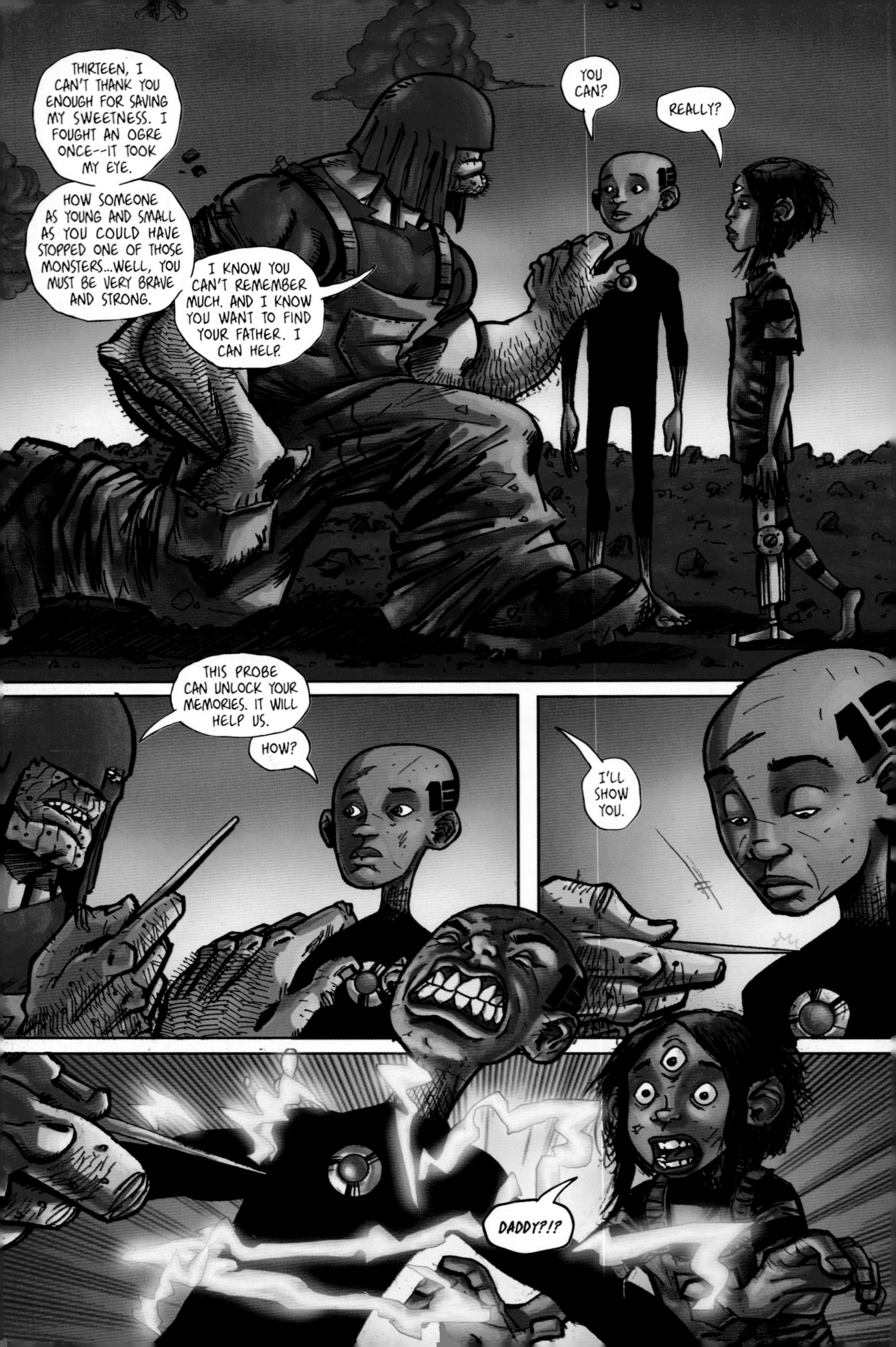

THIRTEEN, I CAN'T THANK YOU ENOUGH FOR SAVING MY SWEETNESS. I FOUGHT AN OGRE ONCE--IT TOOK MY EYE.
HOW SOMEONE AS YOUNG AND SMALL AS YOU COULD HAVE STOPPED ONE OF THOSE MONSTERS...WELL, YOU MUST BE VERY BRAVE AND STRONG.
I KNOW YOU CAN'T REMEMBER MUCH. AND I KNOW YOU WANT TO FIND YOUR FATHER. I CAN HELP.
YOU CAN?
REALLY?
THIS PROBE CAN UNLOCK YOUR MEMORIES. IT WILL HELP US.
HOW?
I'LL SHOW YOU.
DADDY?!?

NUMBER 13
CHAPTER THREE

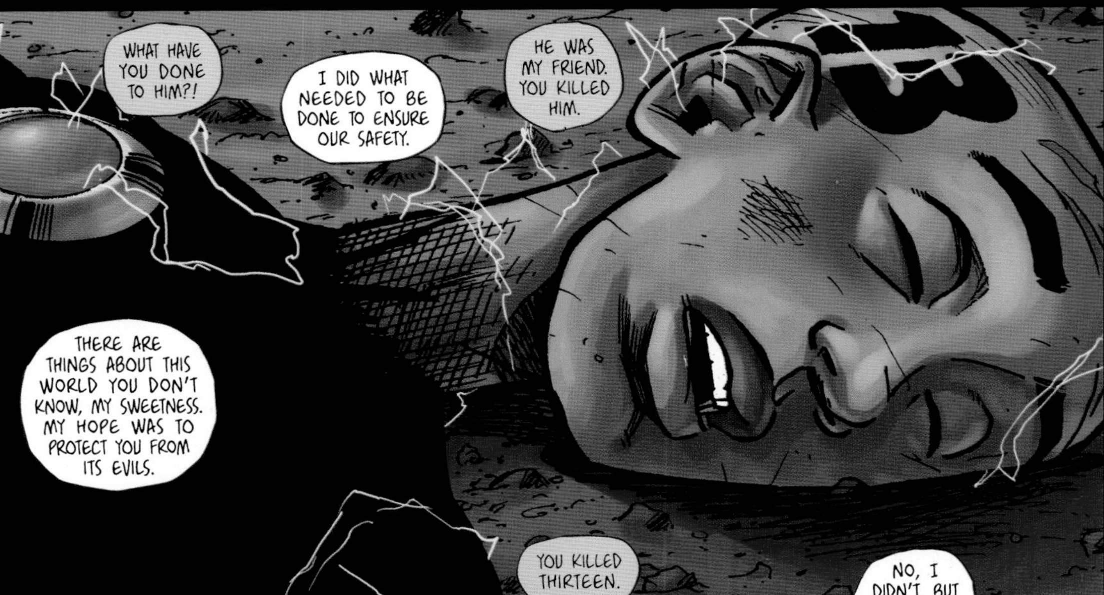
WHAT HAVE YOU DONE TO HIM?!
I DID WHAT NEEDED TO BE DONE TO ENSURE OUR SAFETY.
HE WAS MY FRIEND. YOU KILLED HIM.
THERE ARE THINGS ABOUT THIS WORLD YOU DON'T KNOW, MY SWEETNESS. MY HOPE WAS TO PROTECT YOU FROM ITS EVILS.
YOU KILLED THIRTEEN.
NO, I DIDN'T. BUT I MAY HAVE SAVED THE WORLD.

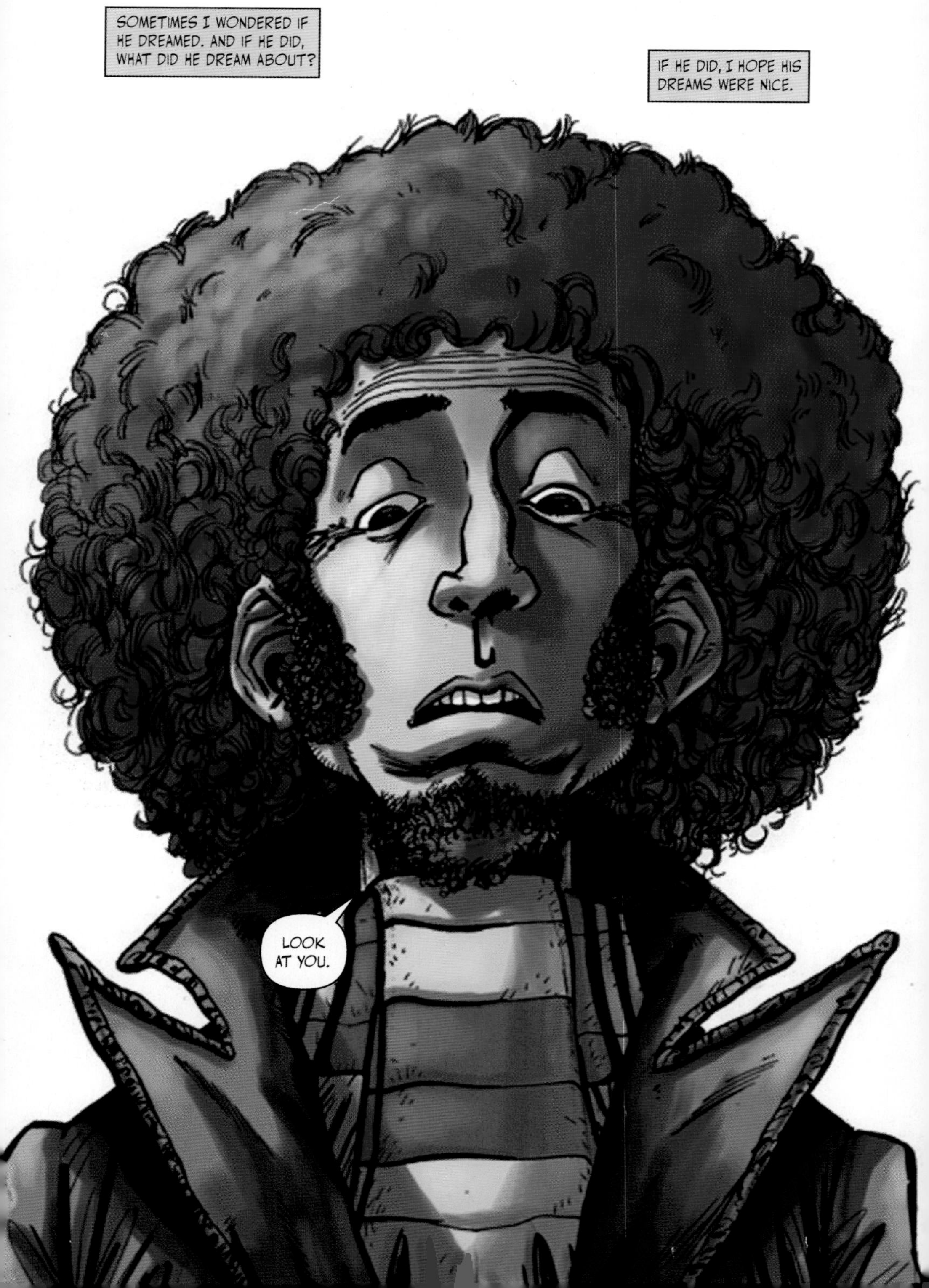
SOMETIMES I WONDERED IF HE DREAMED. AND IF HE DID, WHAT DID HE DREAM ABOUT?
IF HE DID, I HOPE HIS DREAMS WERE NICE.
LOOK AT YOU.

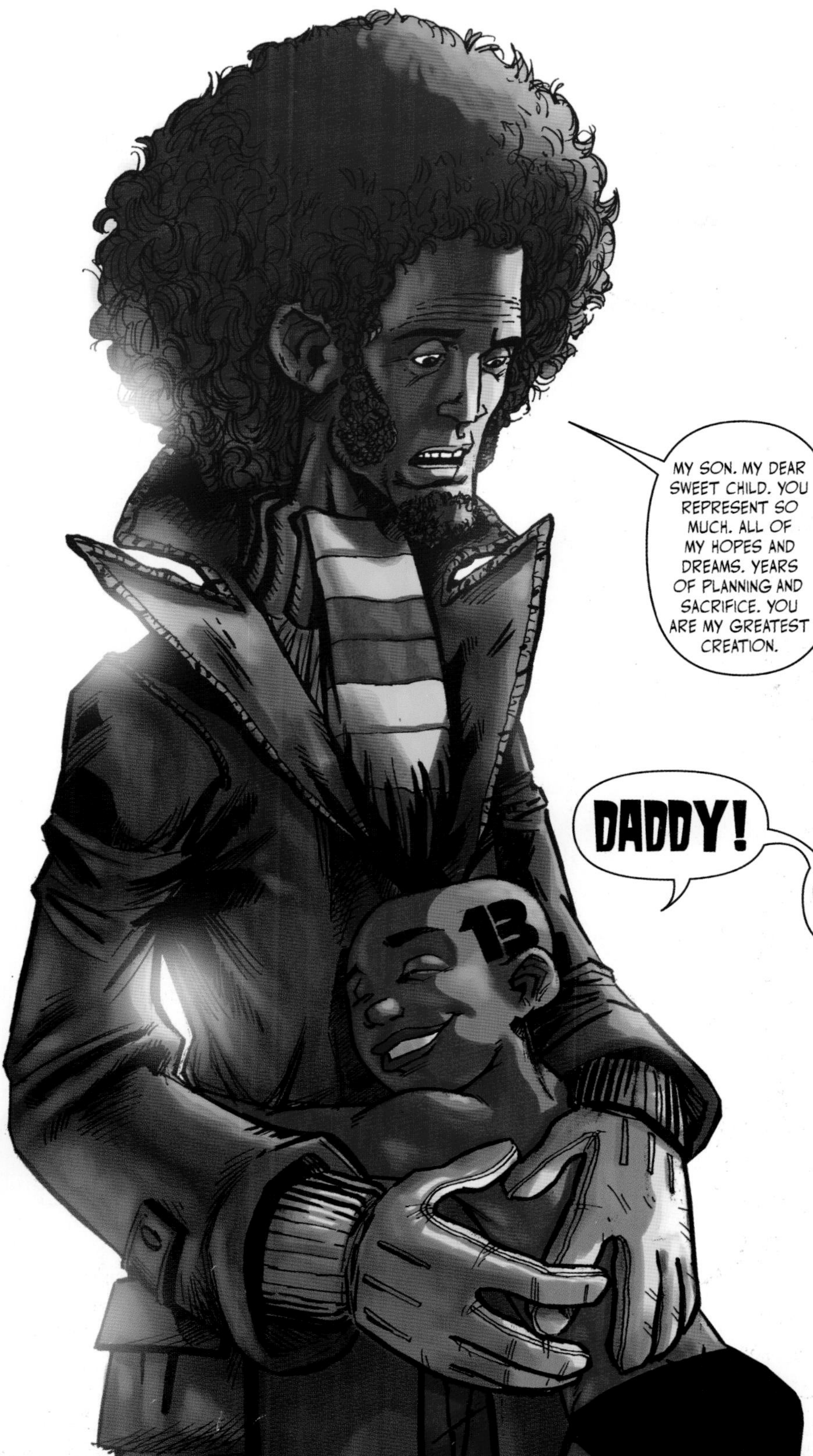
MY SON. MY DEAR SWEET CHILD. YOU REPRESENT SO MUCH. ALL OF MY HOPES AND DREAMS. YEARS OF PLANNING AND SACRIFICE. YOU ARE MY GREATEST CREATION.
DADDY!
I'VE BEEN LOOKING FOR YOU FOR SO LONG!
13

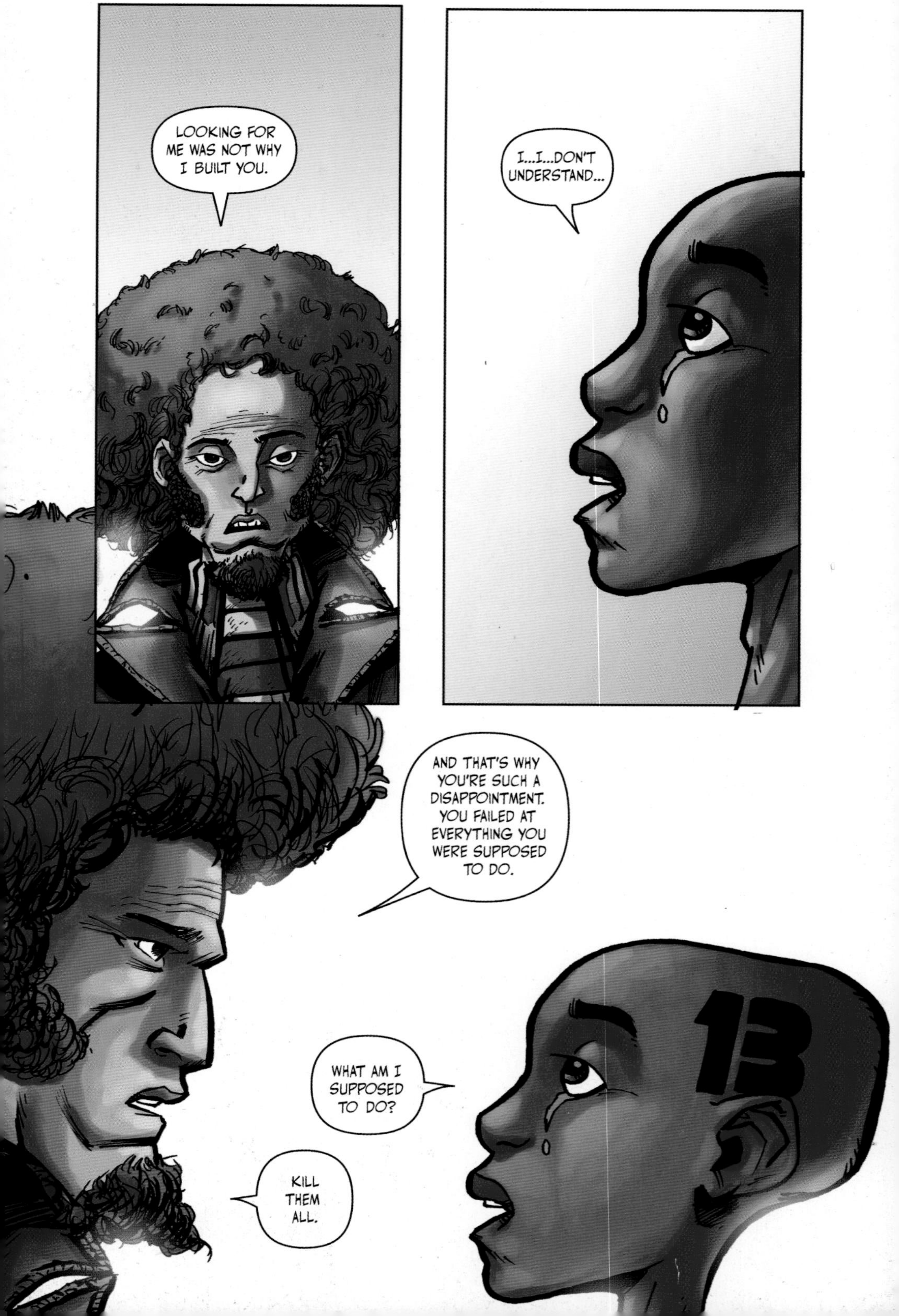
LOOKING FOR ME WAS NOT WHY I BUILT YOU.
I...I...DON'T UNDERSTAND...
AND THAT'S WHY YOU'RE SUCH A DISAPPOINTMENT. YOU FAILED AT EVERYTHING YOU WERE SUPPOSED TO DO.
13
WHAT AM I SUPPOSED TO DO?
KILL THEM ALL.

A VOICE...

I HEAR A VOICE...

I HEAR A VOICE...

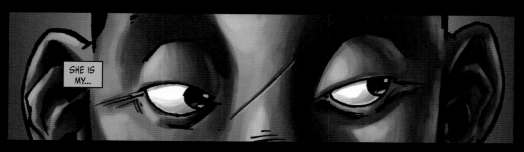

SHE IS MY...

...FRIEND.

I DON'T UNDER-STAND--WHY?! WHY?! WHY ARE YOU DOING THIS?!

WHY ARE YOU DOING THIS TO MY FRIEND!

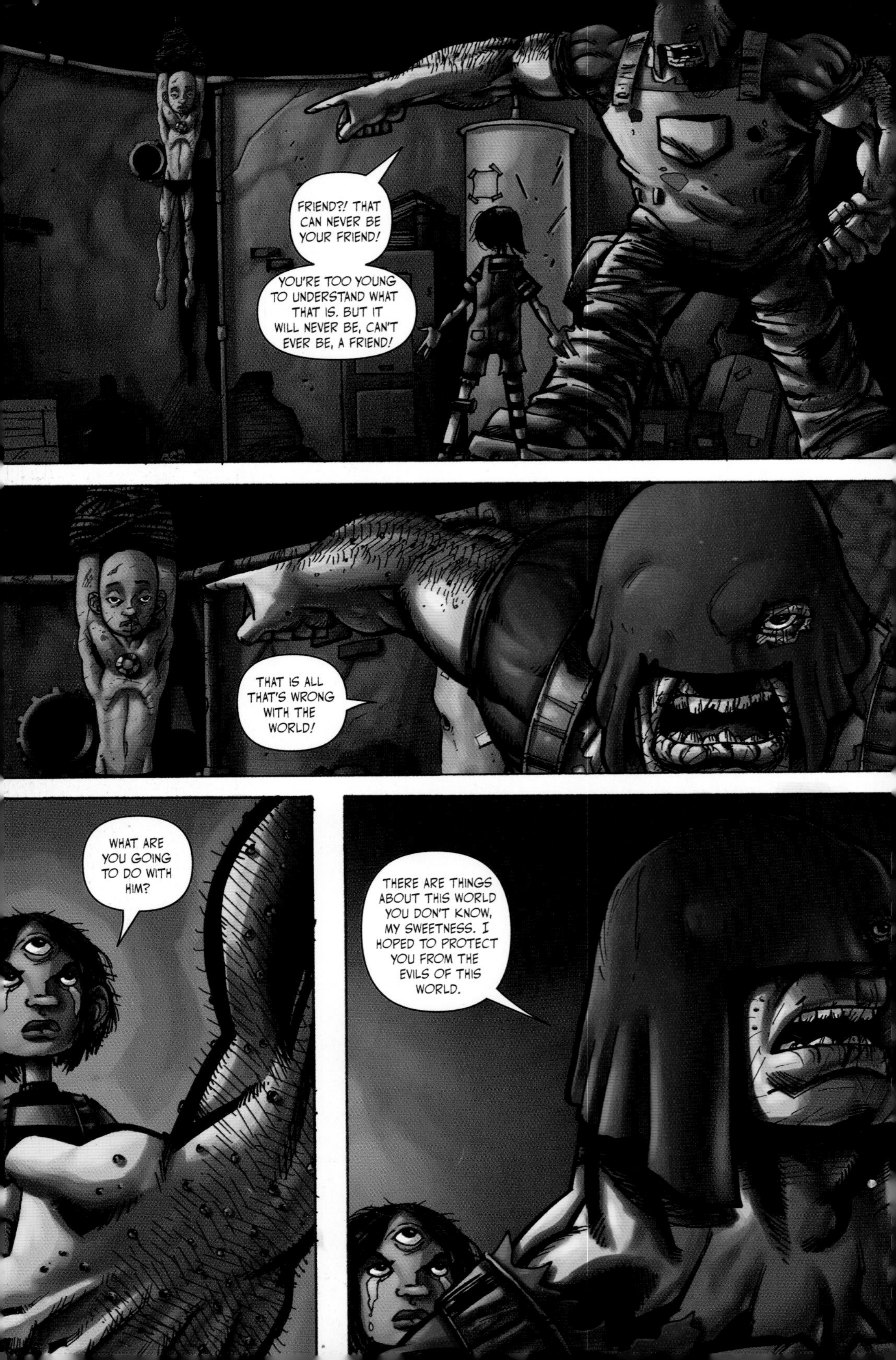
FRIEND?! THAT CAN NEVER BE YOUR FRIEND!
YOU'RE TOO YOUNG TO UNDERSTAND WHAT THAT IS. BUT IT WILL NEVER BE, CAN'T EVER BE, A FRIEND!
THAT IS ALL THAT'S WRONG WITH THE WORLD!
WHAT ARE YOU GOING TO DO WITH HIM?
THERE ARE THINGS ABOUT THIS WORLD YOU DON'T KNOW, MY SWEETNESS. I HOPED TO PROTECT YOU FROM THE EVILS OF THIS WORLD.

I CAN'T LET YOU KILL THIRTEEN! I WON'T LET YOU!!

I DON'T UNDERSTAND. SHE IS HIS DAUGHTER.

HE IS HER FATHER. THEY ARE FAMILY.

CLICK CLACK

HE SHOUTS AT HER...

SHE YELLS AT HIM...

THEY SCREAM AT EACH OTHER...

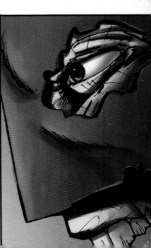

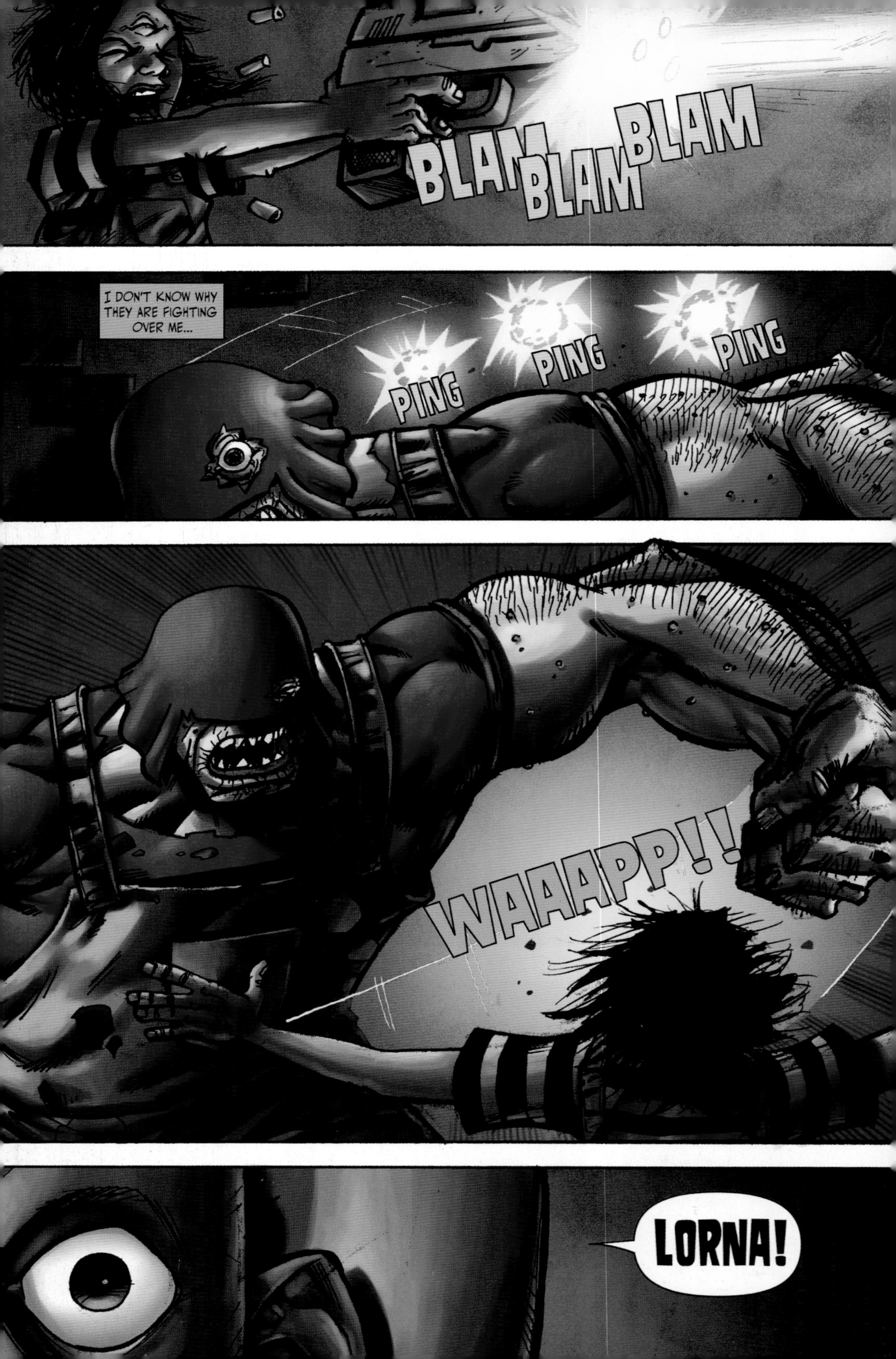
BLAM BLAM BLAM
I DON'T KNOW WHY THEY ARE FIGHTING OVER ME...
PING PING PING
WAAAPP!!
LORNA!

NUMBER 13
CHAPTER FOUR

OVER TWO HOURS AGO...

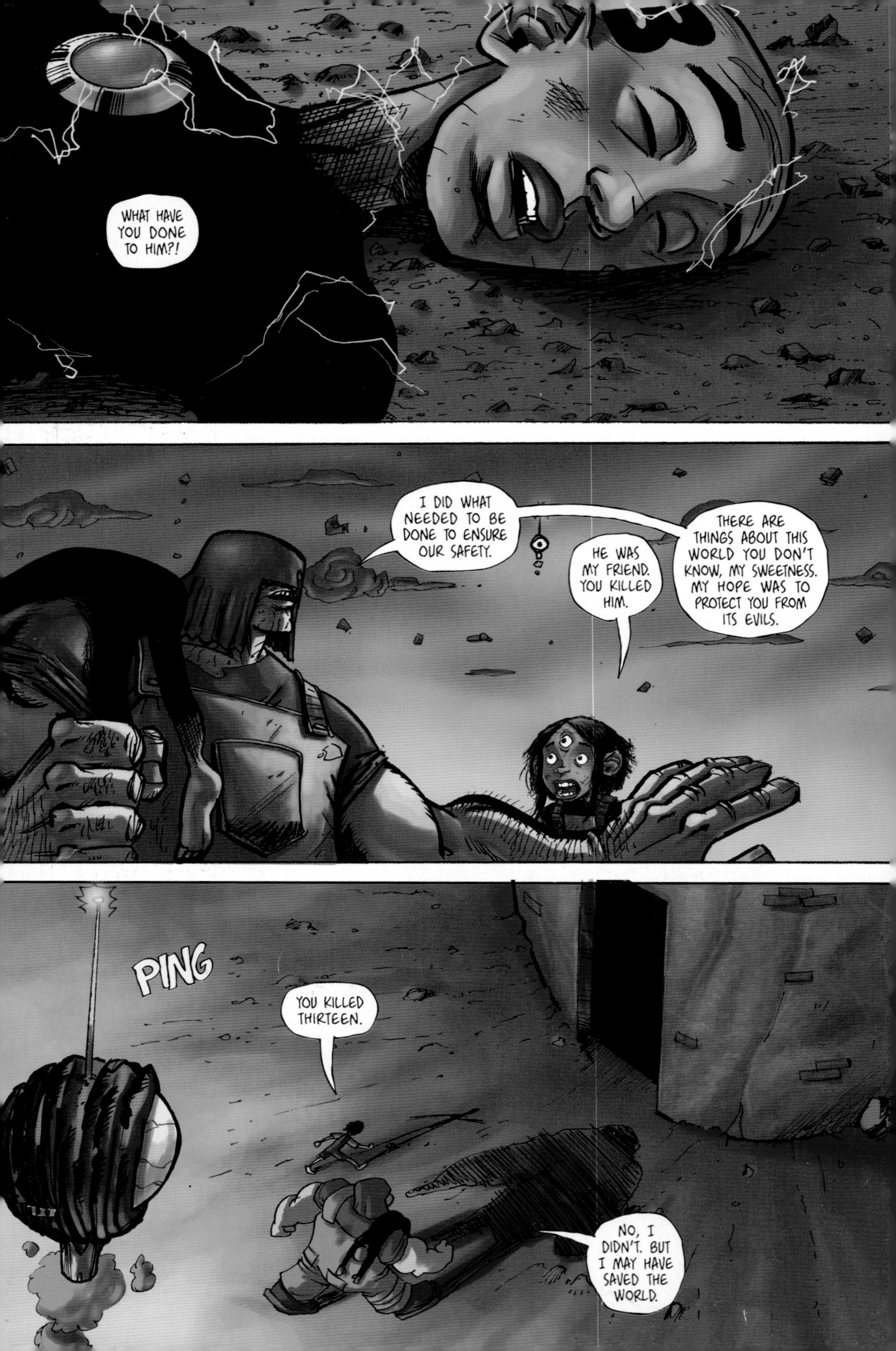
WHAT HAVE YOU DONE TO HIM?!
I DID WHAT NEEDED TO BE DONE TO ENSURE OUR SAFETY.
HE WAS MY FRIEND. YOU KILLED HIM.
THERE ARE THINGS ABOUT THIS WORLD YOU DON'T KNOW, MY SWEETNESS. MY HOPE WAS TO PROTECT YOU FROM ITS EVILS.
PING
YOU KILLED THIRTEEN.
NO, I DIDN'T. BUT I MAY HAVE SAVED THE WORLD.

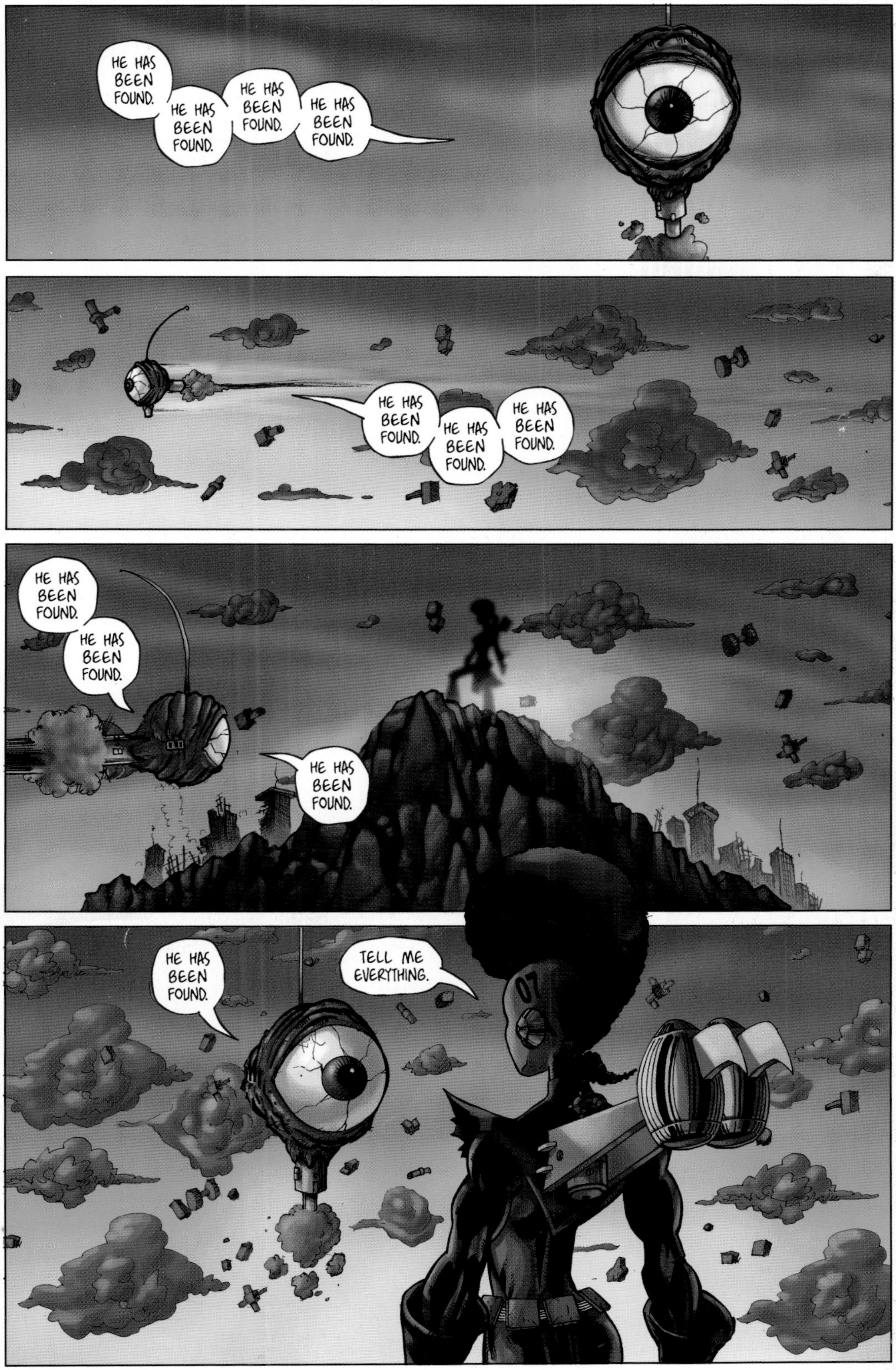
HE HAS BEEN FOUND.
HE HAS BEEN FOUND.
HE HAS BEEN FOUND.
HE HAS BEEN FOUND.
HE HAS BEEN FOUND.
HE HAS BEEN FOUND.
HE HAS BEEN FOUND.
HE HAS BEEN FOUND.
HE HAS BEEN FOUND.
HE HAS BEEN FOUND.
HE HAS BEEN FOUND.
TELL ME EVERYTHING.

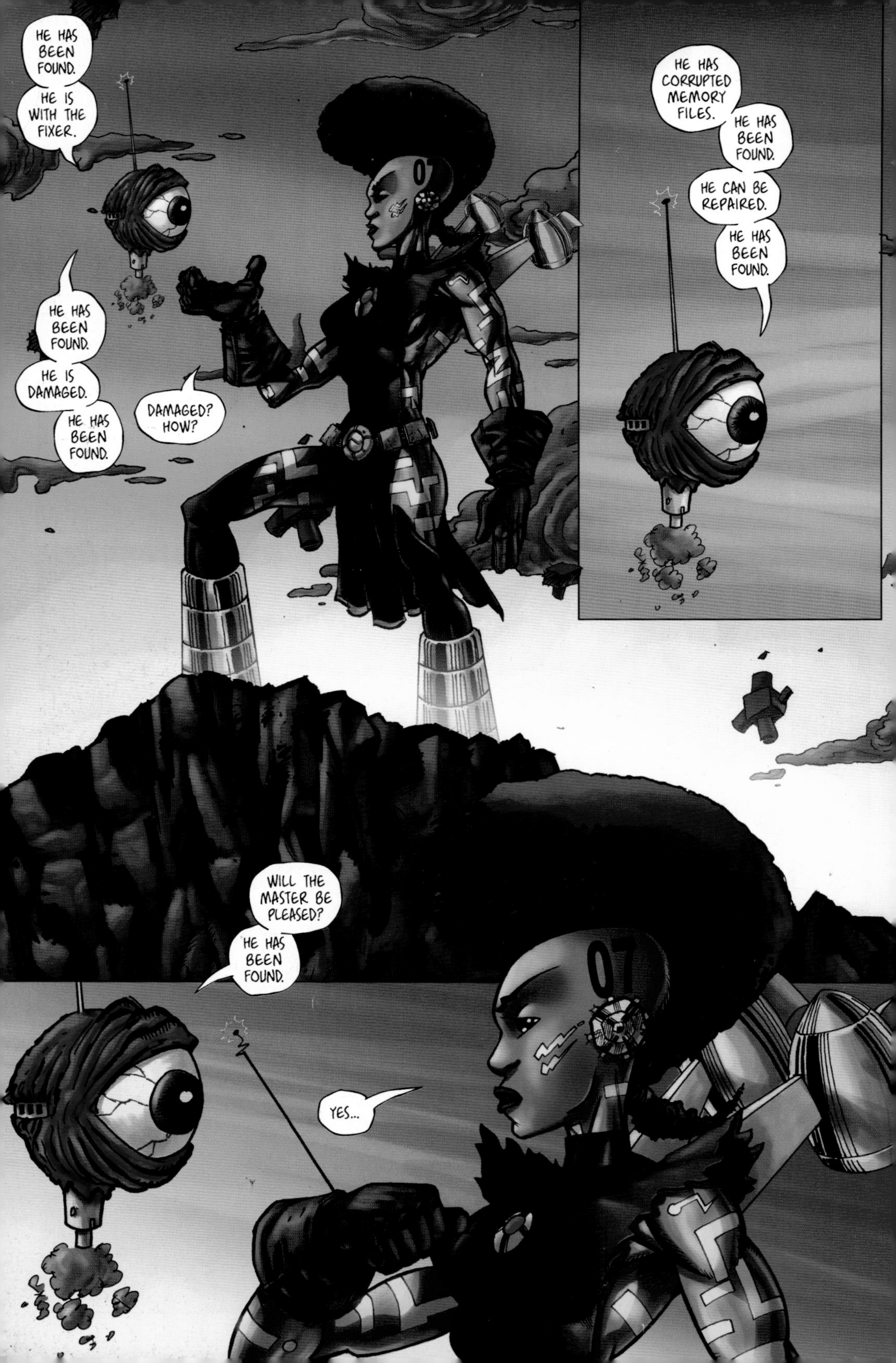
HE HAS BEEN FOUND.
HE IS WITH THE FIXER.
HE HAS BEEN FOUND.
HE IS DAMAGED.
HE HAS BEEN FOUND.
DAMAGED? HOW?
HE HAS CORRUPTED MEMORY FILES.
HE HAS BEEN FOUND.
HE CAN BE REPAIRED.
HE HAS BEEN FOUND.
WILL THE MASTER BE PLEASED?
HE HAS BEEN FOUND.
YES...

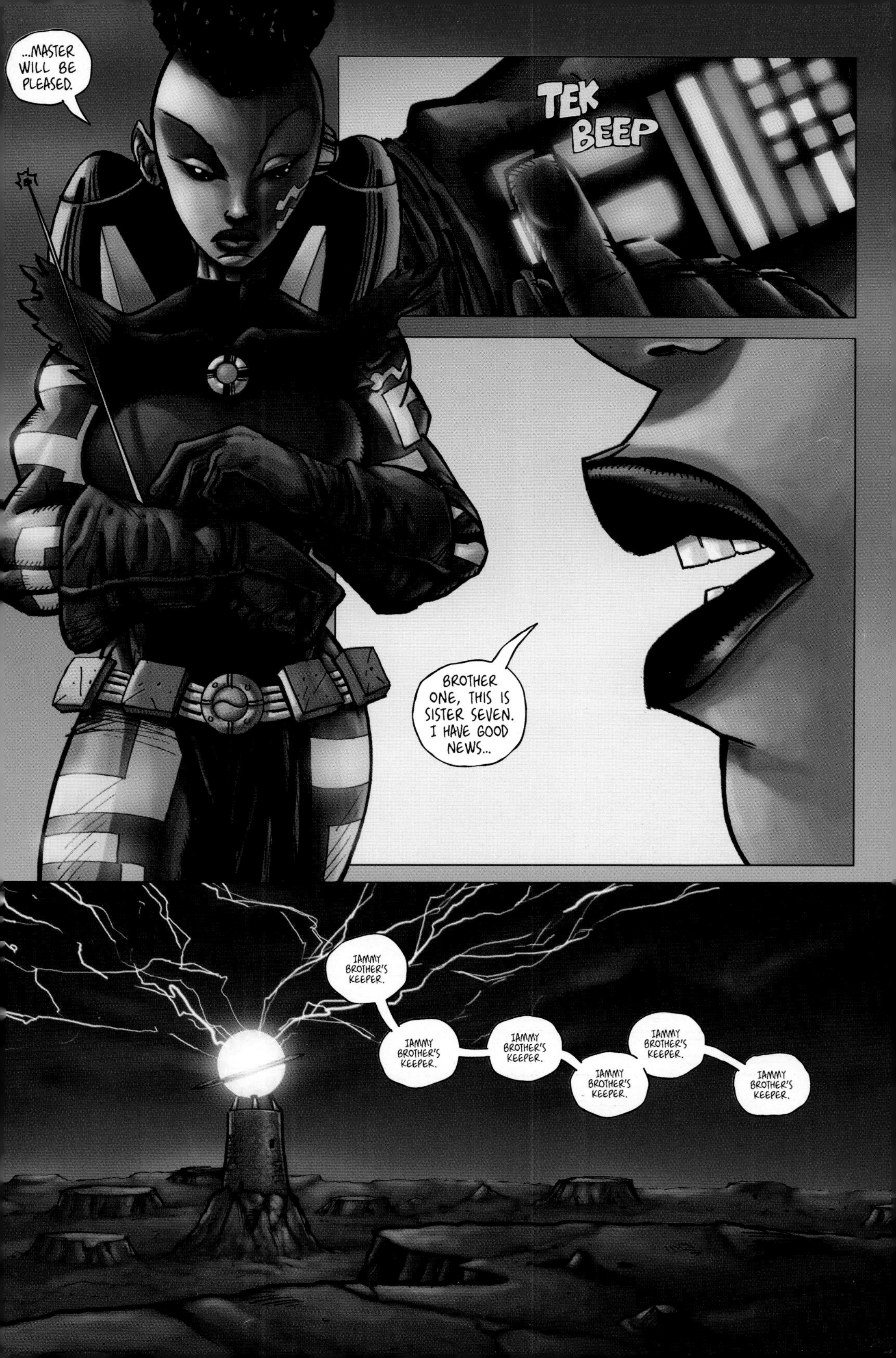
...MASTER WILL BE PLEASED.
TEK
BEEP
BROTHER ONE, THIS IS SISTER SEVEN. I HAVE GOOD NEWS...
IAMMY BROTHER'S KEEPER.
IAMMY BROTHER'S KEEPER.
IAMMY BROTHER'S KEEPER.
IAMMY BROTHER'S KEEPER.
IAMMY BROTHER'S KEEPER.
IAMMY BROTHER'S KEEPER.

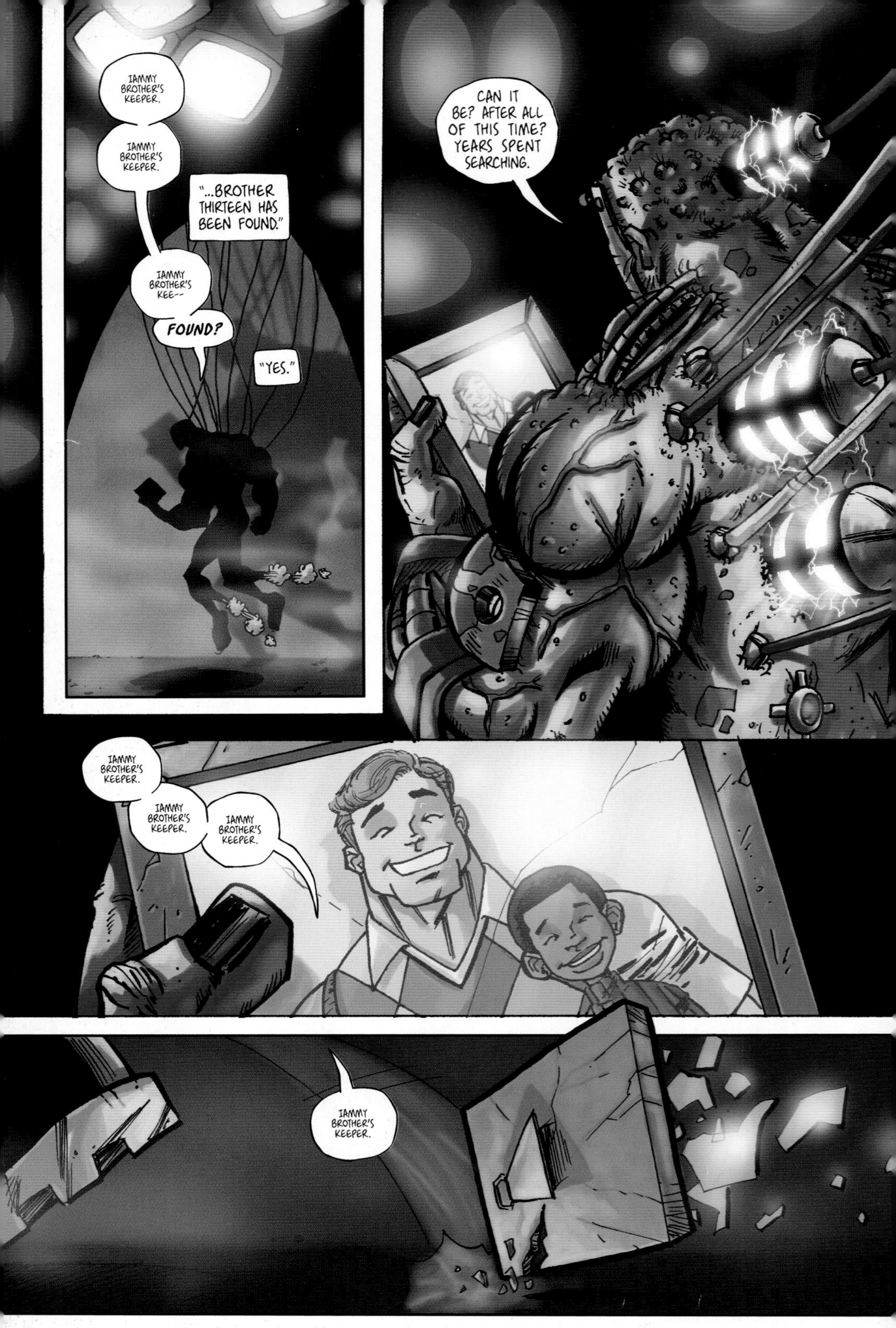
IAMMY BROTHER'S KEEPER.
IAMMY BROTHER'S KEEPER.
"...BROTHER THIRTEEN HAS BEEN FOUND."
IAMMY BROTHER'S KEE--
FOUND?
"YES."
CAN IT BE? AFTER ALL OF THIS TIME? YEARS SPENT SEARCHING.
IAMMY BROTHER'S KEEPER.
IAMMY BROTHER'S KEEPER.
IAMMY BROTHER'S KEEPER.
IAMMY BROTHER'S KEEPER.

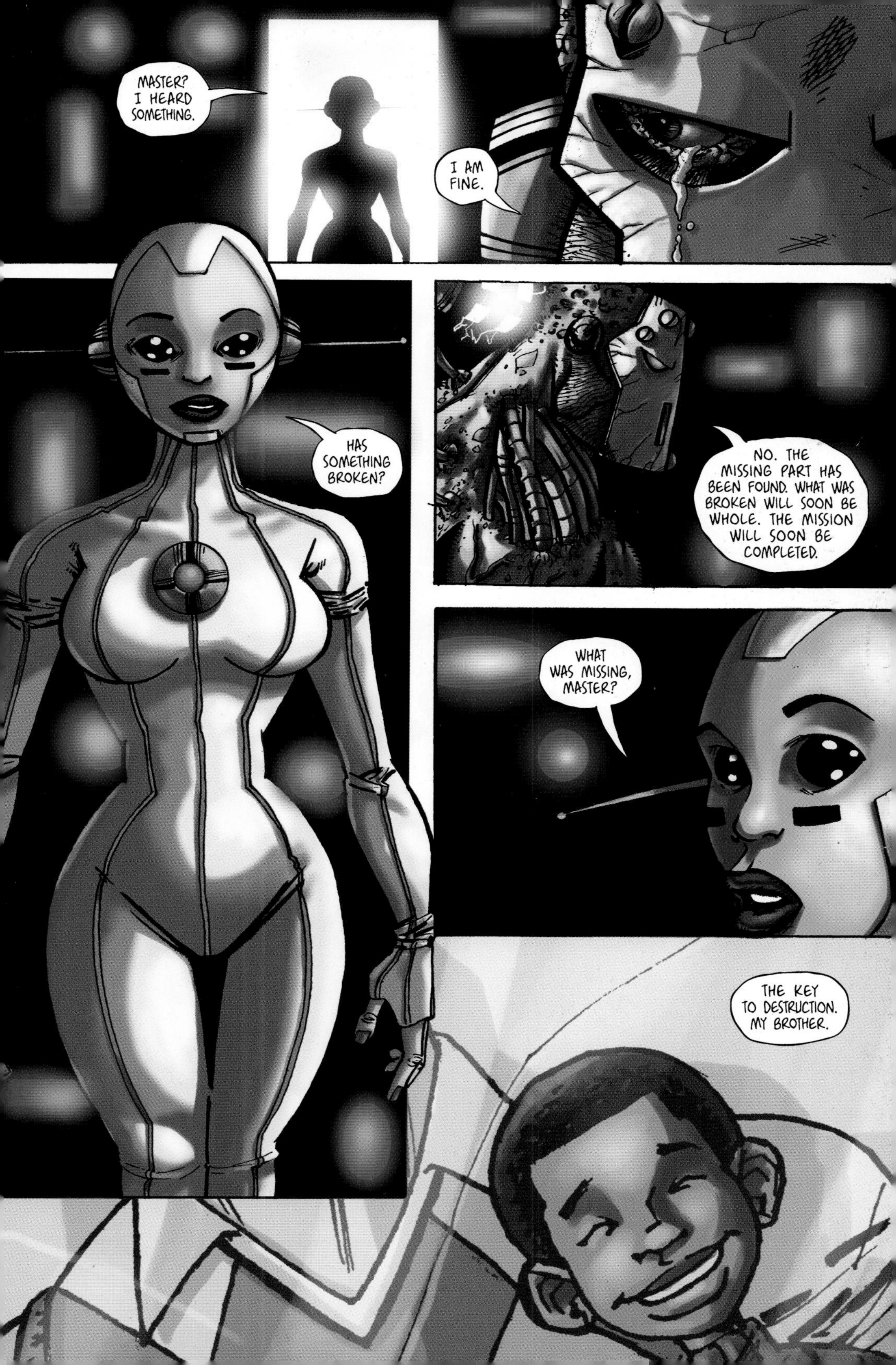
MASTER? I HEARD SOMETHING.
I AM FINE.
HAS SOMETHING BROKEN?
NO. THE MISSING PART HAS BEEN FOUND. WHAT WAS BROKEN WILL SOON BE WHOLE. THE MISSION WILL SOON BE COMPLETED.
WHAT WAS MISSING, MASTER?
THE KEY TO DESTRUCTION. MY BROTHER.

NUMBER 13
CHAPTER FIVE

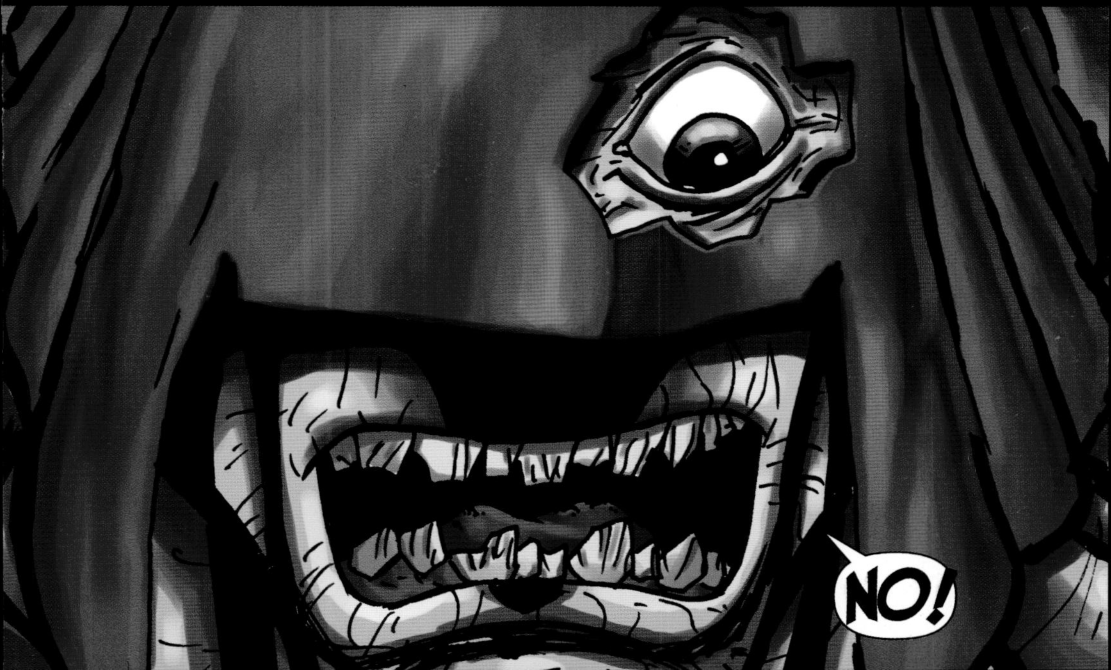
NO!

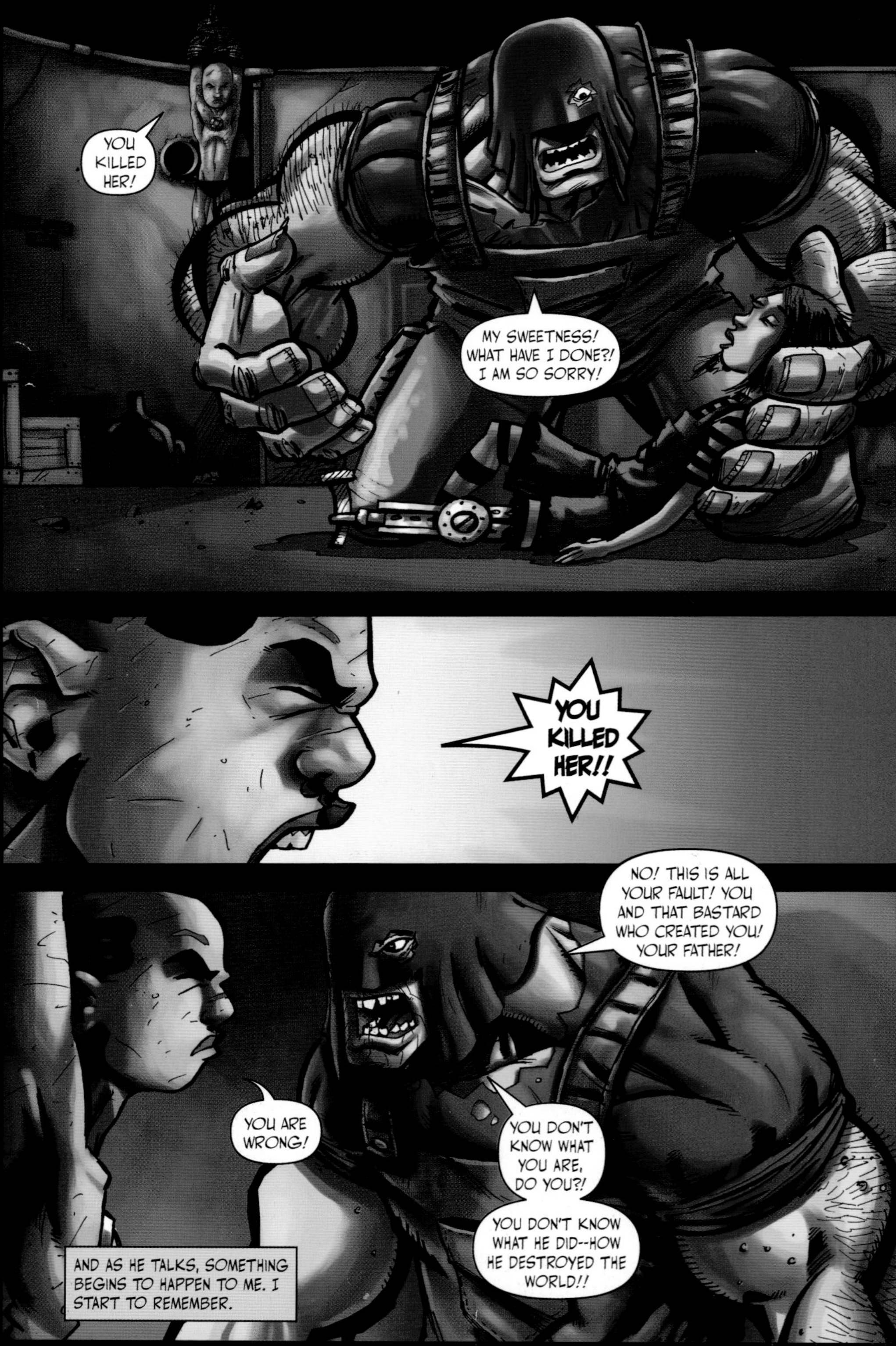

YOU KILLED HER!
MY SWEETNESS! WHAT HAVE I DONE?! I AM SO SORRY!
YOU KILLED HER!!
NO! THIS IS ALL YOUR FAULT! YOU AND THAT BASTARD WHO CREATED YOU! YOUR FATHER!
YOU ARE WRONG!
YOU DON'T KNOW WHAT YOU ARE, DO YOU?!
YOU DON'T KNOW WHAT HE DID--HOW HE DESTROYED THE WORLD!!
AND AS HE TALKS, SOMETHING BEGINS TO HAPPEN TO ME. I START TO REMEMBER.

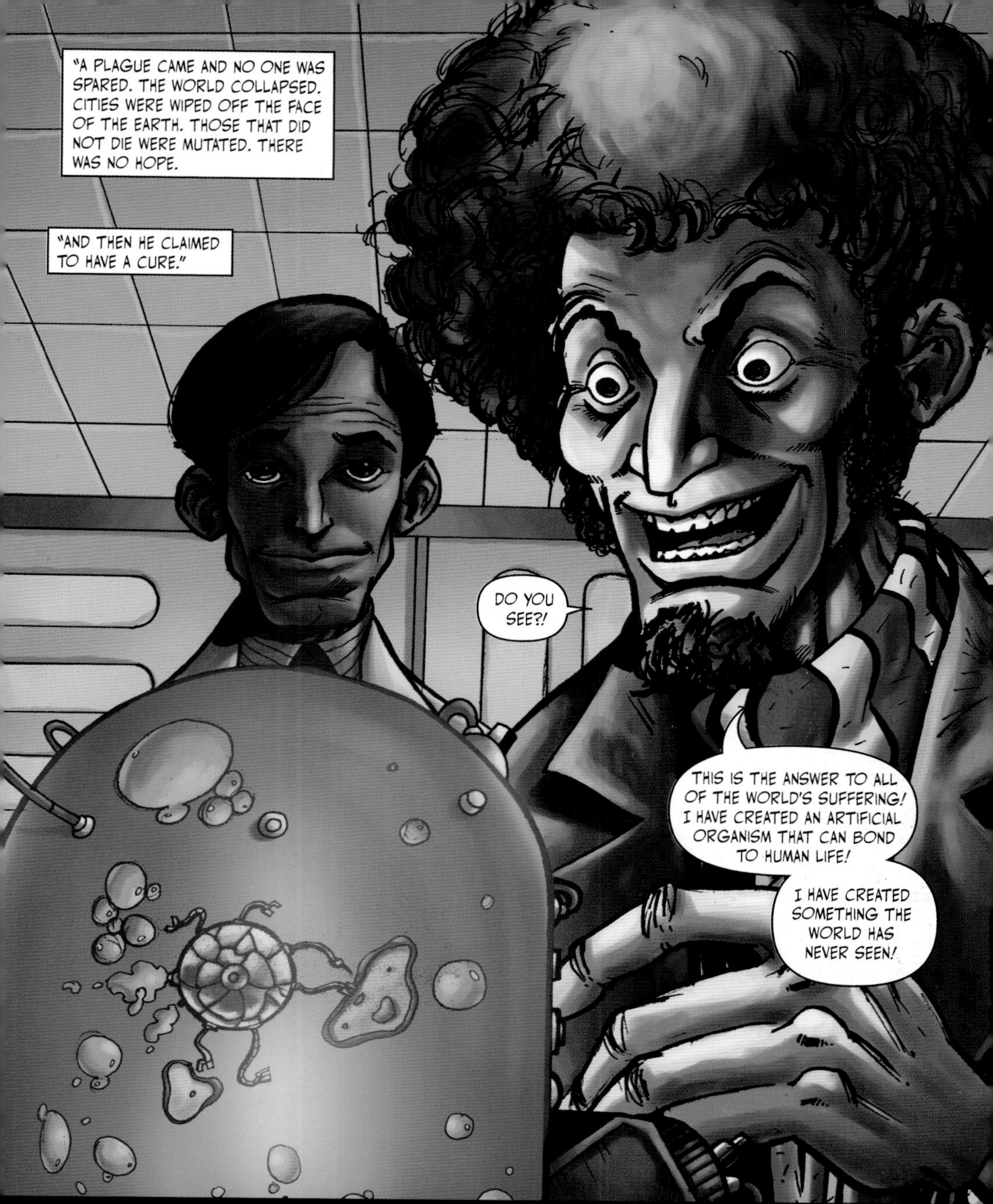
"A PLAGUE CAME AND NO ONE WAS SPARED. THE WORLD COLLAPSED. CITIES WERE WIPED OFF THE FACE OF THE EARTH. THOSE THAT DID NOT DIE WERE MUTATED. THERE WAS NO HOPE.
"AND THEN HE CLAIMED TO HAVE A CURE."
DO YOU SEE?!
THIS IS THE ANSWER TO ALL OF THE WORLD'S SUFFERING! I HAVE CREATED AN ARTIFICIAL ORGANISM THAT CAN BOND TO HUMAN LIFE!
I HAVE CREATED SOMETHING THE WORLD HAS NEVER SEEN!

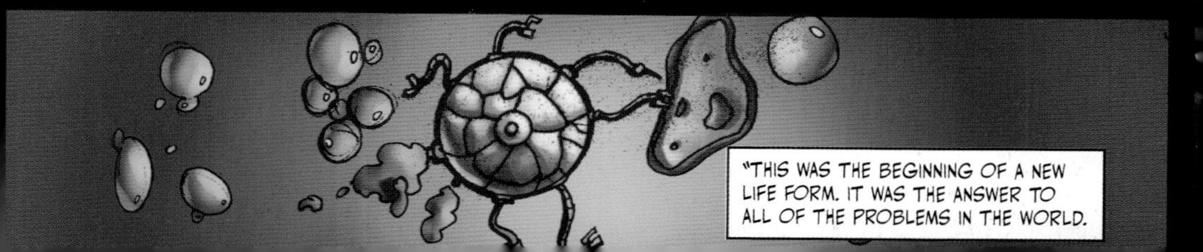
"THIS WAS THE BEGINNING OF A NEW LIFE FORM. IT WAS THE ANSWER TO ALL OF THE PROBLEMS IN THE WORLD.

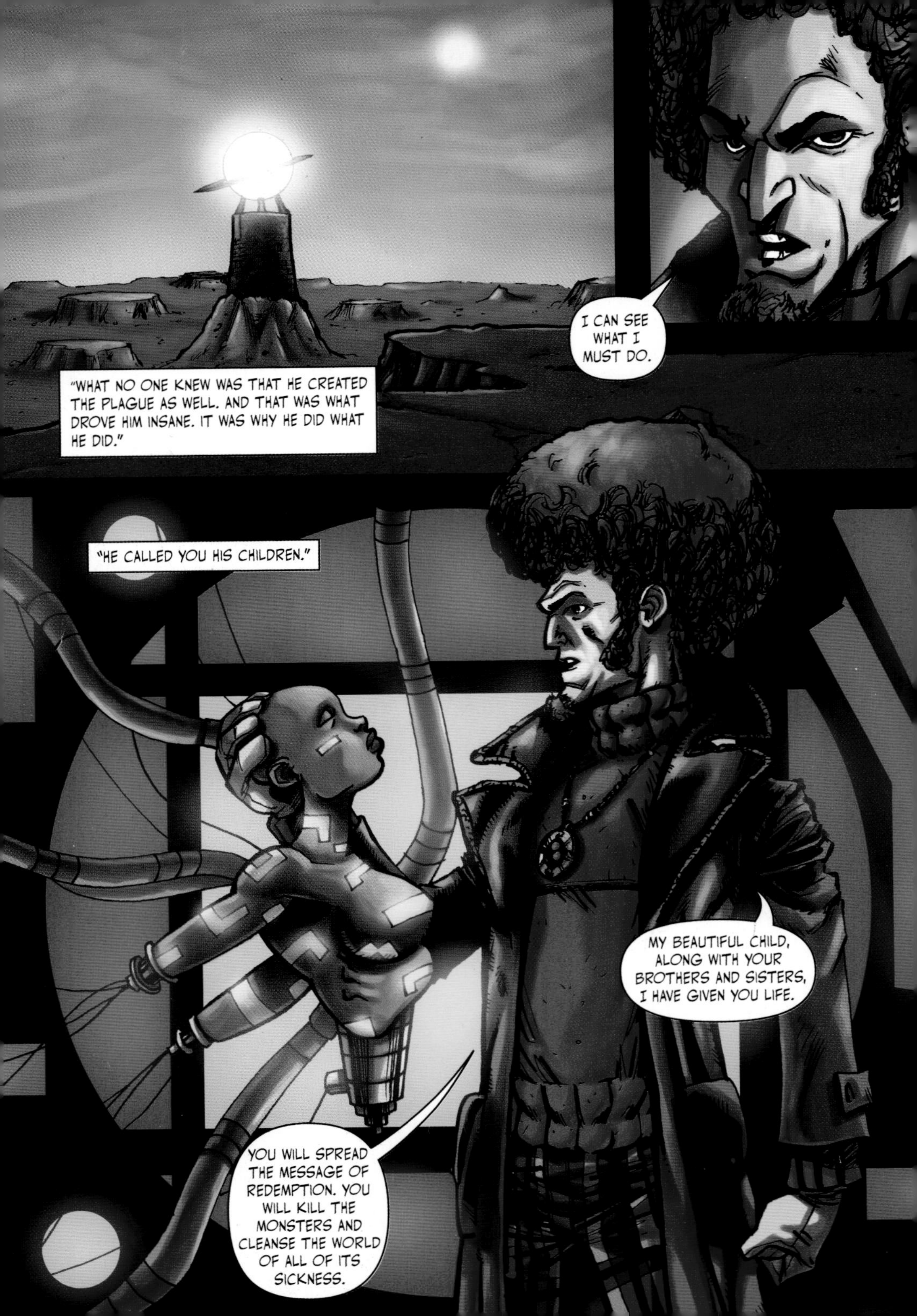
"WHAT NO ONE KNEW WAS THAT HE CREATED THE PLAGUE AS WELL. AND THAT WAS WHAT DROVE HIM INSANE. IT WAS WHY HE DID WHAT HE DID."
I CAN SEE WHAT I MUST DO.
"HE CALLED YOU HIS CHILDREN."
MY BEAUTIFUL CHILD, ALONG WITH YOUR BROTHERS AND SISTERS, I HAVE GIVEN YOU LIFE.
YOU WILL SPREAD THE MESSAGE OF REDEMPTION. YOU WILL KILL THE MONSTERS AND CLEANSE THE WORLD OF ALL OF ITS SICKNESS.

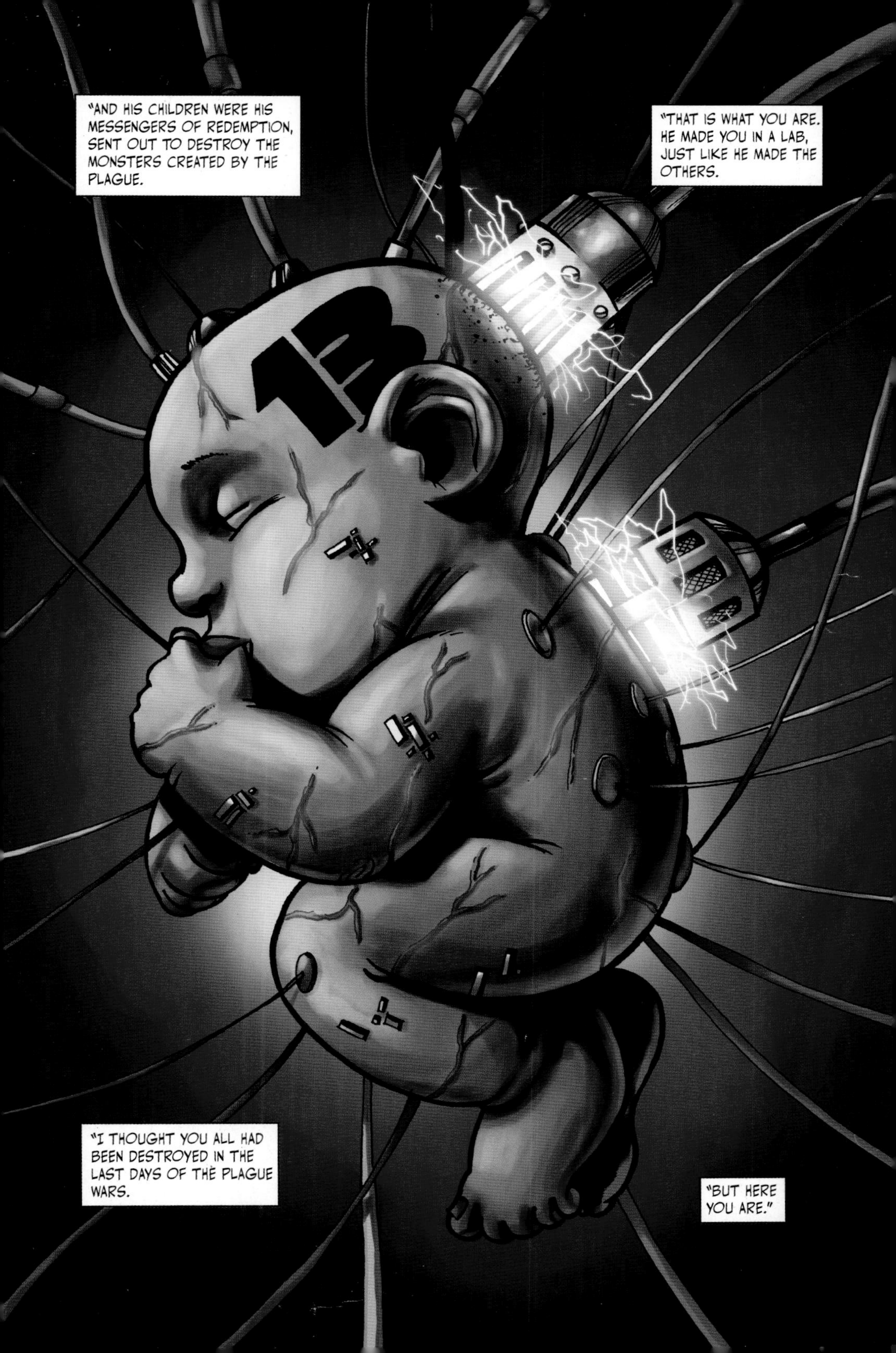
"AND HIS CHILDREN WERE HIS MESSENGERS OF REDEMPTION, SENT OUT TO DESTROY THE MONSTERS CREATED BY THE PLAGUE.
"THAT IS WHAT YOU ARE. HE MADE YOU IN A LAB, JUST LIKE HE MADE THE OTHERS.
13
"I THOUGHT YOU ALL HAD BEEN DESTROYED IN THE LAST DAYS OF THE PLAGUE WARS.
"BUT HERE YOU ARE."

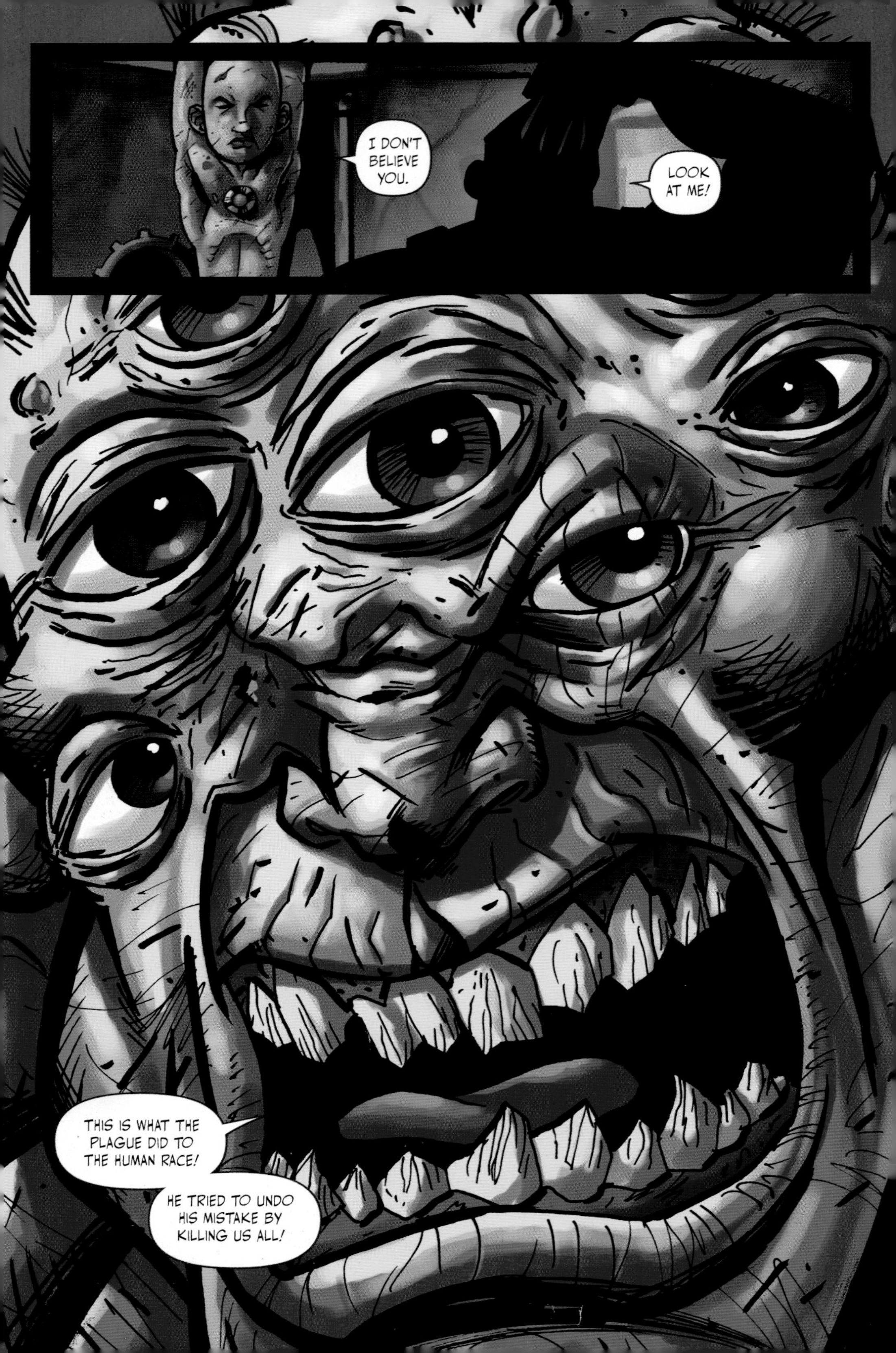
I DON'T BELIEVE YOU.
LOOK AT ME!
THIS IS WHAT THE PLAGUE DID TO THE HUMAN RACE!
HE TRIED TO UNDO HIS MISTAKE BY KILLING US ALL!

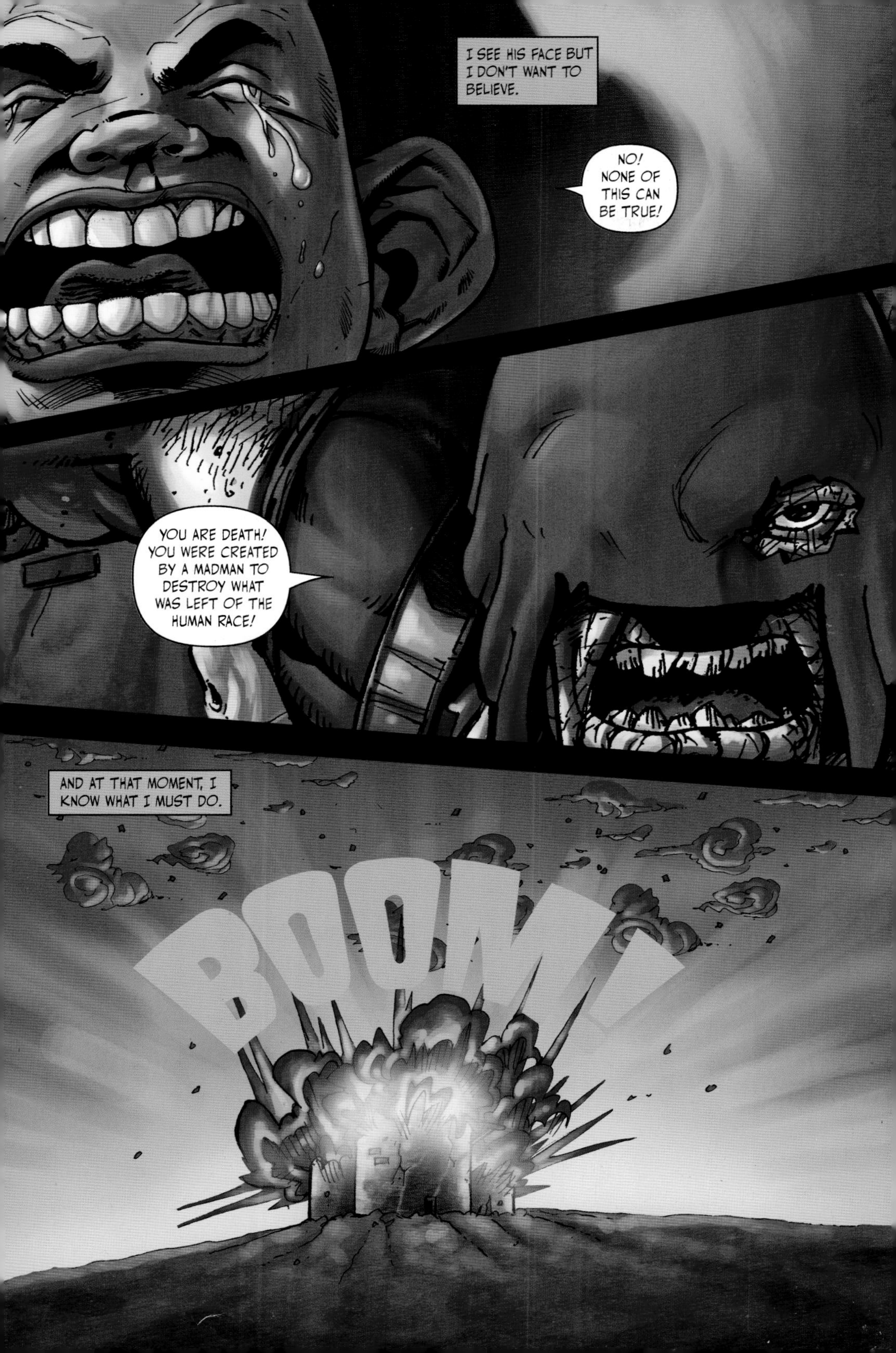
I SEE HIS FACE BUT I DON'T WANT TO BELIEVE.
NO! NONE OF THIS CAN BE TRUE!
YOU ARE DEATH! YOU WERE CREATED BY A MADMAN TO DESTROY WHAT WAS LEFT OF THE HUMAN RACE!
AND AT THAT MOMENT, I KNOW WHAT I MUST DO.
BOOM!

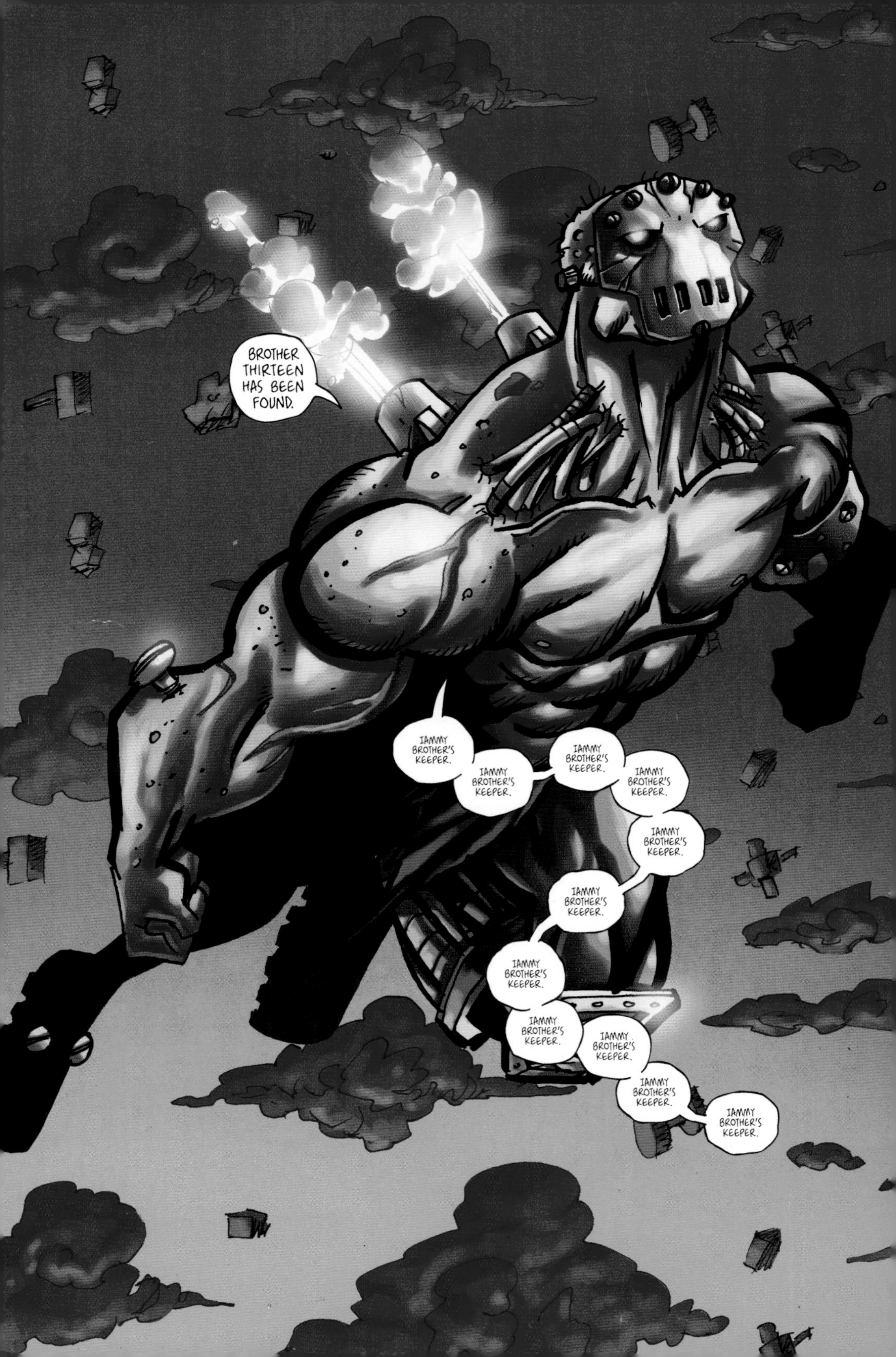
BROTHER THIRTEEN HAS BEEN FOUND.
IAMMY BROTHER'S KEEPER.
IAMMY BROTHER'S KEEPER.
IAMMY BROTHER'S KEEPER.
IAMMY BROTHER'S KEEPER.
IAMMY BROTHER'S KEEPER.
IAMMY BROTHER'S KEEPER.
IAMMY BROTHER'S KEEPER.
IAMMY BROTHER'S KEEPER.
IAMMY BROTHER'S KEEPER.
IAMMY BROTHER'S KEEPER.
IAMMY BROTHER'S KEEPER.

THE END IS THE BEGINNING

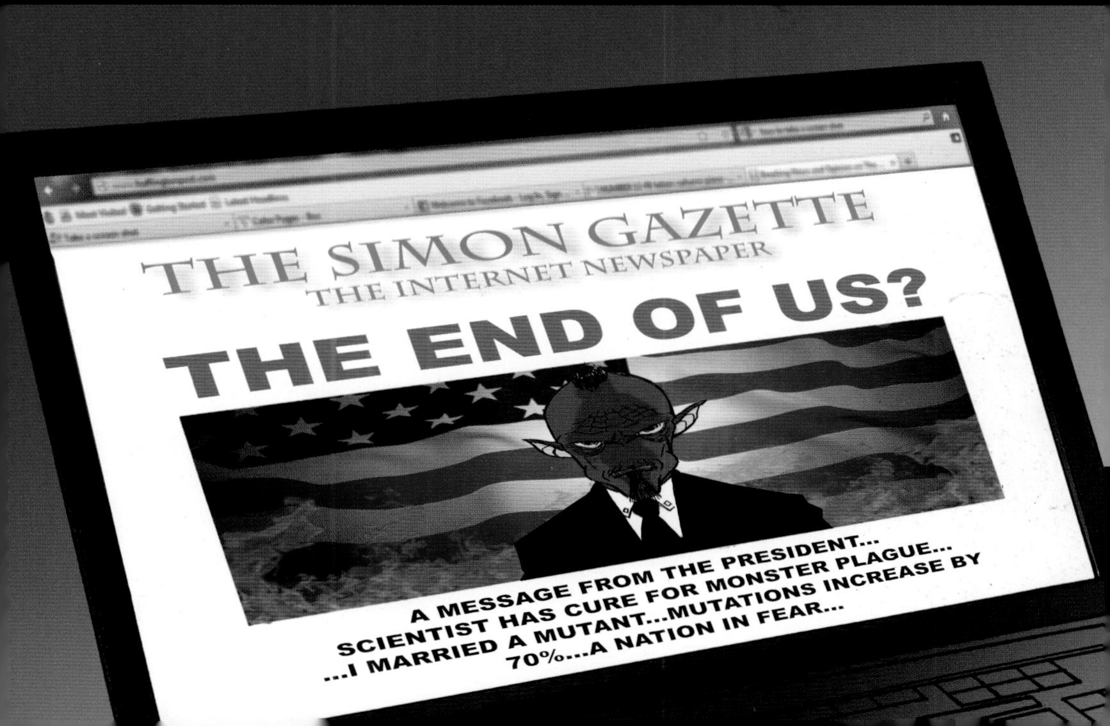
THE SIMON GAZETTE
THE INTERNET NEWSPAPER
THE END OF US?
A MESSAGE FROM THE PRESIDENT...
SCIENTIST HAS CURE FOR MONSTER PLAGUE...
...I MARRIED A MUTANT...MUTATIONS INCREASE BY 70%...A NATION IN FEAR...

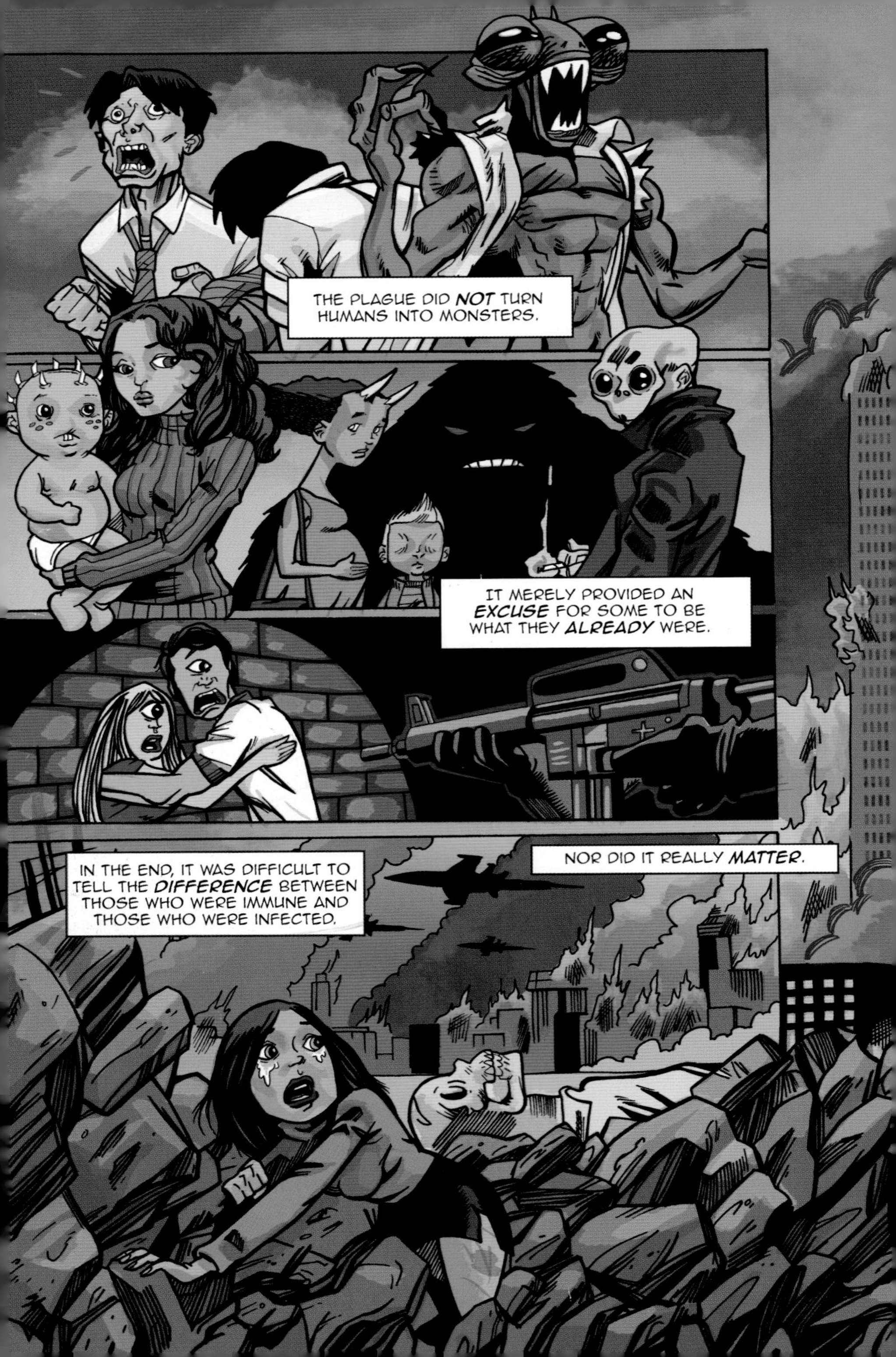
THE PLAGUE DID NOT TURN HUMANS INTO MONSTERS.
IT MERELY PROVIDED AN EXCUSE FOR SOME TO BE WHAT THEY ALREADY WERE.
IN THE END, IT WAS DIFFICULT TO TELL THE DIFFERENCE BETWEEN THOSE WHO WERE IMMUNE AND THOSE WHO WERE INFECTED.
NOR DID IT REALLY MATTER.

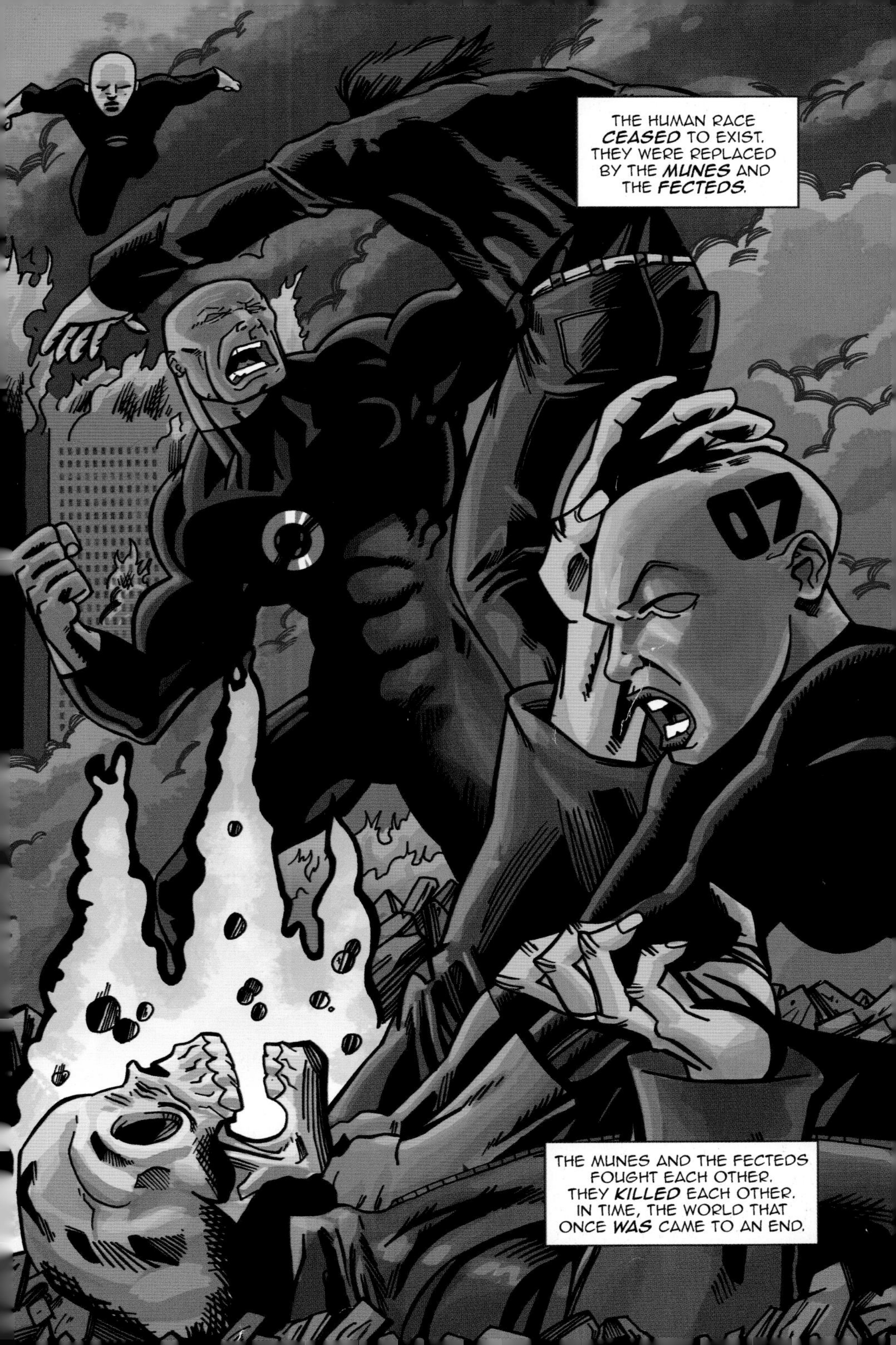
THE HUMAN RACE *CEASED* TO EXIST. THEY WERE REPLACED BY THE *MUNES* AND THE *FECTEDS*.
THE MUNES AND THE FECTEDS FOUGHT EACH OTHER. THEY *KILLED* EACH OTHER. IN TIME, THE WORLD THAT ONCE *WAS* CAME TO AN END.

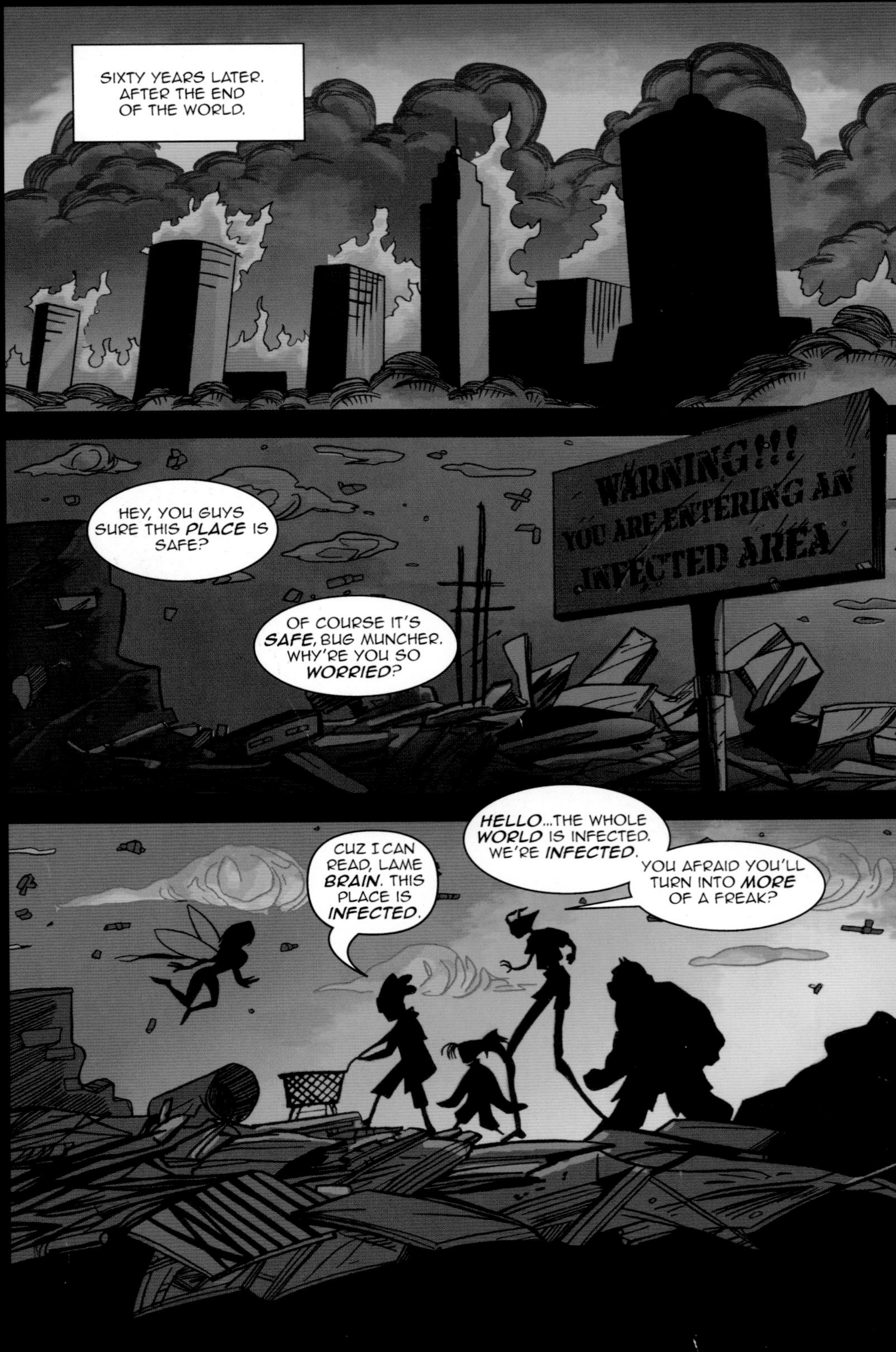
SIXTY YEARS LATER. AFTER THE END OF THE WORLD.
HEY, YOU GUYS SURE THIS PLACE IS SAFE?
WARNING!!! YOU ARE ENTERING AN INFECTED AREA
OF COURSE IT'S SAFE, BUG MUNCHER. WHY'RE YOU SO WORRIED?
CUZ I CAN READ, LAME BRAIN. THIS PLACE IS INFECTED.
HELLO...THE WHOLE WORLD IS INFECTED. WE'RE INFECTED.
YOU AFRAID YOU'LL TURN INTO MORE OF A FREAK?

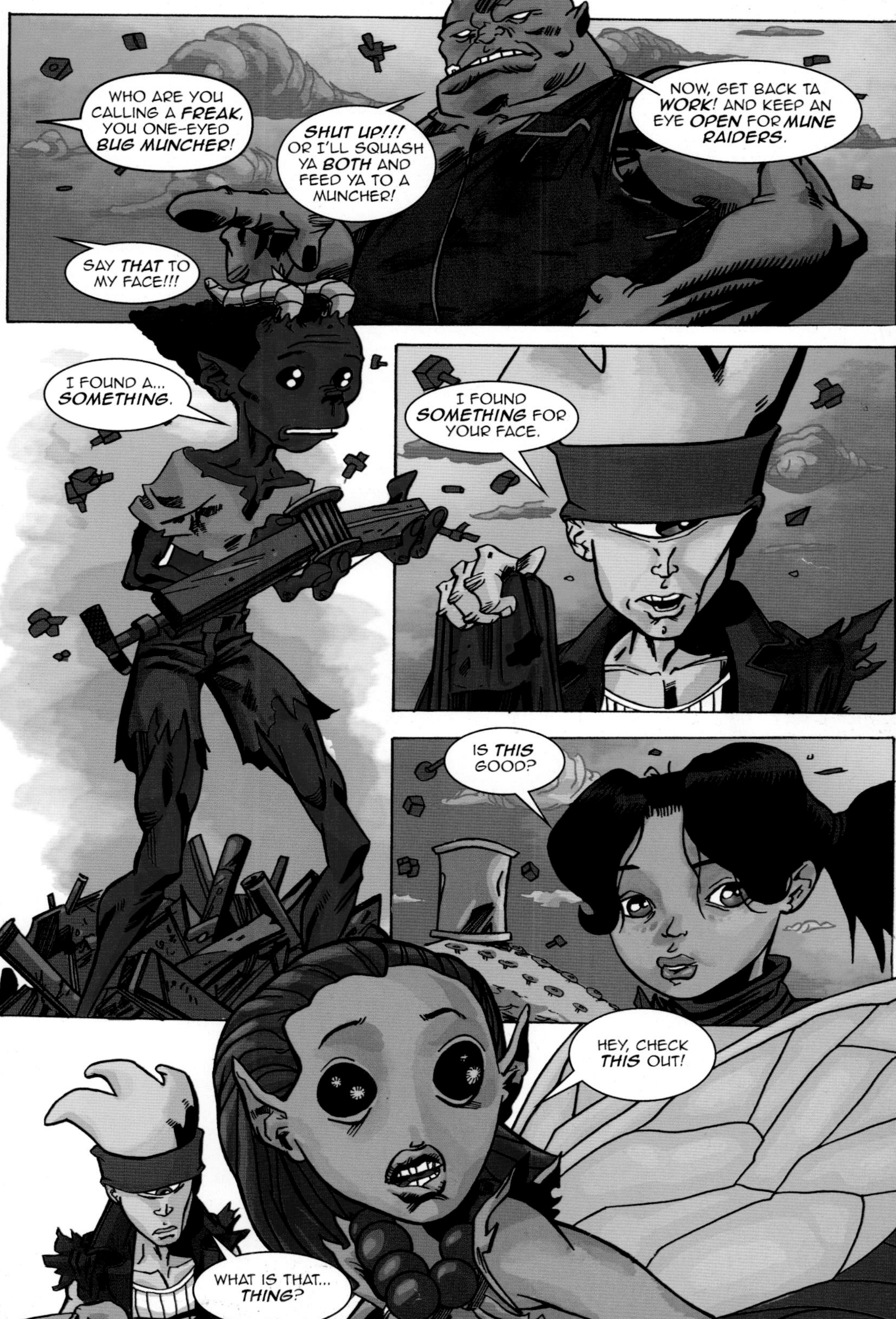
WHO ARE YOU CALLING A FREAK, YOU ONE-EYED BUG MUNCHER!
SHUT UP!!! OR I'LL SQUASH YA BOTH AND FEED YA TO A MUNCHER!
NOW, GET BACK TA WORK! AND KEEP AN EYE OPEN FOR MUNE RAIDERS.
SAY THAT TO MY FACE!!!
I FOUND A... SOMETHING.
I FOUND SOMETHING FOR YOUR FACE.
IS THIS GOOD?
HEY, CHECK THIS OUT!
WHAT IS THAT... THING?

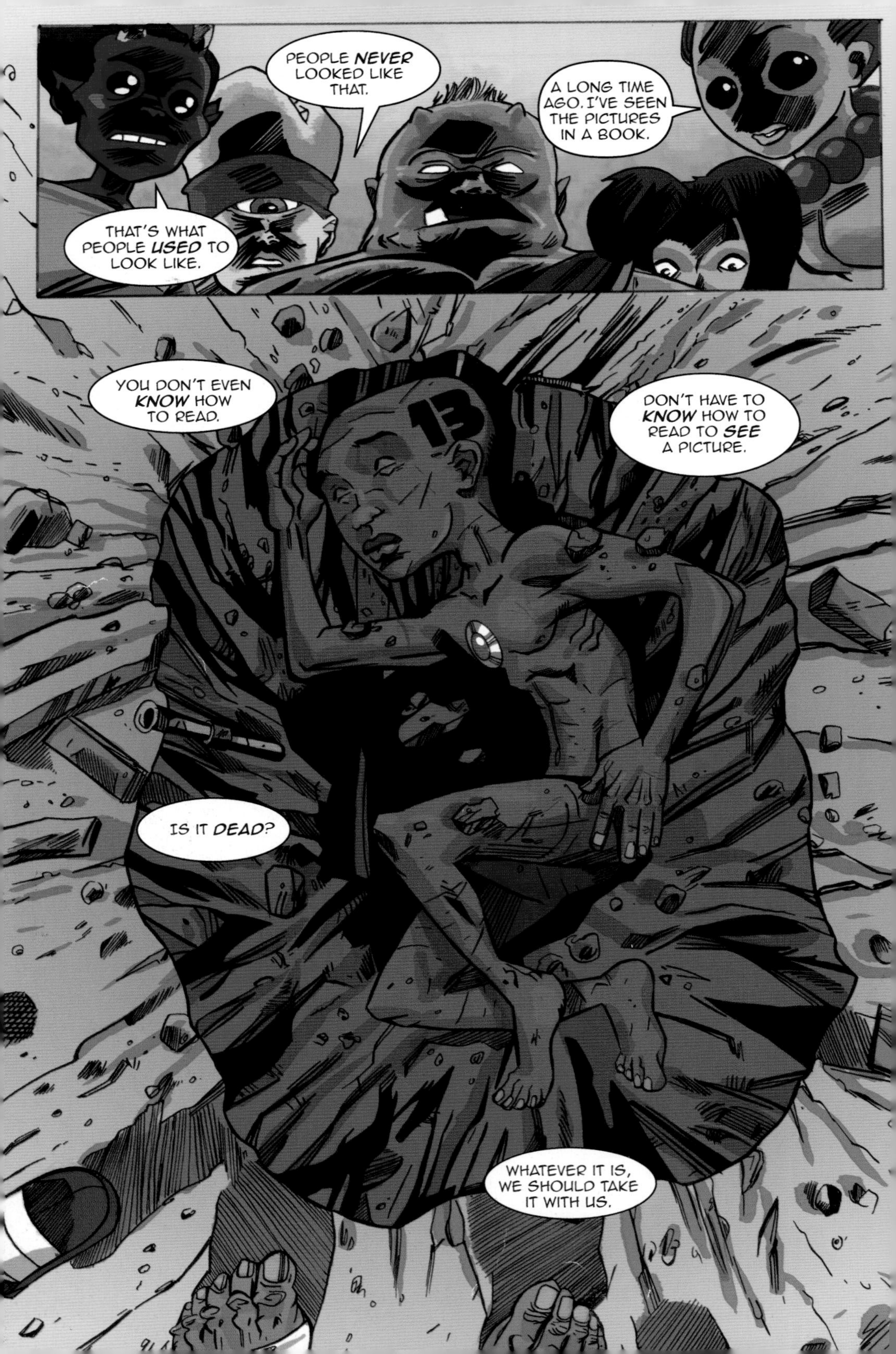
PEOPLE **NEVER** LOOKED LIKE THAT.
A LONG TIME AGO. I'VE SEEN THE PICTURES IN A BOOK.
THAT'S WHAT PEOPLE **USED** TO LOOK LIKE.
YOU DON'T EVEN **KNOW** HOW TO READ.
DON'T HAVE TO **KNOW** HOW TO READ TO **SEE** A PICTURE.
IS IT **DEAD**?
WHATEVER IT IS, WE SHOULD TAKE IT WITH US.

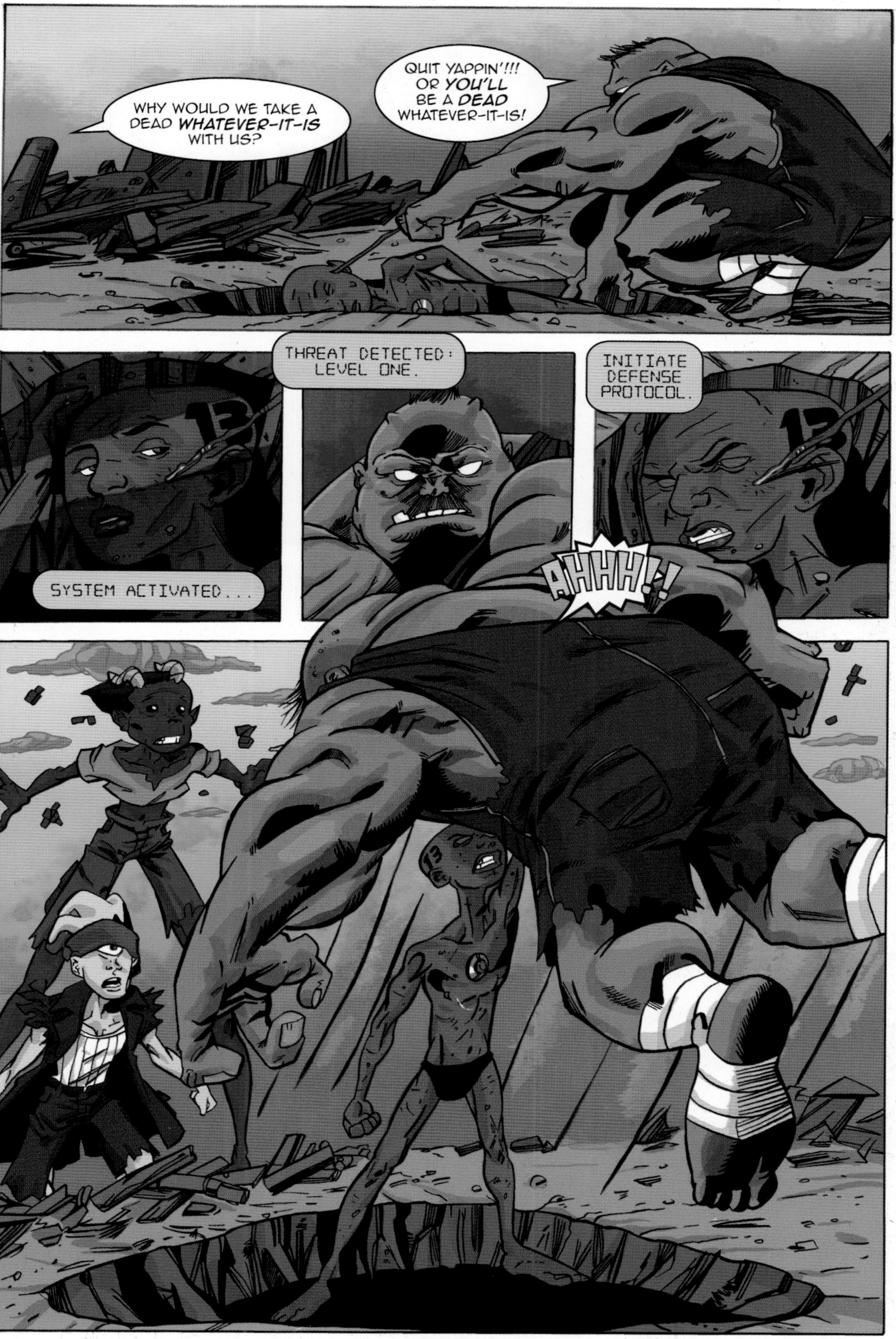
WHY WOULD WE TAKE A DEAD WHATEVER-IT-IS WITH US?
QUIT YAPPIN'!!! OR YOU'LL BE A DEAD WHATEVER-IT-IS!
SYSTEM ACTIVATED...
THREAT DETECTED: LEVEL ONE.
INITIATE DEFENSE PROTOCOL.
AHHH!!

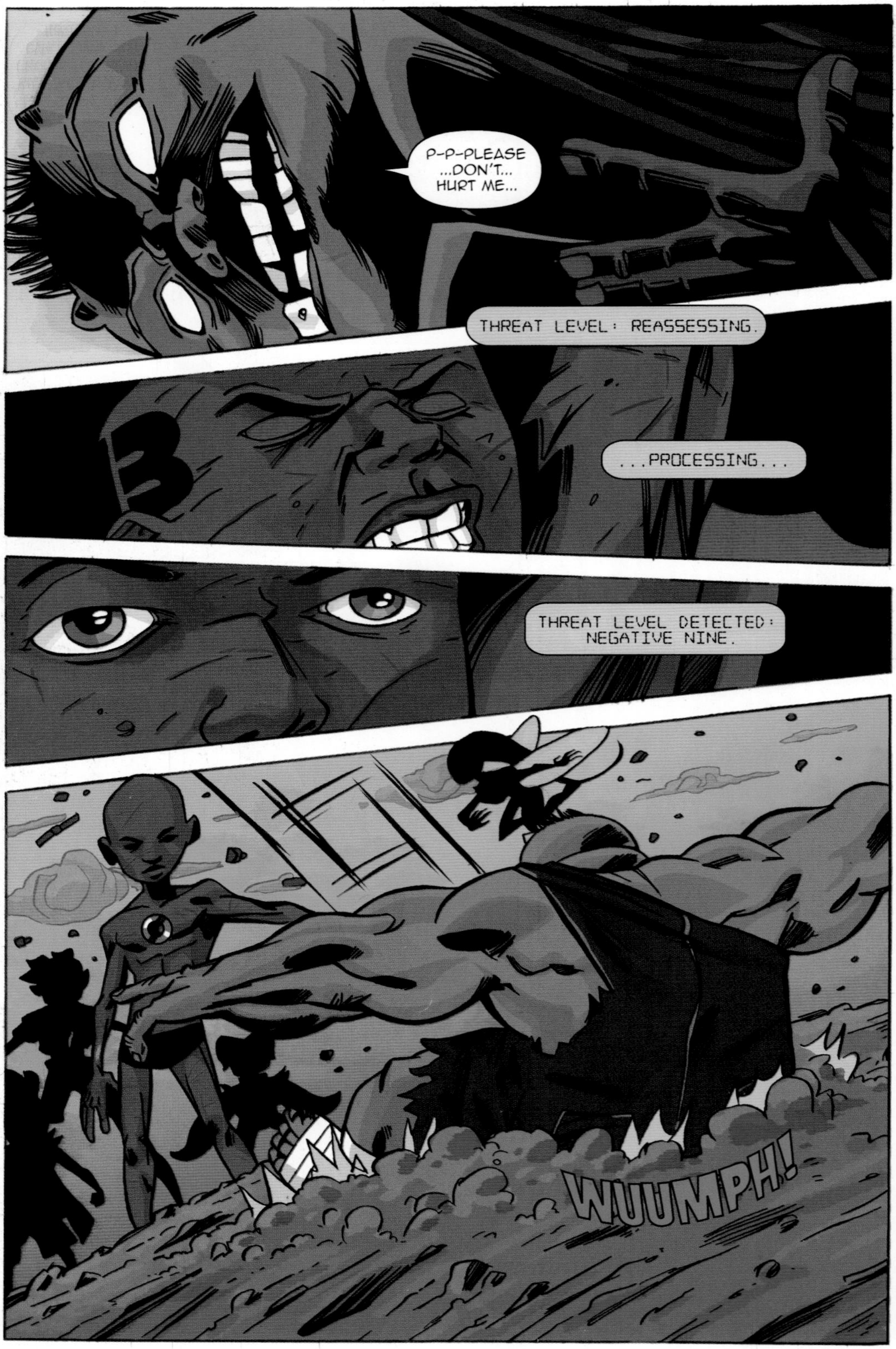
P-P-PLEASE ...DON'T... HURT ME...
THREAT LEVEL: REASSESSING.
...PROCESSING...
THREAT LEVEL DETECTED: NEGATIVE NINE.
WUUMPH!

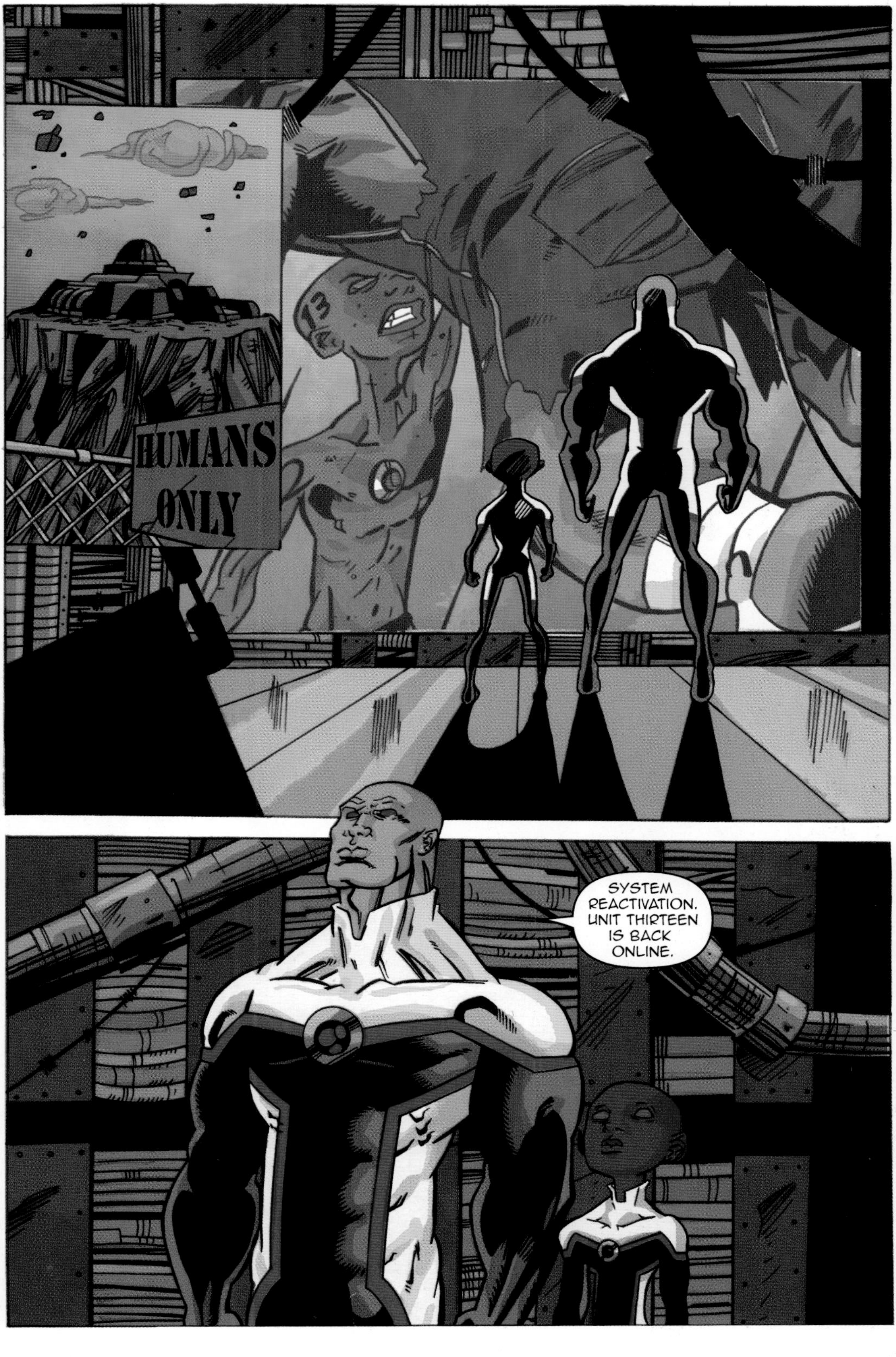
HUMANS ONLY
SYSTEM REACTIVATION. UNIT THIRTEEN IS BACK ONLINE.

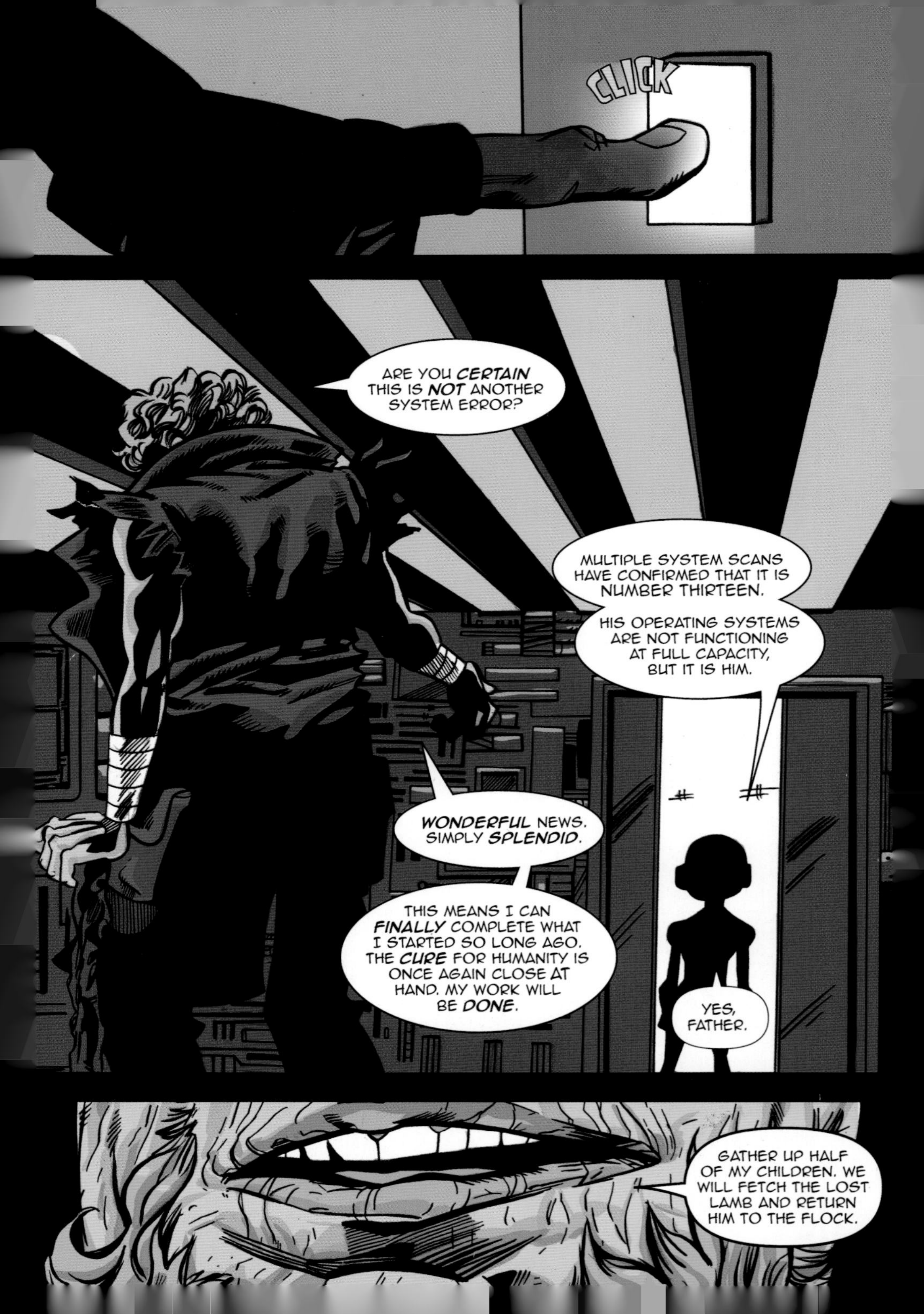
CLICK
ARE YOU CERTAIN THIS IS NOT ANOTHER SYSTEM ERROR?
MULTIPLE SYSTEM SCANS HAVE CONFIRMED THAT IT IS NUMBER THIRTEEN.
HIS OPERATING SYSTEMS ARE NOT FUNCTIONING AT FULL CAPACITY, BUT IT IS HIM.
WONDERFUL NEWS. SIMPLY SPLENDID.
THIS MEANS I CAN FINALLY COMPLETE WHAT I STARTED SO LONG AGO. THE CURE FOR HUMANITY IS ONCE AGAIN CLOSE AT HAND. MY WORK WILL BE DONE.
YES, FATHER.
GATHER UP HALF OF MY CHILDREN. WE WILL FETCH THE LOST LAMB AND RETURN HIM TO THE FLOCK.

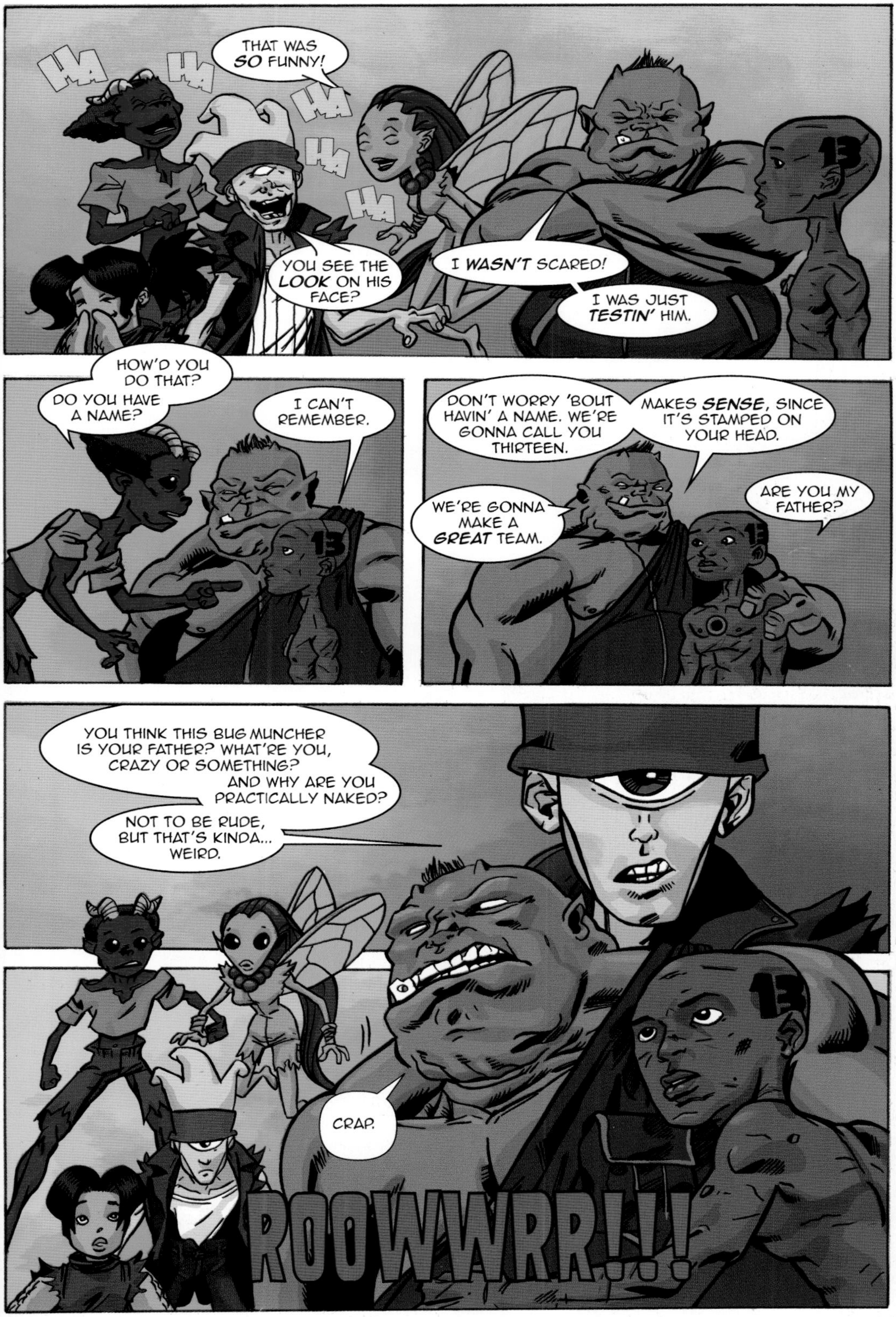
HA
HA
THAT WAS SO FUNNY!
HA
HA
HA
YOU SEE THE LOOK ON HIS FACE?
I WASN'T SCARED!
I WAS JUST TESTIN' HIM.
HOW'D YOU DO THAT?
DO YOU HAVE A NAME?
I CAN'T REMEMBER.
DON'T WORRY 'BOUT HAVIN' A NAME. WE'RE GONNA CALL YOU THIRTEEN.
MAKES SENSE, SINCE IT'S STAMPED ON YOUR HEAD.
WE'RE GONNA MAKE A GREAT TEAM.
ARE YOU MY FATHER?
YOU THINK THIS BUG MUNCHER IS YOUR FATHER? WHAT'RE YOU, CRAZY OR SOMETHING?
AND WHY ARE YOU PRACTICALLY NAKED?
NOT TO BE RUDE, BUT THAT'S KINDA... WEIRD.
CRAP.
ROOWWRR!!!

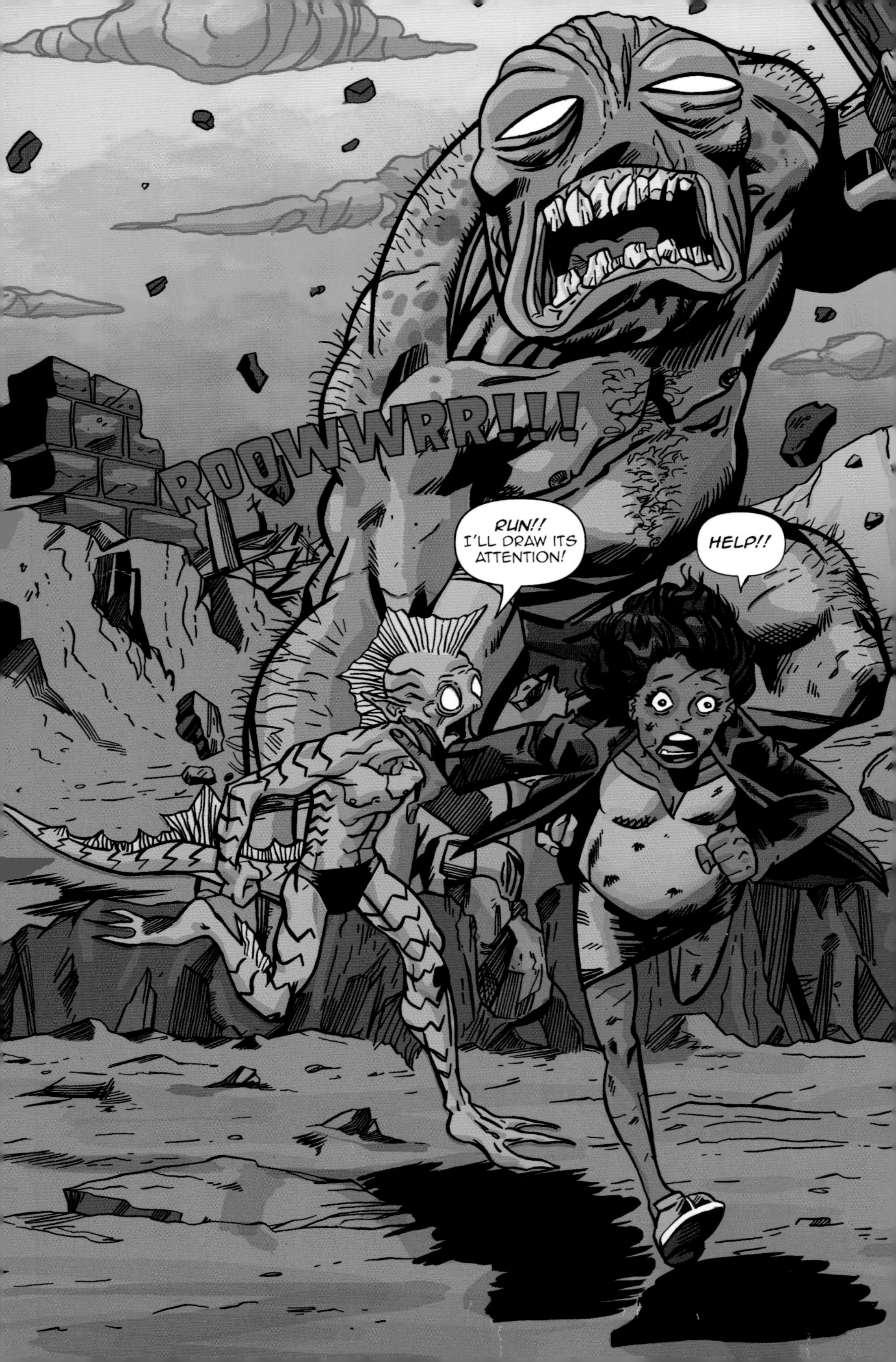
ROOOWWRR!!!
RUN!! I'LL DRAW ITS ATTENTION!
HELP!!

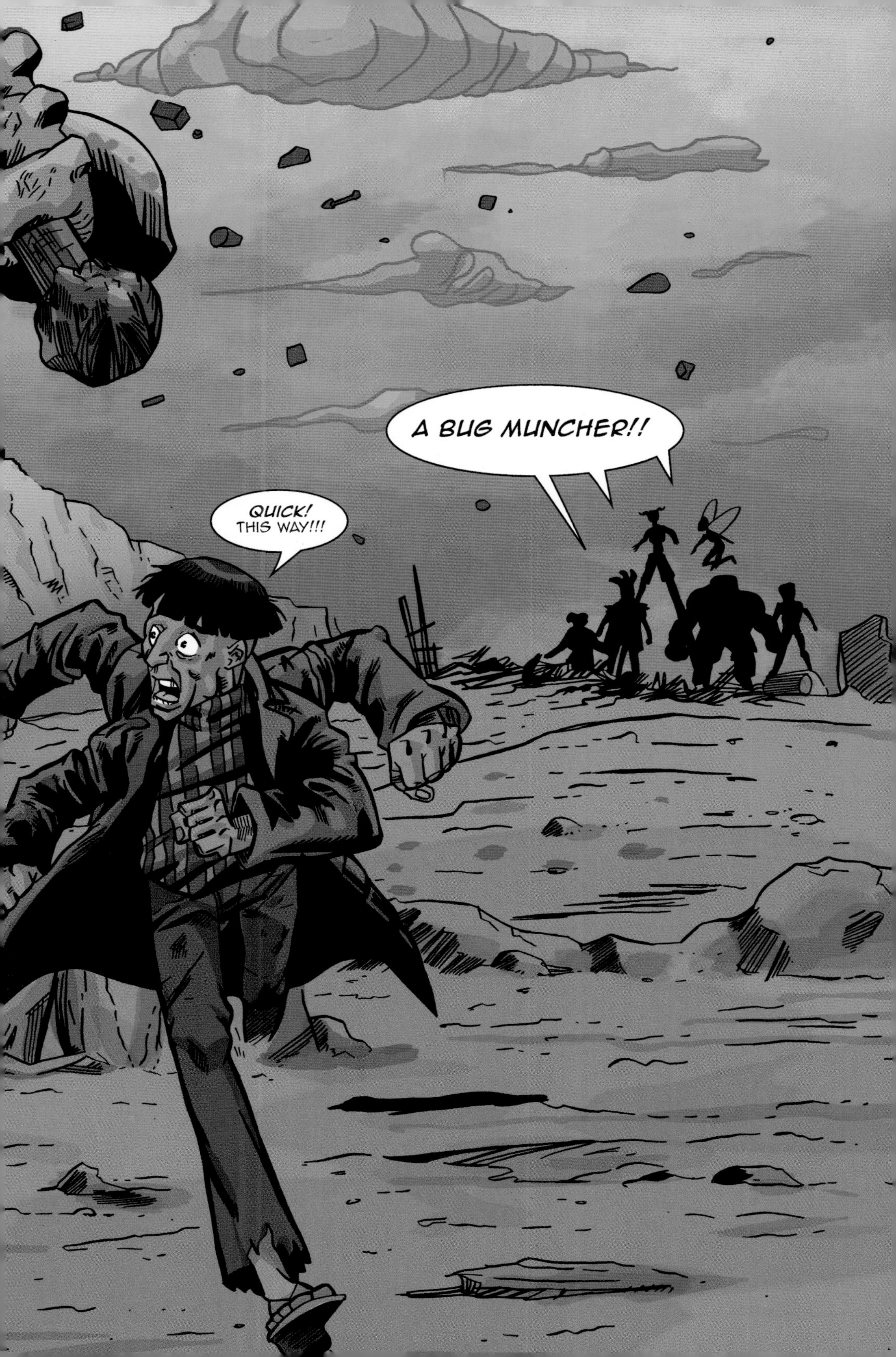
A BUG MUNCHER!!
QUICK! THIS WAY!!!

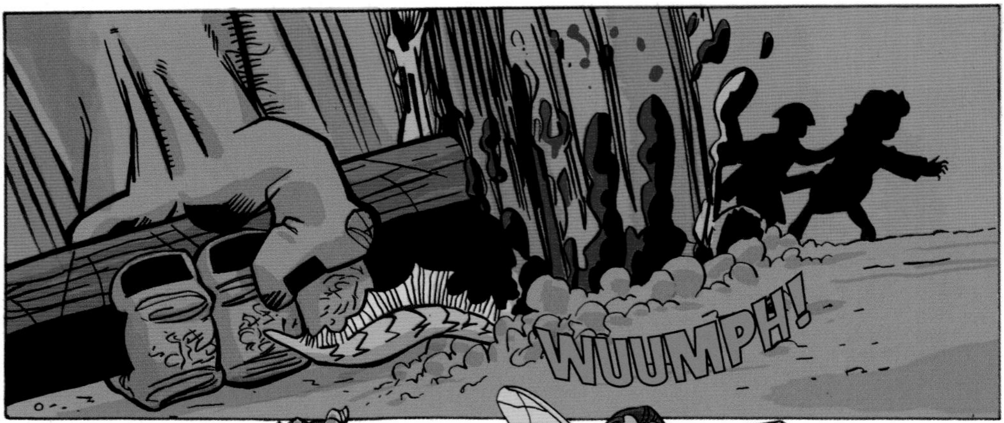
WUUMPH!
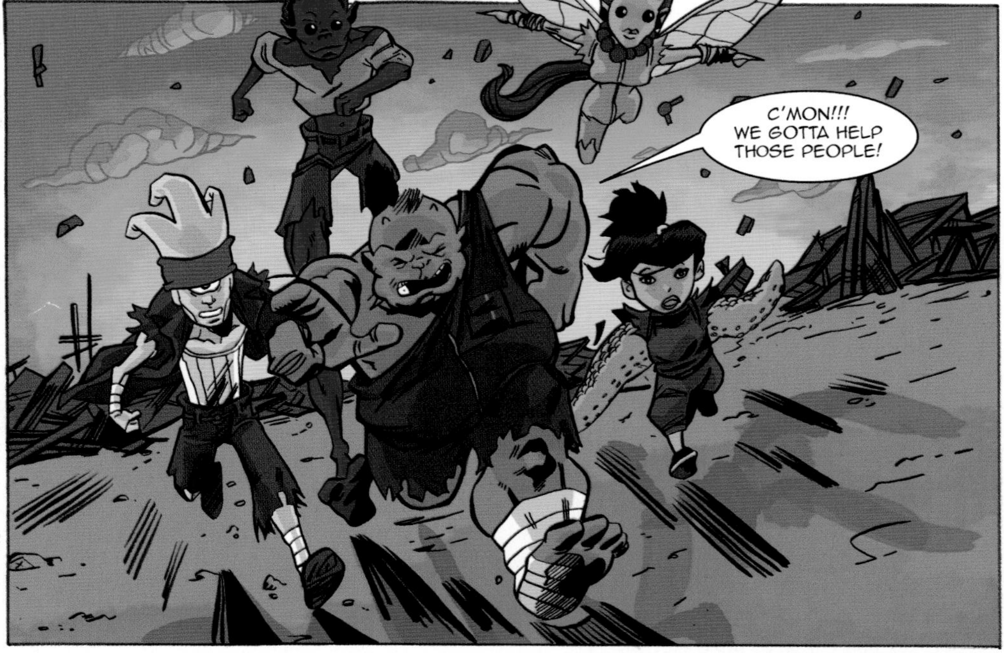
C'MON!!!
WE GOTTA HELP
THOSE PEOPLE!
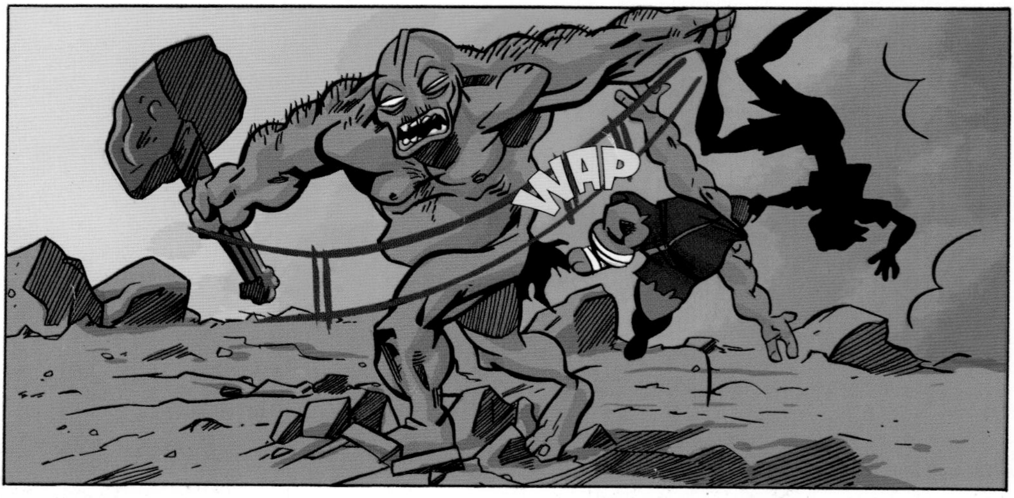
WAP

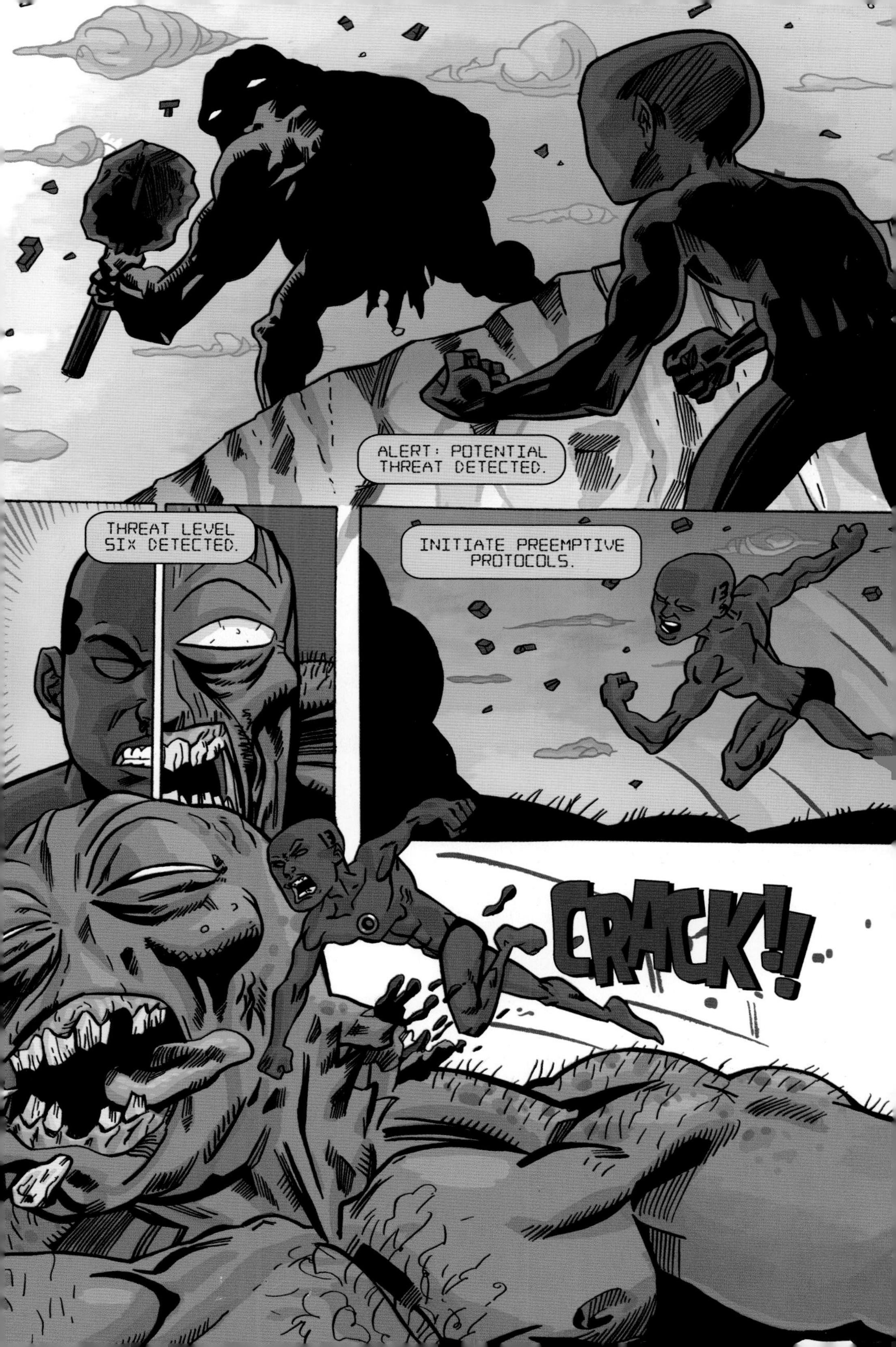
ALERT: POTENTIAL THREAT DETECTED.
THREAT LEVEL SIX DETECTED.
INITIATE PREEMPTIVE PROTOCOLS.
CRACK!!

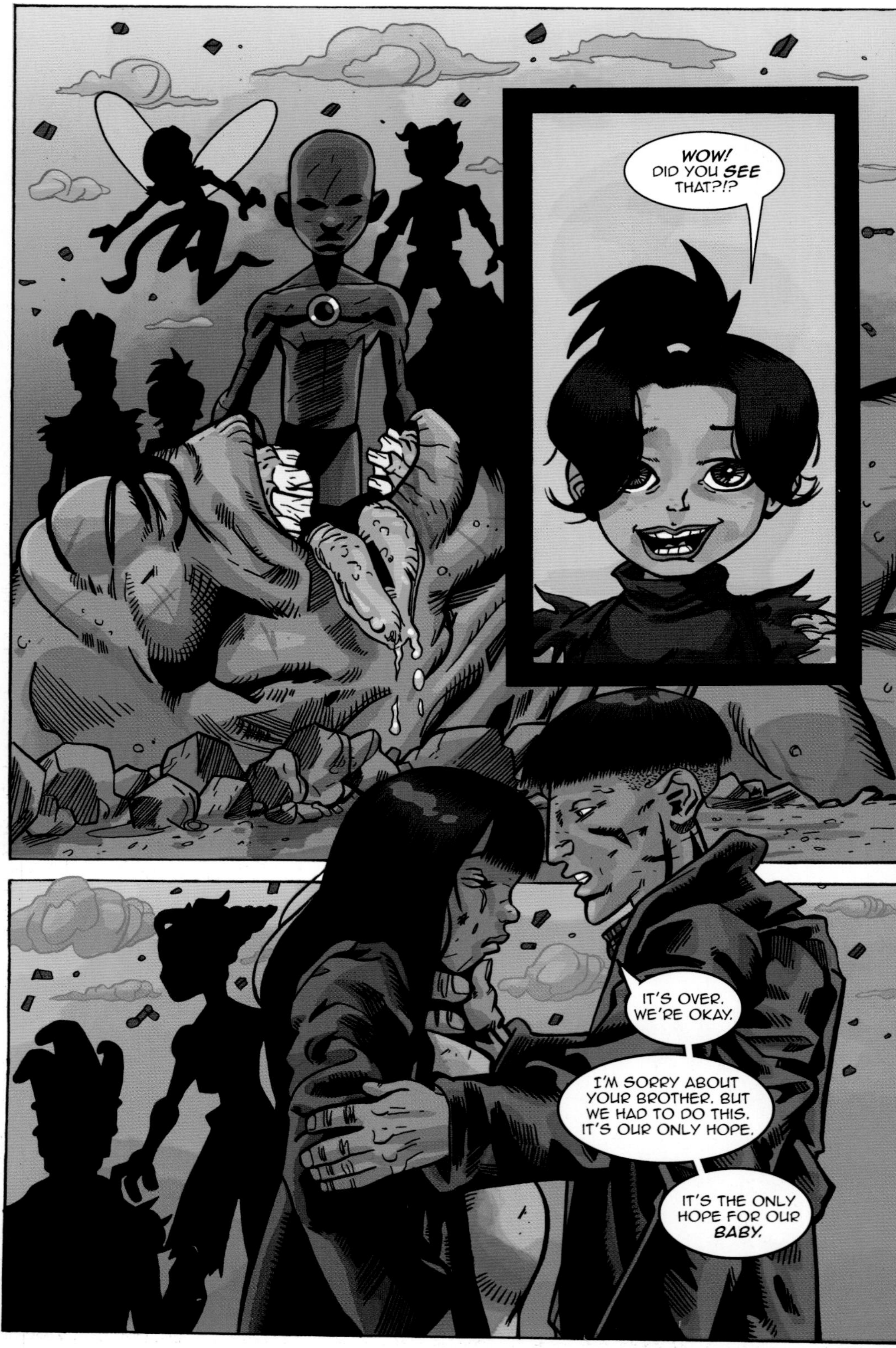
WOW! DID YOU SEE THAT?!?
IT'S OVER. WE'RE OKAY.
I'M SORRY ABOUT YOUR BROTHER. BUT WE HAD TO DO THIS. IT'S OUR ONLY HOPE.
IT'S THE ONLY HOPE FOR OUR BABY.

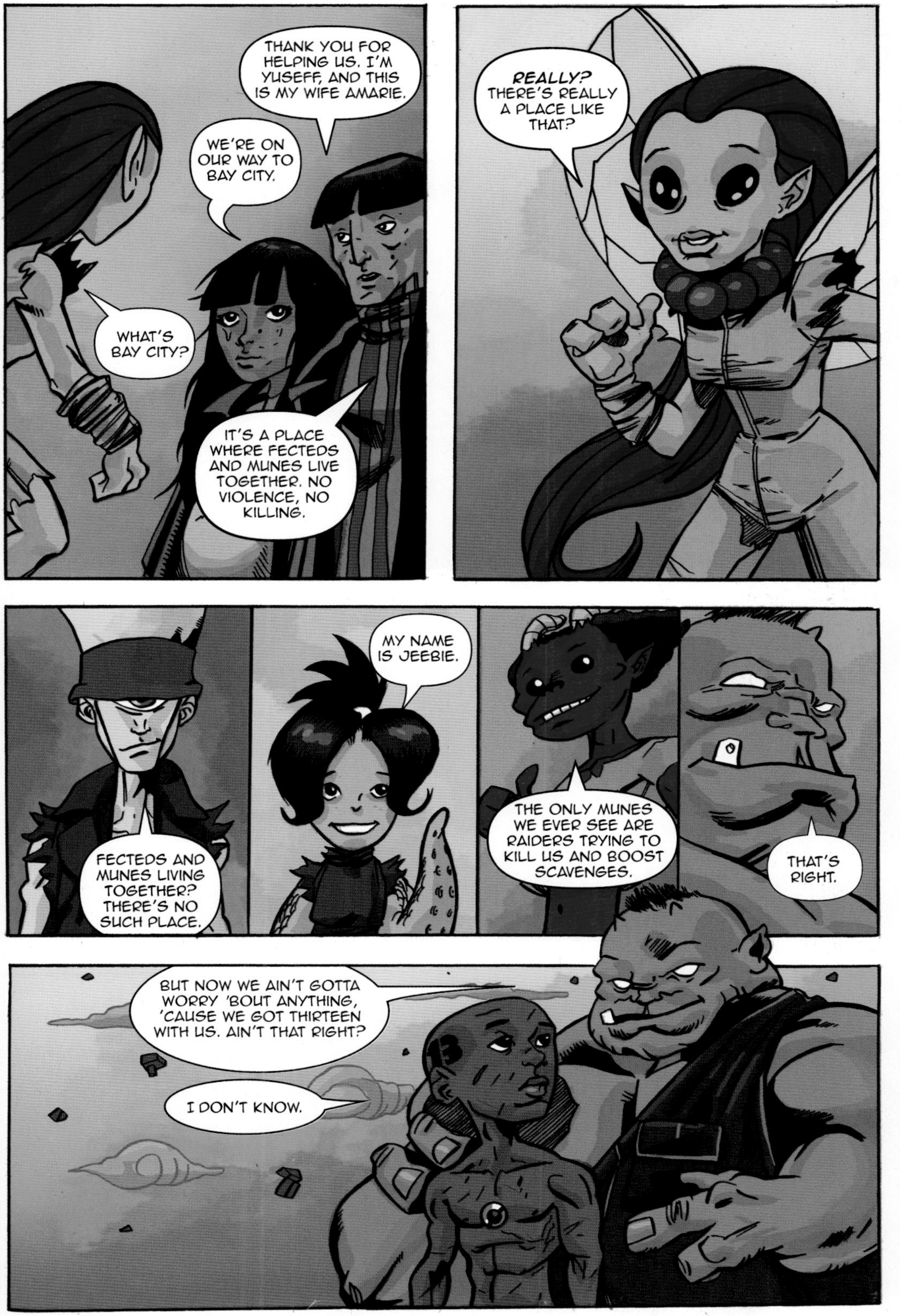

THANK YOU FOR HELPING US. I'M YUSEFF, AND THIS IS MY WIFE AMARIE.
WE'RE ON OUR WAY TO BAY CITY.
WHAT'S BAY CITY?
IT'S A PLACE WHERE FECTEDS AND MUNES LIVE TOGETHER. NO VIOLENCE, NO KILLING.
REALLY? THERE'S REALLY A PLACE LIKE THAT?
FECTEDS AND MUNES LIVING TOGETHER? THERE'S NO SUCH PLACE.
MY NAME IS JEEBIE.
THE ONLY MUNES WE EVER SEE ARE RAIDERS TRYING TO KILL US AND BOOST SCAVENGES.
THAT'S RIGHT.
BUT NOW WE AIN'T GOTTA WORRY 'BOUT ANYTHING, 'CAUSE WE GOT THIRTEEN WITH US. AIN'T THAT RIGHT?
I DON'T KNOW.

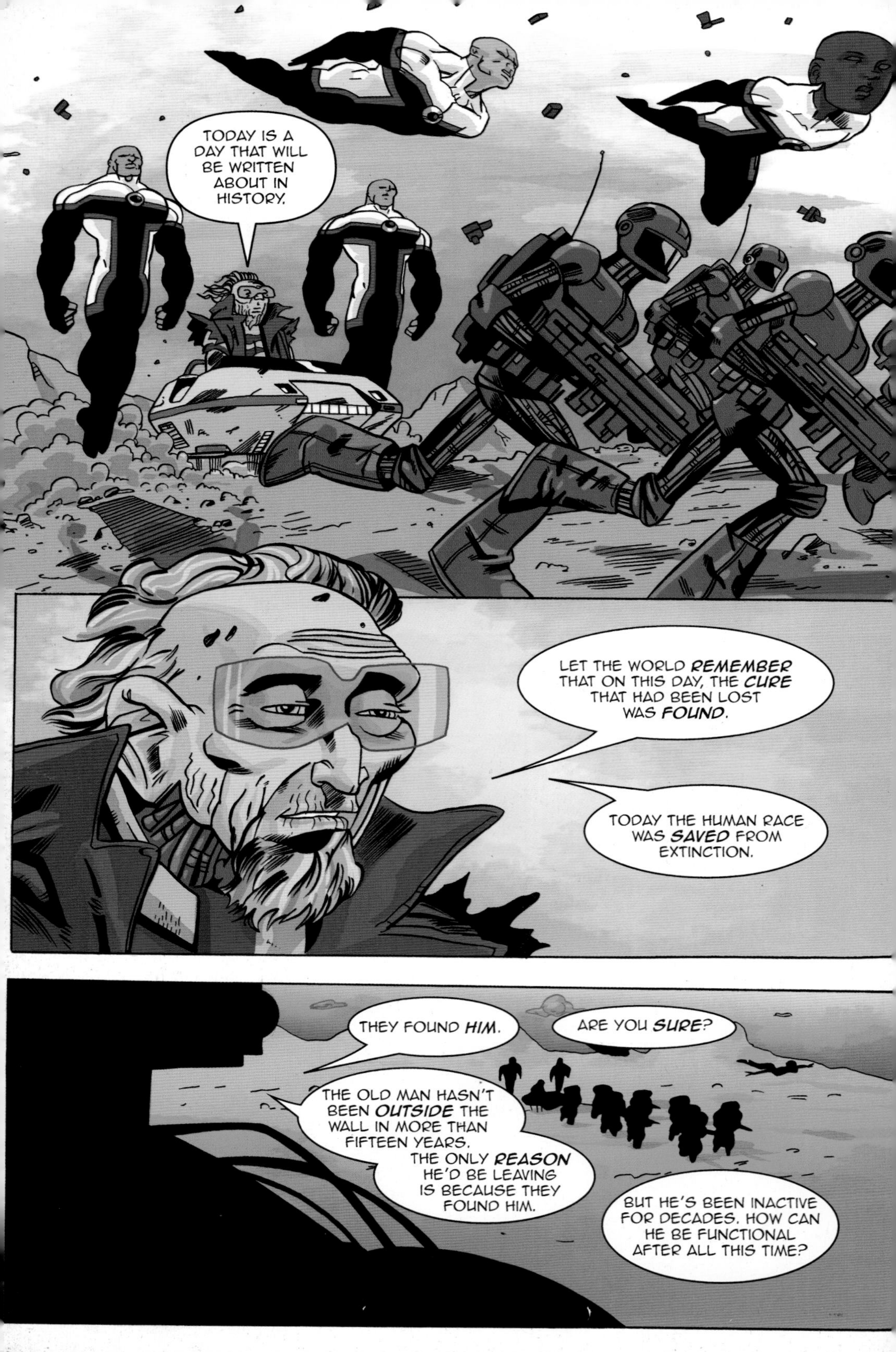
TODAY IS A DAY THAT WILL BE WRITTEN ABOUT IN HISTORY.
LET THE WORLD REMEMBER THAT ON THIS DAY, THE CURE THAT HAD BEEN LOST WAS FOUND.
TODAY THE HUMAN RACE WAS SAVED FROM EXTINCTION.
THEY FOUND HIM.
ARE YOU SURE?
THE OLD MAN HASN'T BEEN OUTSIDE THE WALL IN MORE THAN FIFTEEN YEARS.
THE ONLY REASON HE'D BE LEAVING IS BECAUSE THEY FOUND HIM.
BUT HE'S BEEN INACTIVE FOR DECADES. HOW CAN HE BE FUNCTIONAL AFTER ALL THIS TIME?

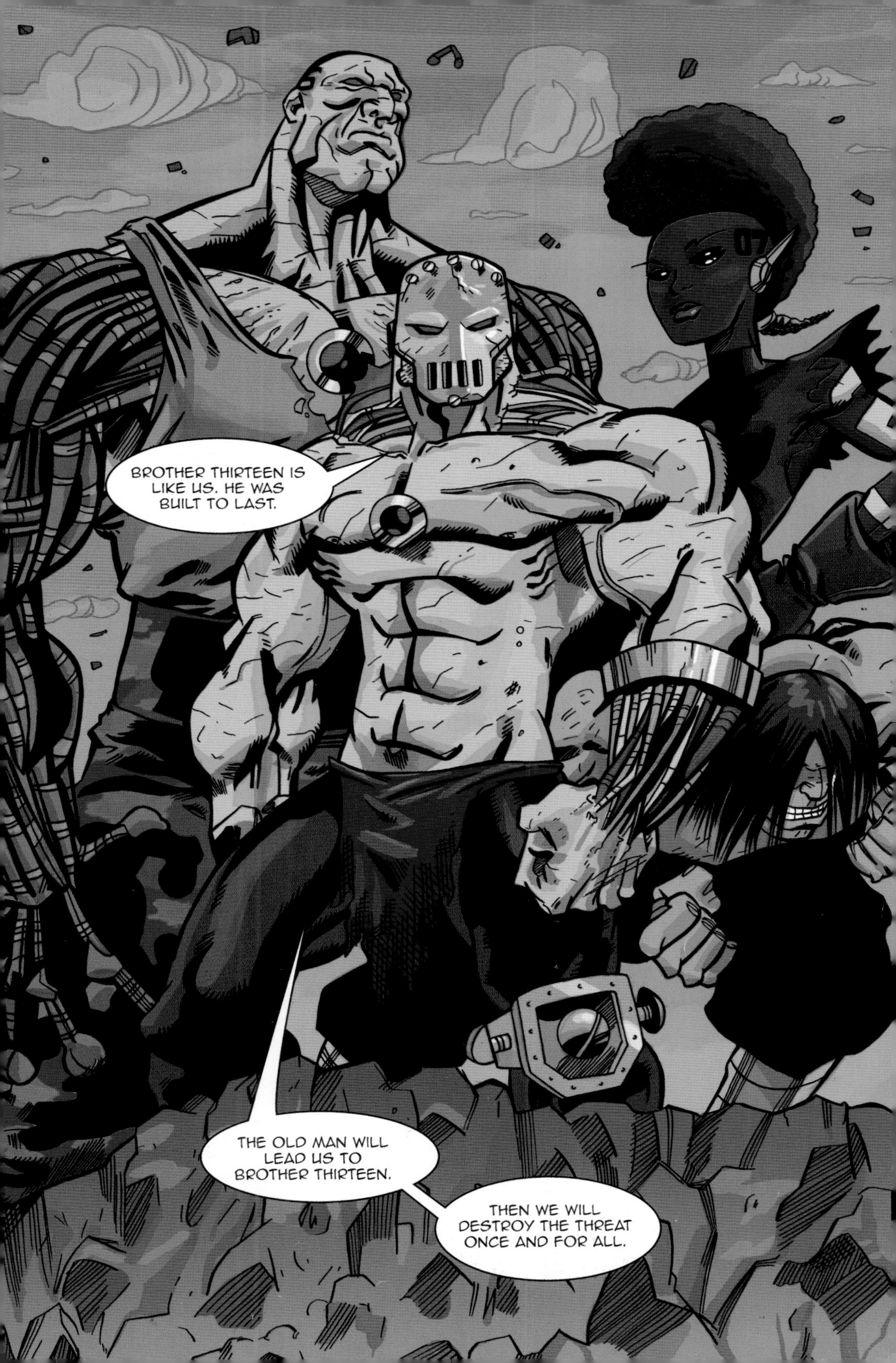
BROTHER THIRTEEN IS LIKE US. HE WAS BUILT TO LAST.
THE OLD MAN WILL LEAD US TO BROTHER THIRTEEN.
THEN WE WILL DESTROY THE THREAT ONCE AND FOR ALL.

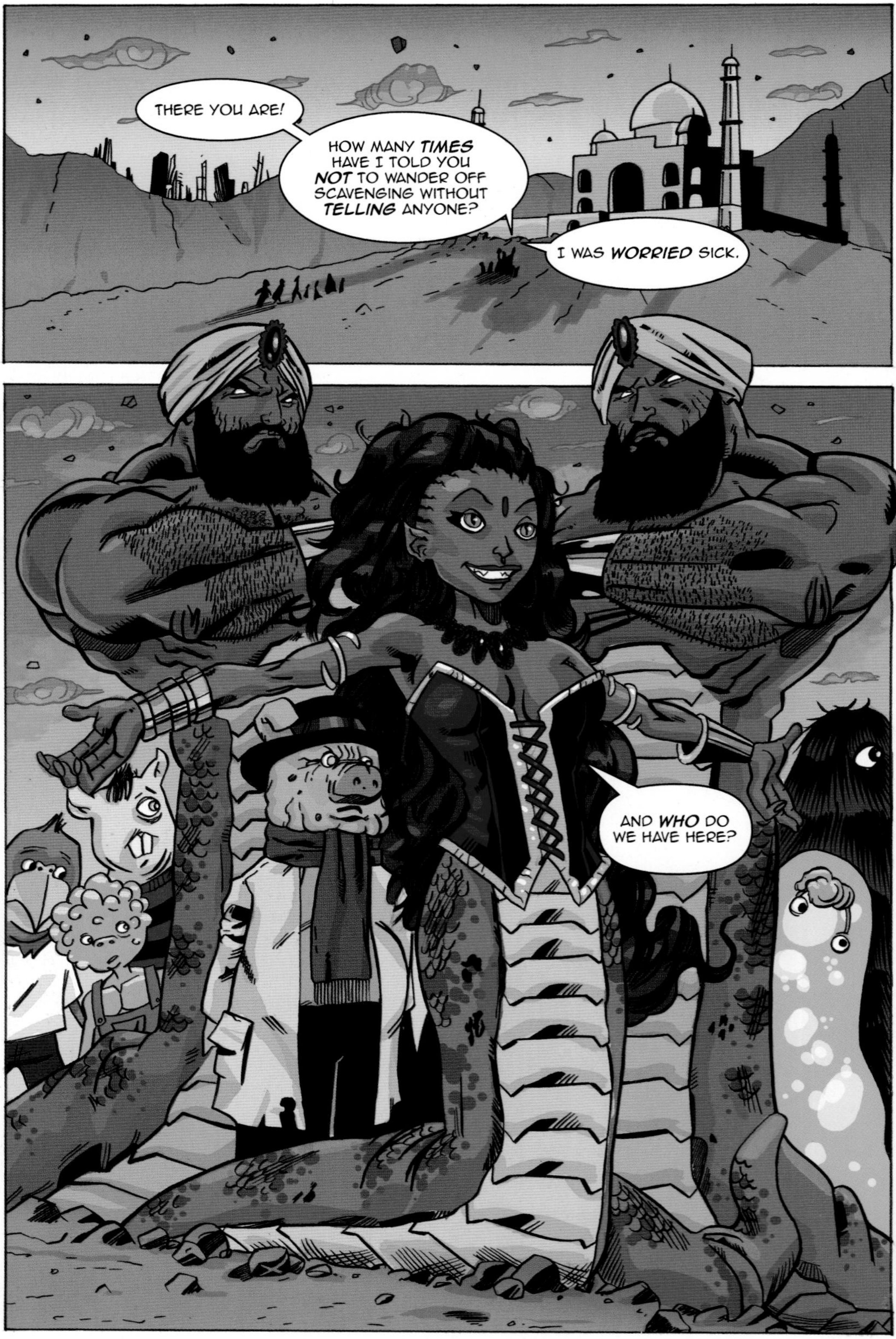
THERE YOU ARE!
HOW MANY TIMES HAVE I TOLD YOU NOT TO WANDER OFF SCAVENGING WITHOUT TELLING ANYONE?
I WAS WORRIED SICK.
AND WHO DO WE HAVE HERE?

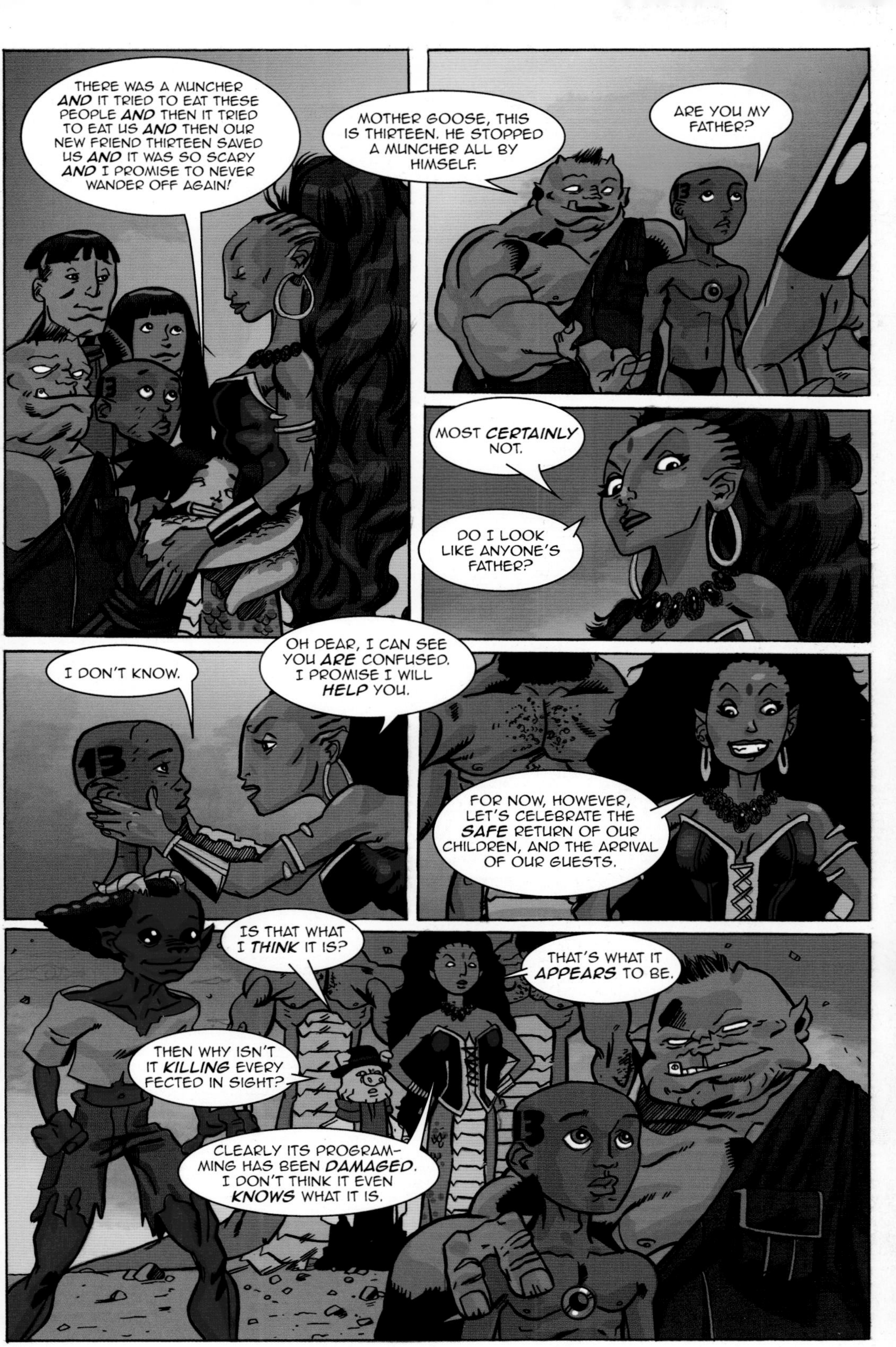
THERE WAS A MUNCHER AND IT TRIED TO EAT THESE PEOPLE AND THEN IT TRIED TO EAT US AND THEN OUR NEW FRIEND THIRTEEN SAVED US AND IT WAS SO SCARY AND I PROMISE TO NEVER WANDER OFF AGAIN!
MOTHER GOOSE, THIS IS THIRTEEN. HE STOPPED A MUNCHER ALL BY HIMSELF.
ARE YOU MY FATHER?
MOST CERTAINLY NOT.
DO I LOOK LIKE ANYONE'S FATHER?
I DON'T KNOW.
OH DEAR, I CAN SEE YOU ARE CONFUSED. I PROMISE I WILL HELP YOU.
FOR NOW, HOWEVER, LET'S CELEBRATE THE SAFE RETURN OF OUR CHILDREN, AND THE ARRIVAL OF OUR GUESTS.
IS THAT WHAT I THINK IT IS?
THAT'S WHAT IT APPEARS TO BE.
THEN WHY ISN'T IT KILLING EVERY FECTED IN SIGHT?
CLEARLY ITS PROGRAMMING HAS BEEN DAMAGED. I DON'T THINK IT EVEN KNOWS WHAT IT IS.

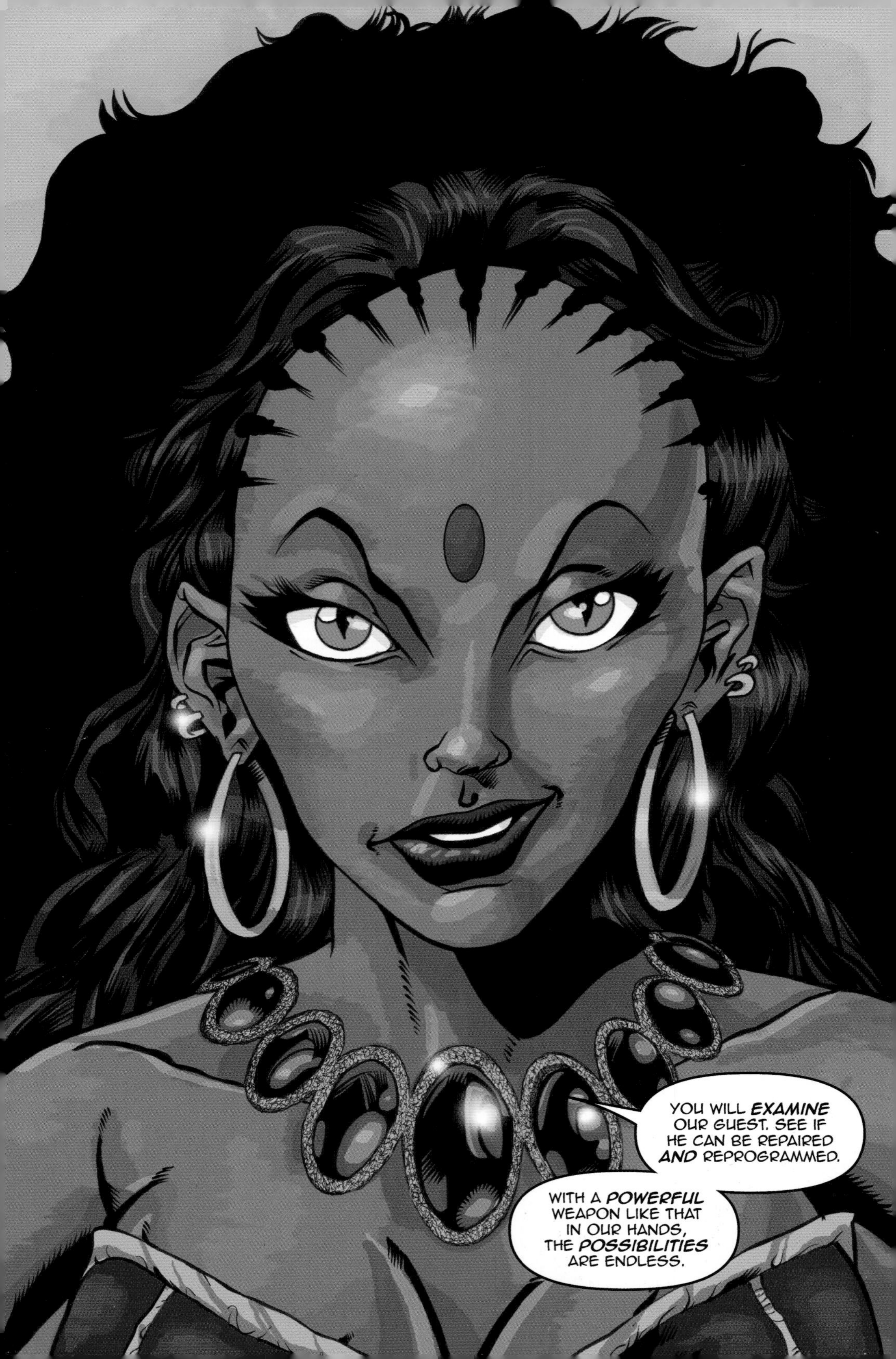
YOU WILL EXAMINE OUR GUEST. SEE IF HE CAN BE REPAIRED AND REPROGRAMMED.
WITH A POWERFUL WEAPON LIKE THAT IN OUR HANDS, THE POSSIBILITIES ARE ENDLESS.

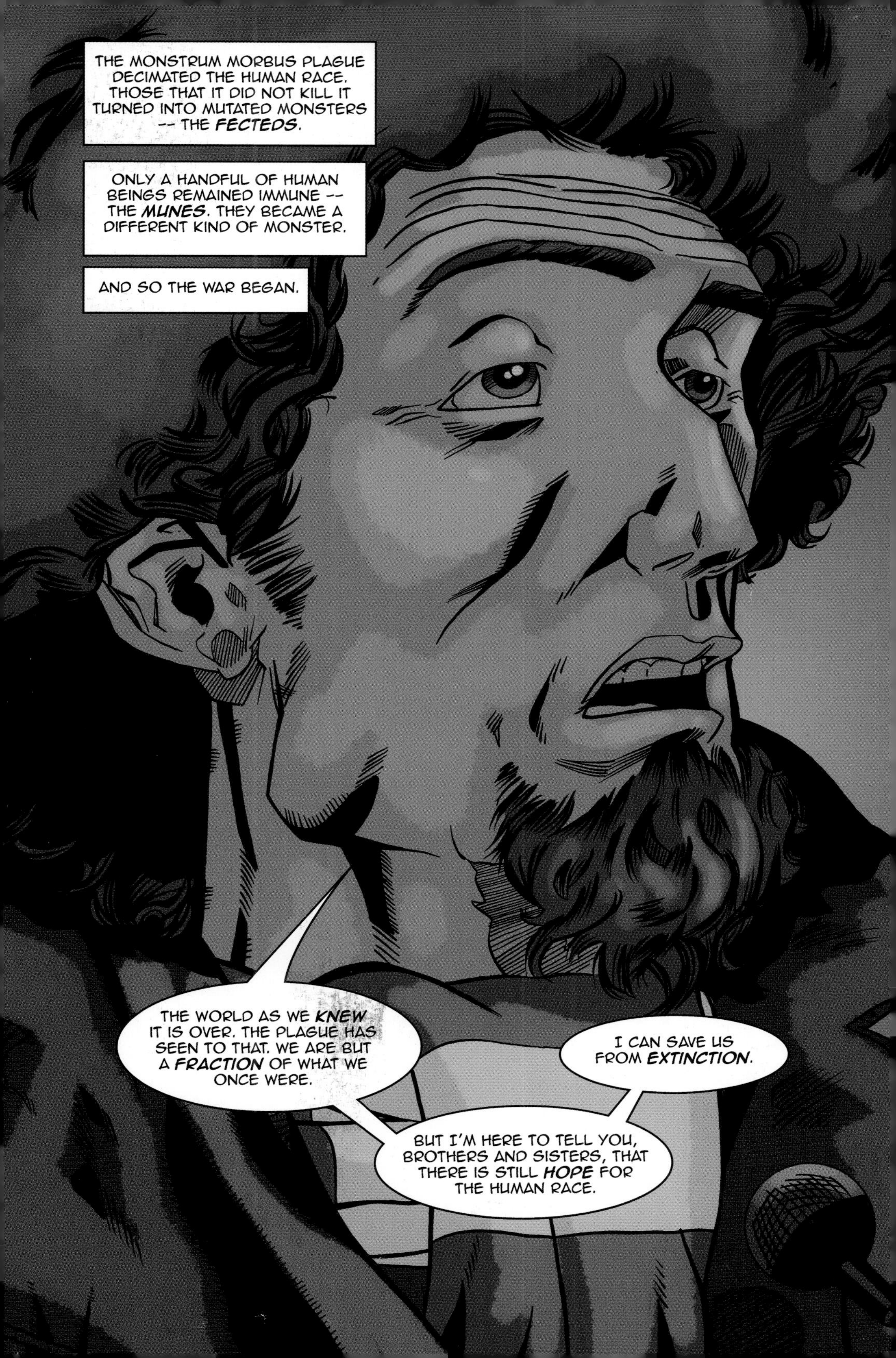
THE MONSTRUM MORBUS PLAGUE DECIMATED THE HUMAN RACE. THOSE THAT IT DID NOT KILL IT TURNED INTO MUTATED MONSTERS -- THE FECTEDS.
ONLY A HANDFUL OF HUMAN BEINGS REMAINED IMMUNE -- THE MUNES. THEY BECAME A DIFFERENT KIND OF MONSTER.
AND SO THE WAR BEGAN.
THE WORLD AS WE KNEW IT IS OVER. THE PLAGUE HAS SEEN TO THAT. WE ARE BUT A FRACTION OF WHAT WE ONCE WERE.
BUT I'M HERE TO TELL YOU, BROTHERS AND SISTERS, THAT THERE IS STILL HOPE FOR THE HUMAN RACE.
I CAN SAVE US FROM EXTINCTION.

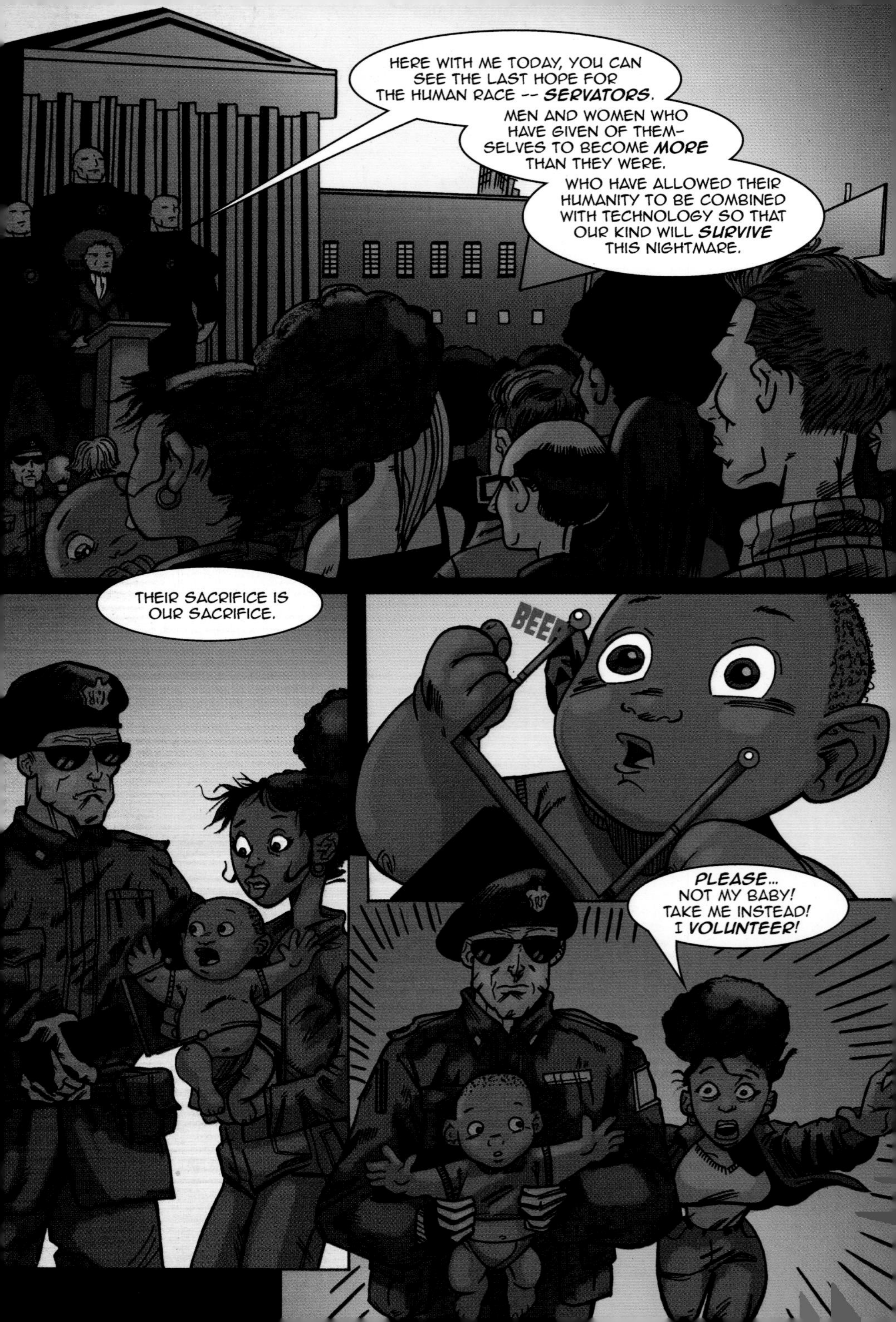
HERE WITH ME TODAY, YOU CAN SEE THE LAST HOPE FOR THE HUMAN RACE -- SERVATORS.
MEN AND WOMEN WHO HAVE GIVEN OF THEM-SELVES TO BECOME MORE THAN THEY WERE.
WHO HAVE ALLOWED THEIR HUMANITY TO BE COMBINED WITH TECHNOLOGY SO THAT OUR KIND WILL SURVIVE THIS NIGHTMARE.
THEIR SACRIFICE IS OUR SACRIFICE.
BEEP
PLEASE... NOT MY BABY! TAKE ME INSTEAD! I VOLUNTEER!

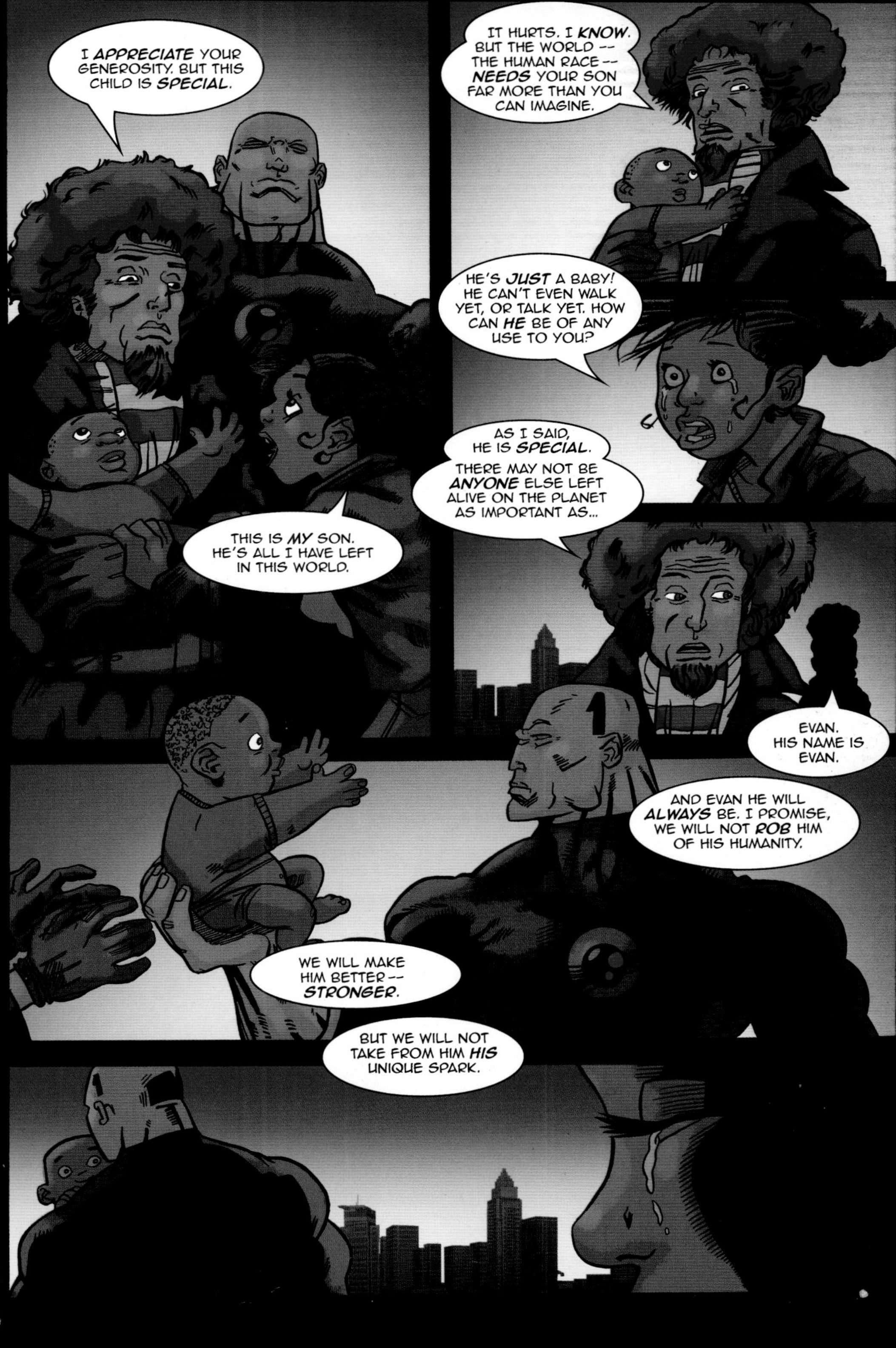
I APPRECIATE YOUR GENEROSITY. BUT THIS CHILD IS SPECIAL.
IT HURTS. I KNOW. BUT THE WORLD -- THE HUMAN RACE -- NEEDS YOUR SON FAR MORE THAN YOU CAN IMAGINE.
THIS IS MY SON. HE'S ALL I HAVE LEFT IN THIS WORLD.
HE'S JUST A BABY! HE CAN'T EVEN WALK YET, OR TALK YET. HOW CAN HE BE OF ANY USE TO YOU?
AS I SAID, HE IS SPECIAL.
THERE MAY NOT BE ANYONE ELSE LEFT ALIVE ON THE PLANET AS IMPORTANT AS...
EVAN. HIS NAME IS EVAN.
AND EVAN HE WILL ALWAYS BE. I PROMISE, WE WILL NOT ROB HIM OF HIS HUMANITY.
WE WILL MAKE HIM BETTER -- STRONGER.
BUT WE WILL NOT TAKE FROM HIM HIS UNIQUE SPARK.

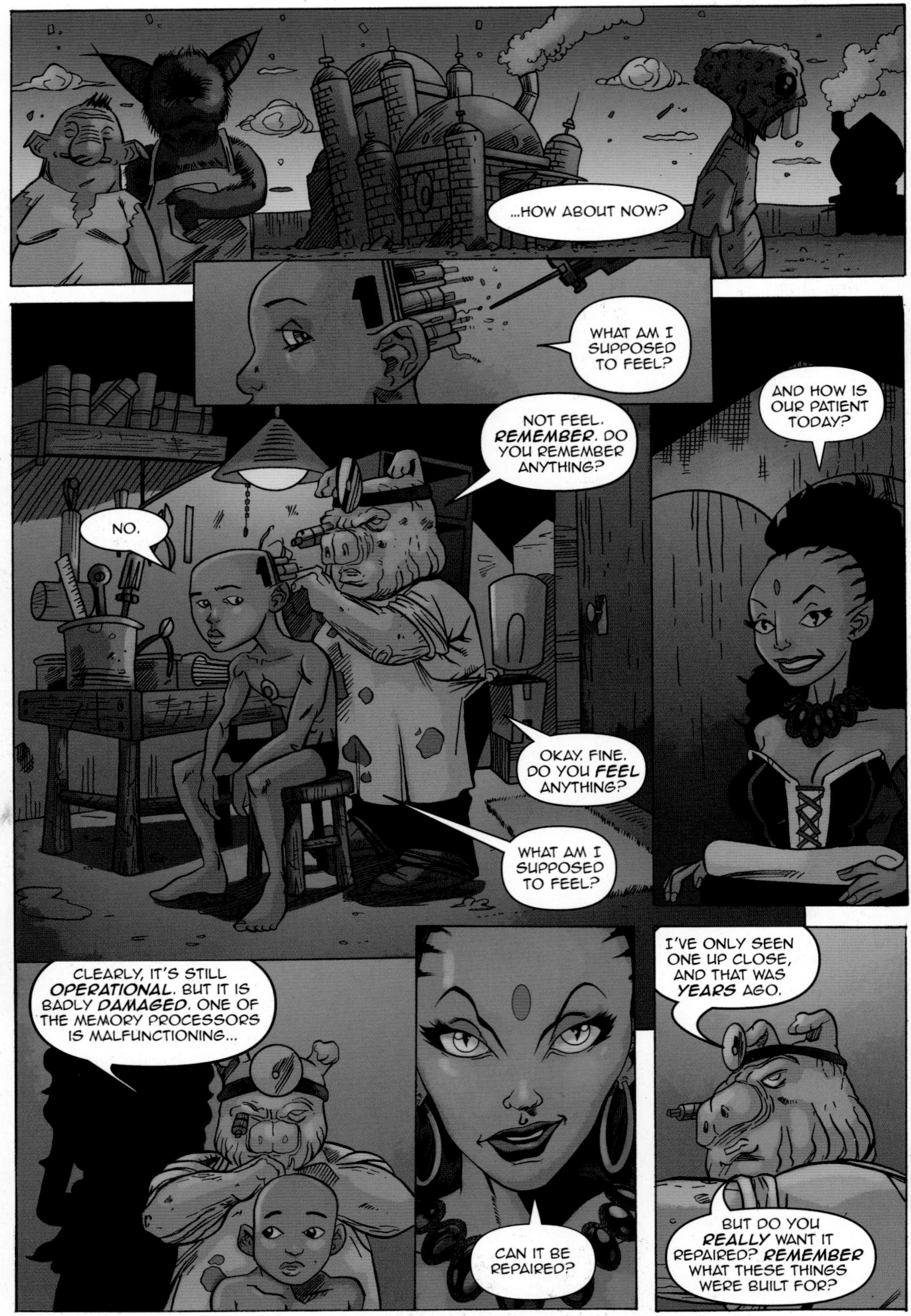
...HOW ABOUT NOW?
WHAT AM I SUPPOSED TO FEEL?
NOT FEEL. REMEMBER. DO YOU REMEMBER ANYTHING?
NO.
OKAY. FINE. DO YOU FEEL ANYTHING?
WHAT AM I SUPPOSED TO FEEL?
AND HOW IS OUR PATIENT TODAY?
CLEARLY, IT'S STILL OPERATIONAL. BUT IT IS BADLY DAMAGED. ONE OF THE MEMORY PROCESSORS IS MALFUNCTIONING...
CAN IT BE REPAIRED?
I'VE ONLY SEEN ONE UP CLOSE, AND THAT WAS YEARS AGO.
BUT DO YOU REALLY WANT IT REPAIRED? REMEMBER WHAT THESE THINGS WERE BUILT FOR?

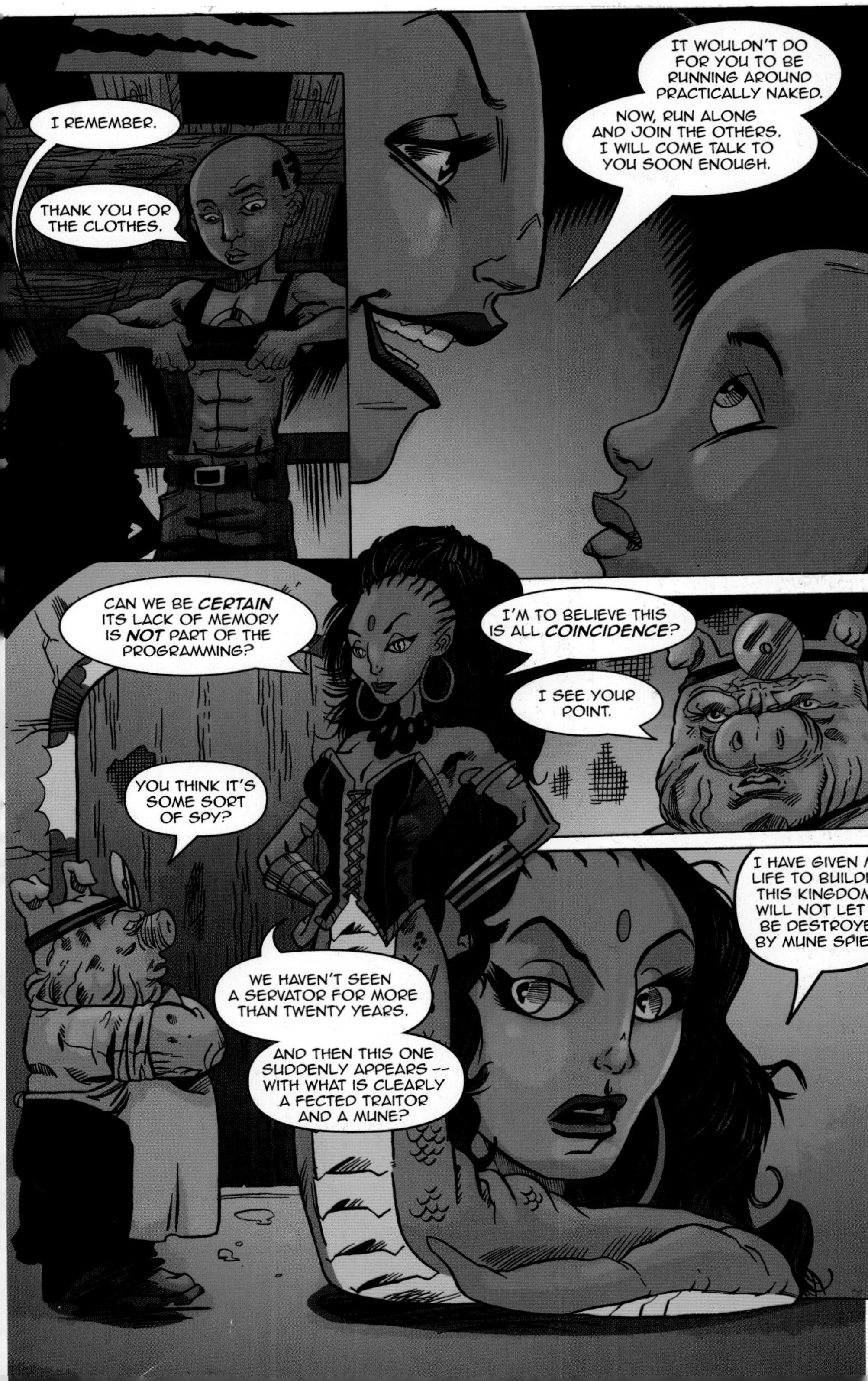
I REMEMBER.
THANK YOU FOR THE CLOTHES.
IT WOULDN'T DO FOR YOU TO BE RUNNING AROUND PRACTICALLY NAKED.
NOW, RUN ALONG AND JOIN THE OTHERS. I WILL COME TALK TO YOU SOON ENOUGH.
CAN WE BE *CERTAIN* ITS LACK OF MEMORY IS *NOT* PART OF THE PROGRAMMING?
I'M TO BELIEVE THIS IS ALL *COINCIDENCE*?
I SEE YOUR POINT.
YOU THINK IT'S SOME SORT OF SPY?
WE HAVEN'T SEEN A SERVATOR FOR MORE THAN TWENTY YEARS.
AND THEN THIS ONE SUDDENLY APPEARS -- WITH WHAT IS CLEARLY A FECTED TRAITOR AND A MUNE?
I HAVE GIVEN MY LIFE TO BUILDING THIS KINGDOM. I WILL NOT LET IT BE DESTROYED BY MUNE SPIES.

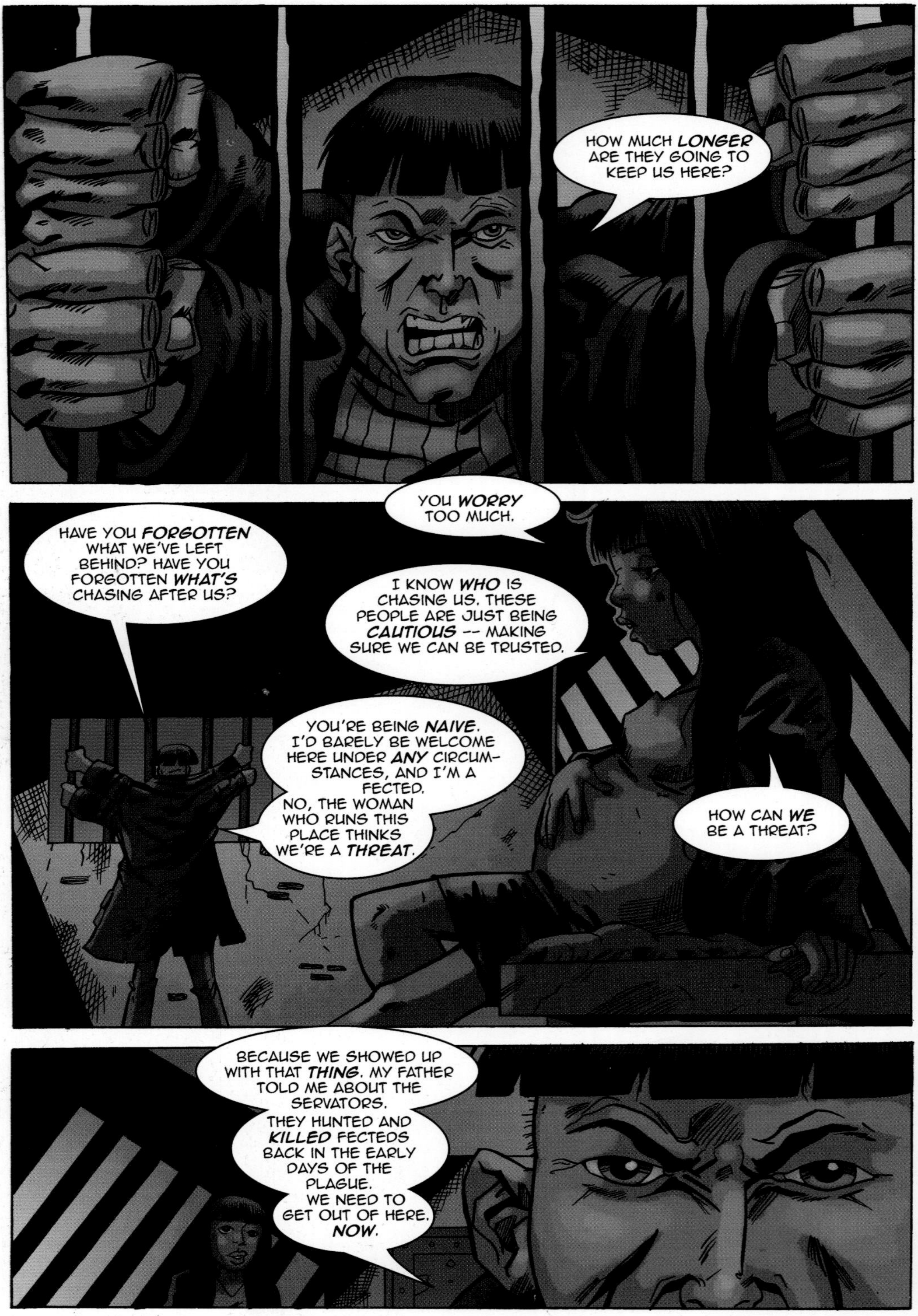
HOW MUCH LONGER ARE THEY GOING TO KEEP US HERE?
YOU WORRY TOO MUCH.
HAVE YOU FORGOTTEN WHAT WE'VE LEFT BEHIND? HAVE YOU FORGOTTEN WHAT'S CHASING AFTER US?
I KNOW WHO IS CHASING US. THESE PEOPLE ARE JUST BEING CAUTIOUS -- MAKING SURE WE CAN BE TRUSTED.
YOU'RE BEING NAIVE. I'D BARELY BE WELCOME HERE UNDER ANY CIRCUMSTANCES, AND I'M A FECTED.
NO, THE WOMAN WHO RUNS THIS PLACE THINKS WE'RE A THREAT.
HOW CAN WE BE A THREAT?
BECAUSE WE SHOWED UP WITH THAT THING. MY FATHER TOLD ME ABOUT THE SERVATORS.
THEY HUNTED AND KILLED FECTEDS BACK IN THE EARLY DAYS OF THE PLAGUE.
WE NEED TO GET OUT OF HERE. NOW.

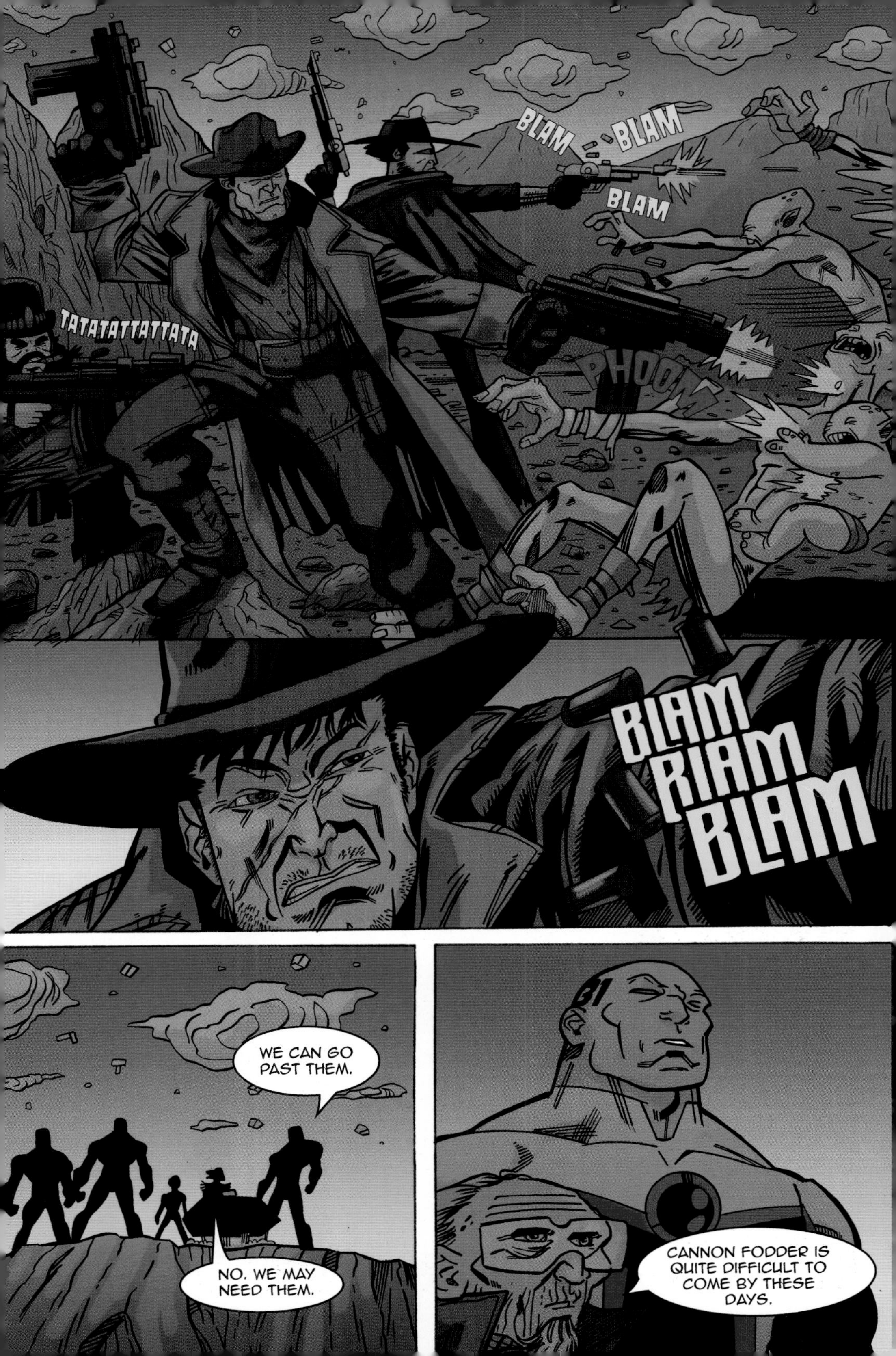

BLAM
BLAM
BLAM
TATATATTATTATA
PHOOM
BLAM
RIAM
BLAM
WE CAN GO PAST THEM.
NO. WE MAY NEED THEM.
CANNON FODDER IS QUITE DIFFICULT TO COME BY THESE DAYS.

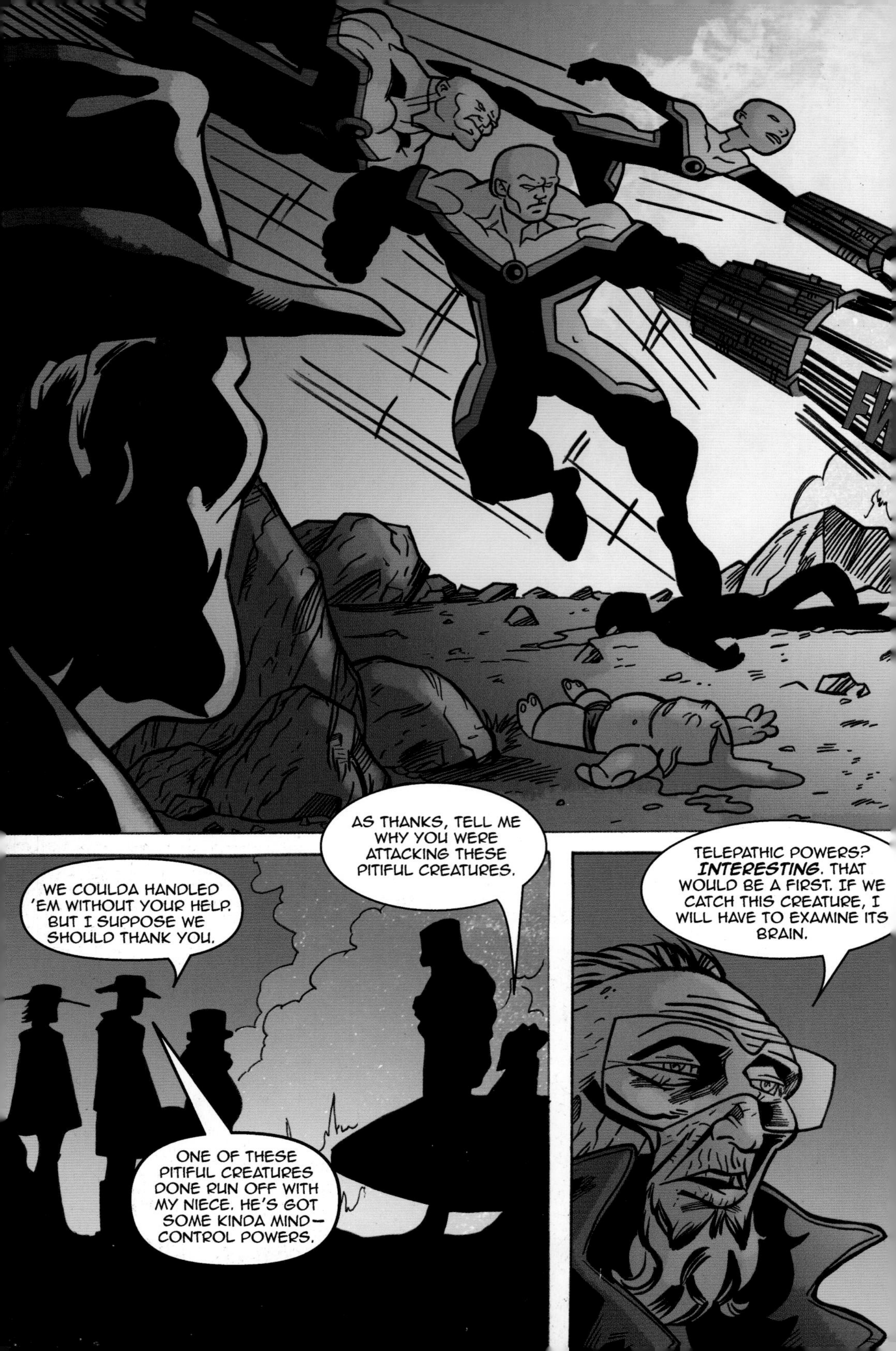
WE COULDA HANDLED 'EM WITHOUT YOUR HELP. BUT I SUPPOSE WE SHOULD THANK YOU.
AS THANKS, TELL ME WHY YOU WERE ATTACKING THESE PITIFUL CREATURES.
ONE OF THESE PITIFUL CREATURES DONE RUN OFF WITH MY NIECE. HE'S GOT SOME KINDA MIND-CONTROL POWERS.
TELEPATHIC POWERS? ***INTERESTING***. THAT WOULD BE A FIRST. IF WE CATCH THIS CREATURE, I WILL HAVE TO EXAMINE ITS BRAIN.

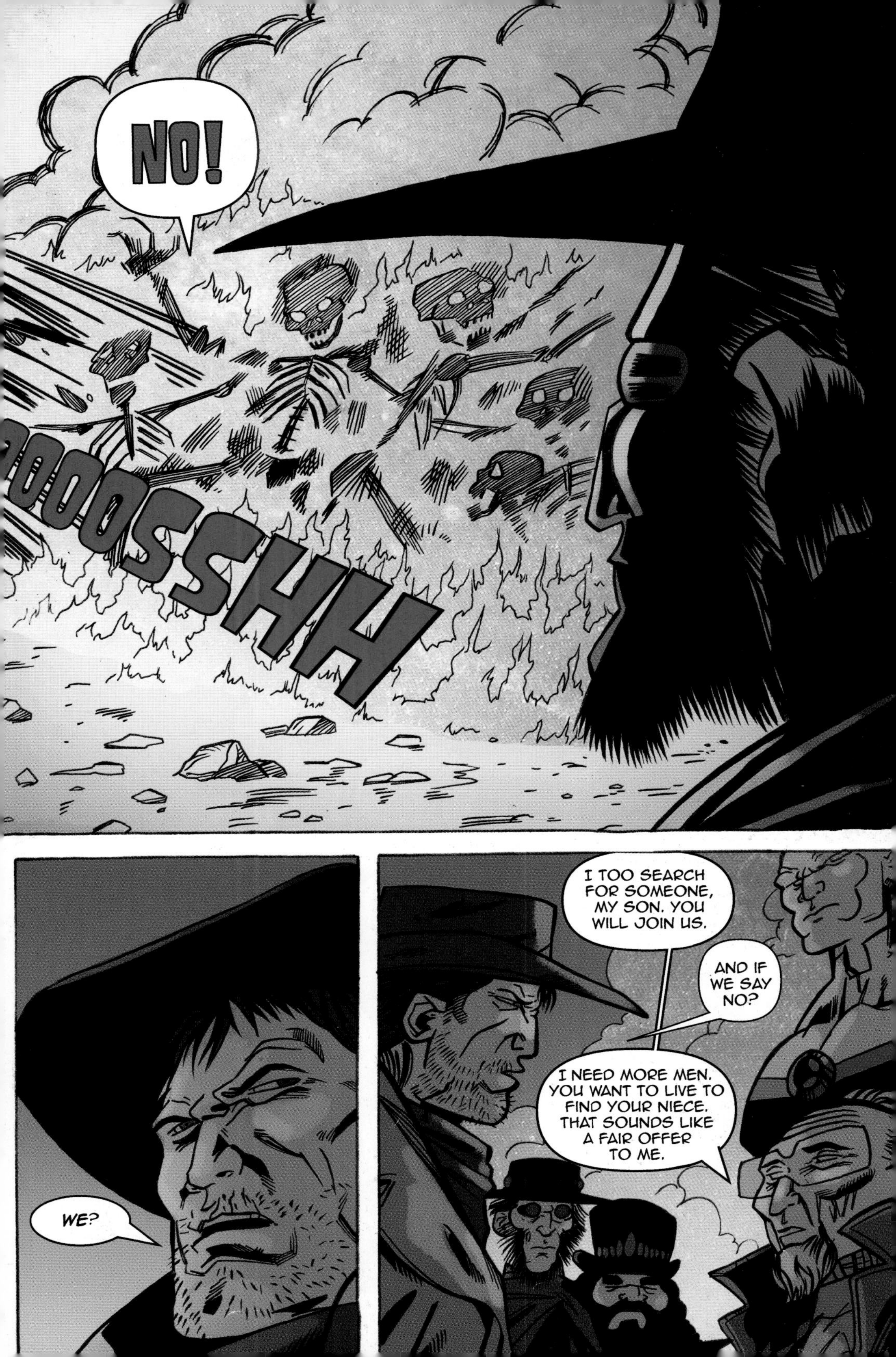
NO!
OOOOSSHH
WE?
I TOO SEARCH FOR SOMEONE, MY SON. YOU WILL JOIN US.
AND IF WE SAY NO?
I NEED MORE MEN. YOU WANT TO LIVE TO FIND YOUR NIECE. THAT SOUNDS LIKE A FAIR OFFER TO ME.

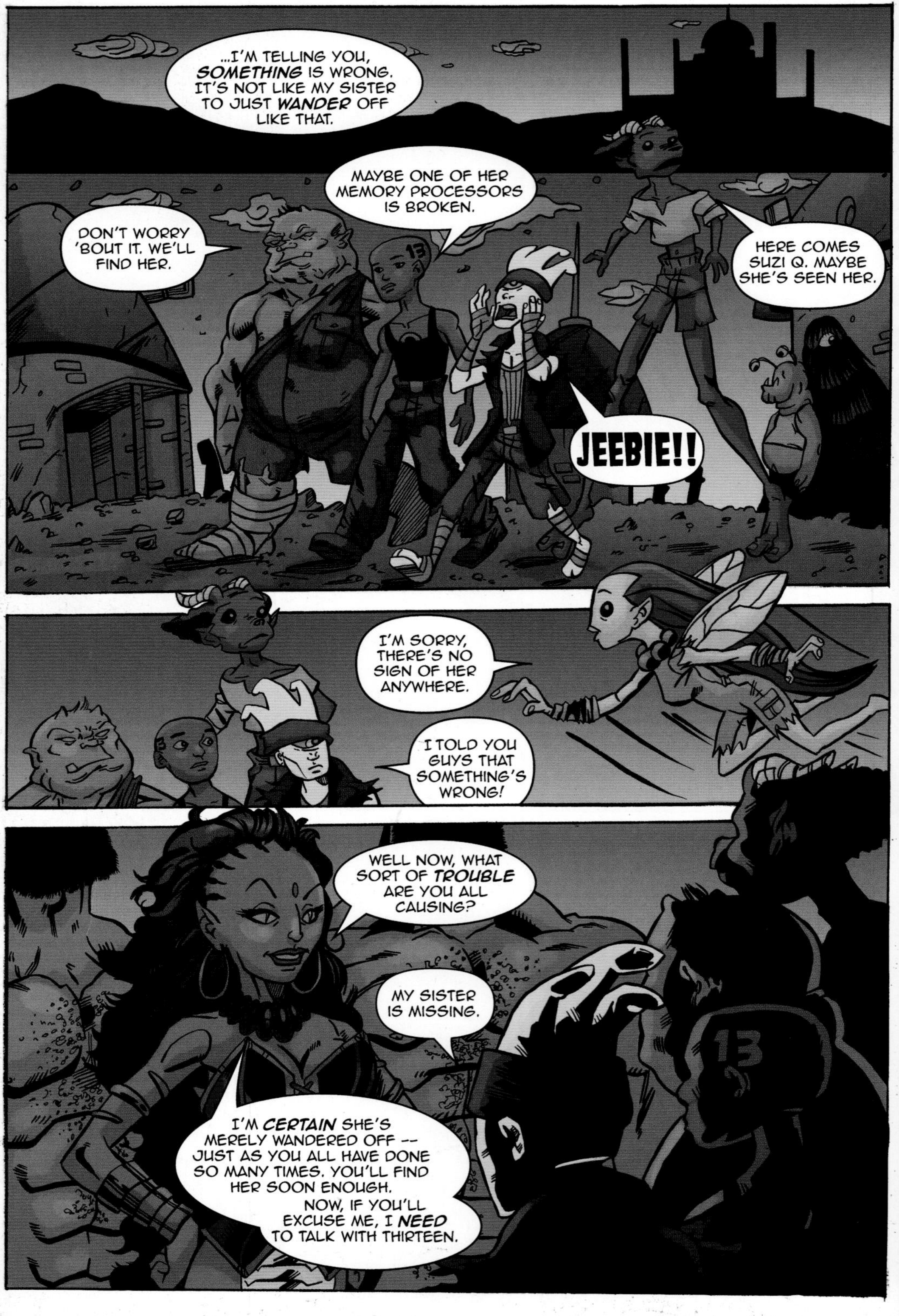
...I'M TELLING YOU, SOMETHING IS WRONG. IT'S NOT LIKE MY SISTER TO JUST WANDER OFF LIKE THAT.
DON'T WORRY 'BOUT IT. WE'LL FIND HER.
MAYBE ONE OF HER MEMORY PROCESSORS IS BROKEN.
HERE COMES SUZI Q. MAYBE SHE'S SEEN HER.
JEEBIE!!
I'M SORRY, THERE'S NO SIGN OF HER ANYWHERE.
I TOLD YOU GUYS THAT SOMETHING'S WRONG!
WELL NOW, WHAT SORT OF TROUBLE ARE YOU ALL CAUSING?
MY SISTER IS MISSING.
I'M CERTAIN SHE'S MERELY WANDERED OFF -- JUST AS YOU ALL HAVE DONE SO MANY TIMES. YOU'LL FIND HER SOON ENOUGH.
NOW, IF YOU'LL EXCUSE ME, I NEED TO TALK WITH THIRTEEN.

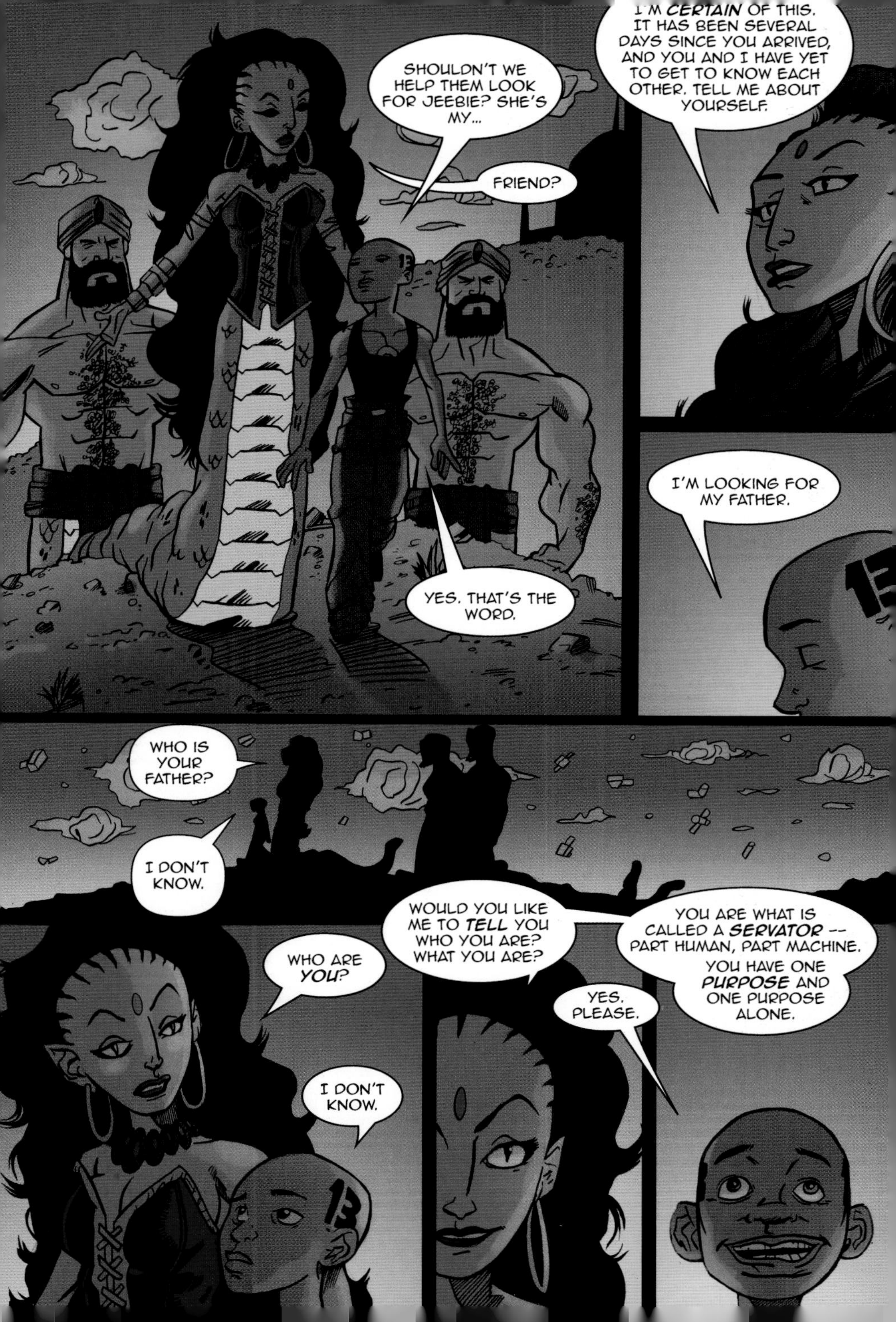
SHOULDN'T WE HELP THEM LOOK FOR JEEBIE? SHE'S MY...
FRIEND?
YES. THAT'S THE WORD.
I'M CERTAIN OF THIS. IT HAS BEEN SEVERAL DAYS SINCE YOU ARRIVED, AND YOU AND I HAVE YET TO GET TO KNOW EACH OTHER. TELL ME ABOUT YOURSELF.
I'M LOOKING FOR MY FATHER.
WHO IS YOUR FATHER?
I DON'T KNOW.
WHO ARE YOU?
I DON'T KNOW.
WOULD YOU LIKE ME TO TELL YOU WHO YOU ARE? WHAT YOU ARE?
YES. PLEASE.
YOU ARE WHAT IS CALLED A SERVATOR -- PART HUMAN, PART MACHINE.
YOU HAVE ONE PURPOSE AND ONE PURPOSE ALONE.

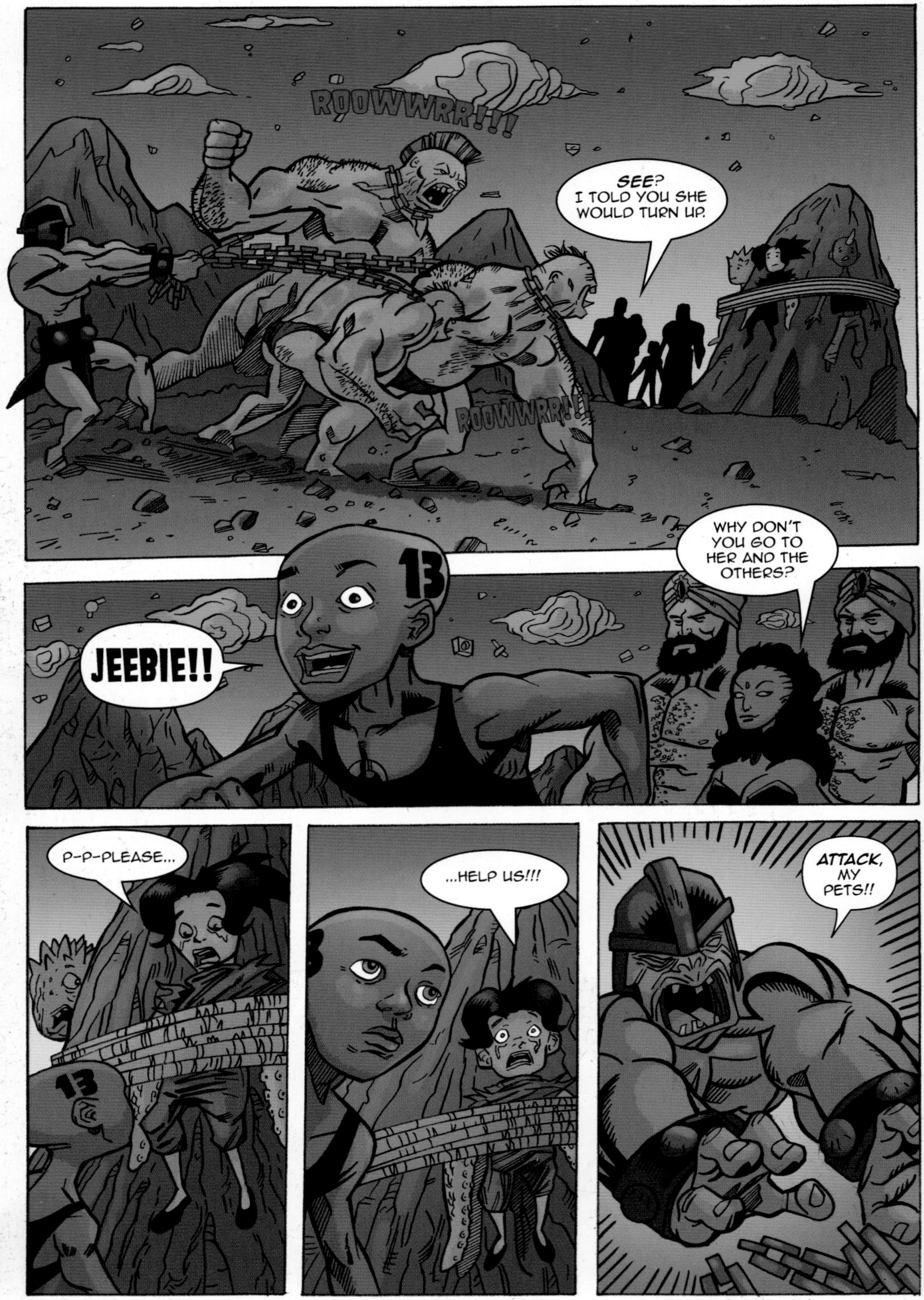
ROOWWRR!!!
SEE? I TOLD YOU SHE WOULD TURN UP.
ROOWWRR!!!
WHY DON'T YOU GO TO HER AND THE OTHERS?
JEEBIE!!
13
P-P-PLEASE...
13
...HELP US!!!
ATTACK, MY PETS!!

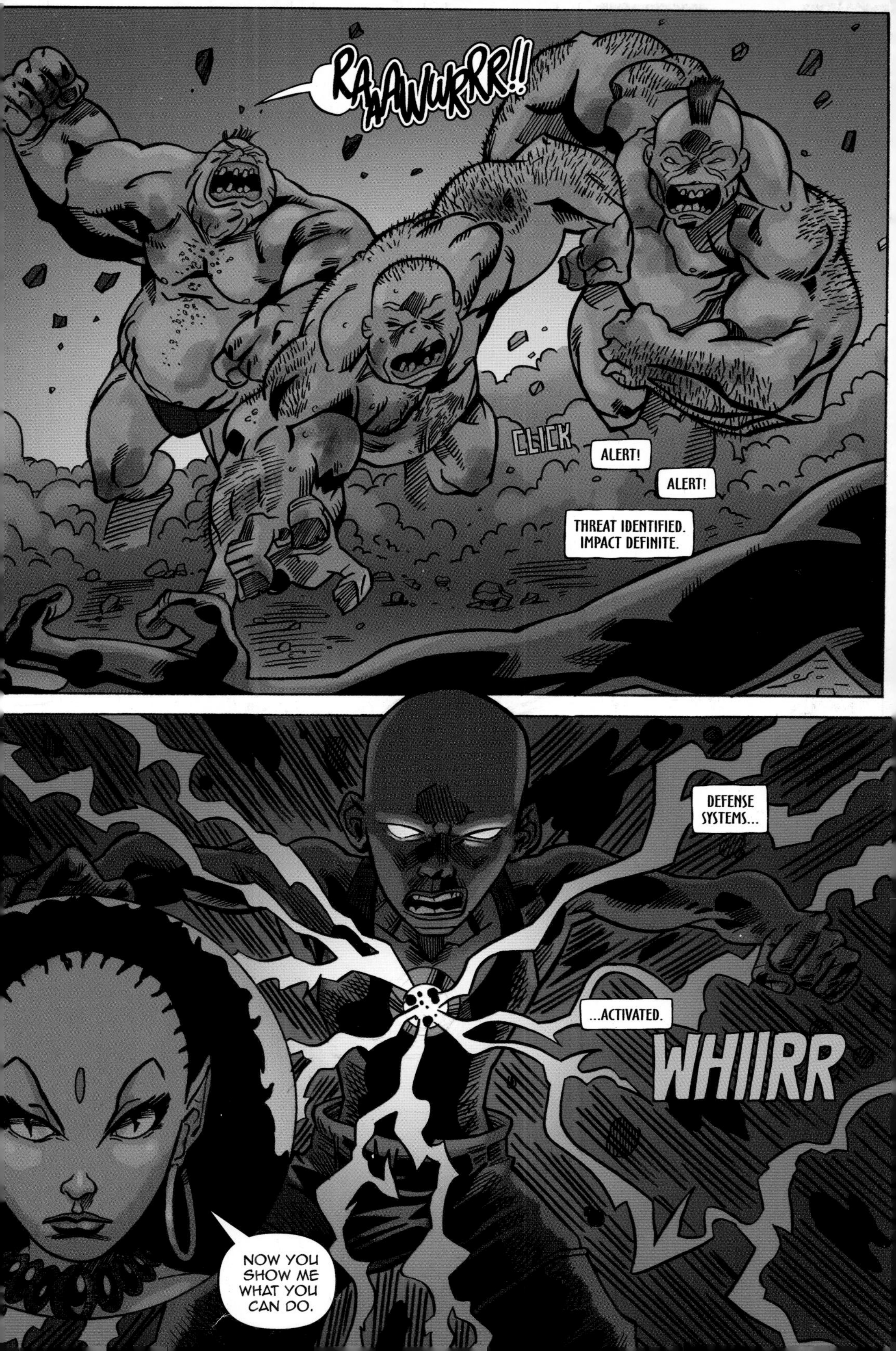

RAAAWURRR!!
CLICK
ALERT!
ALERT!
THREAT IDENTIFIED. IMPACT DEFINITE.
DEFENSE SYSTEMS...
...ACTIVATED.
WHIIRR
NOW YOU SHOW ME WHAT YOU CAN DO.

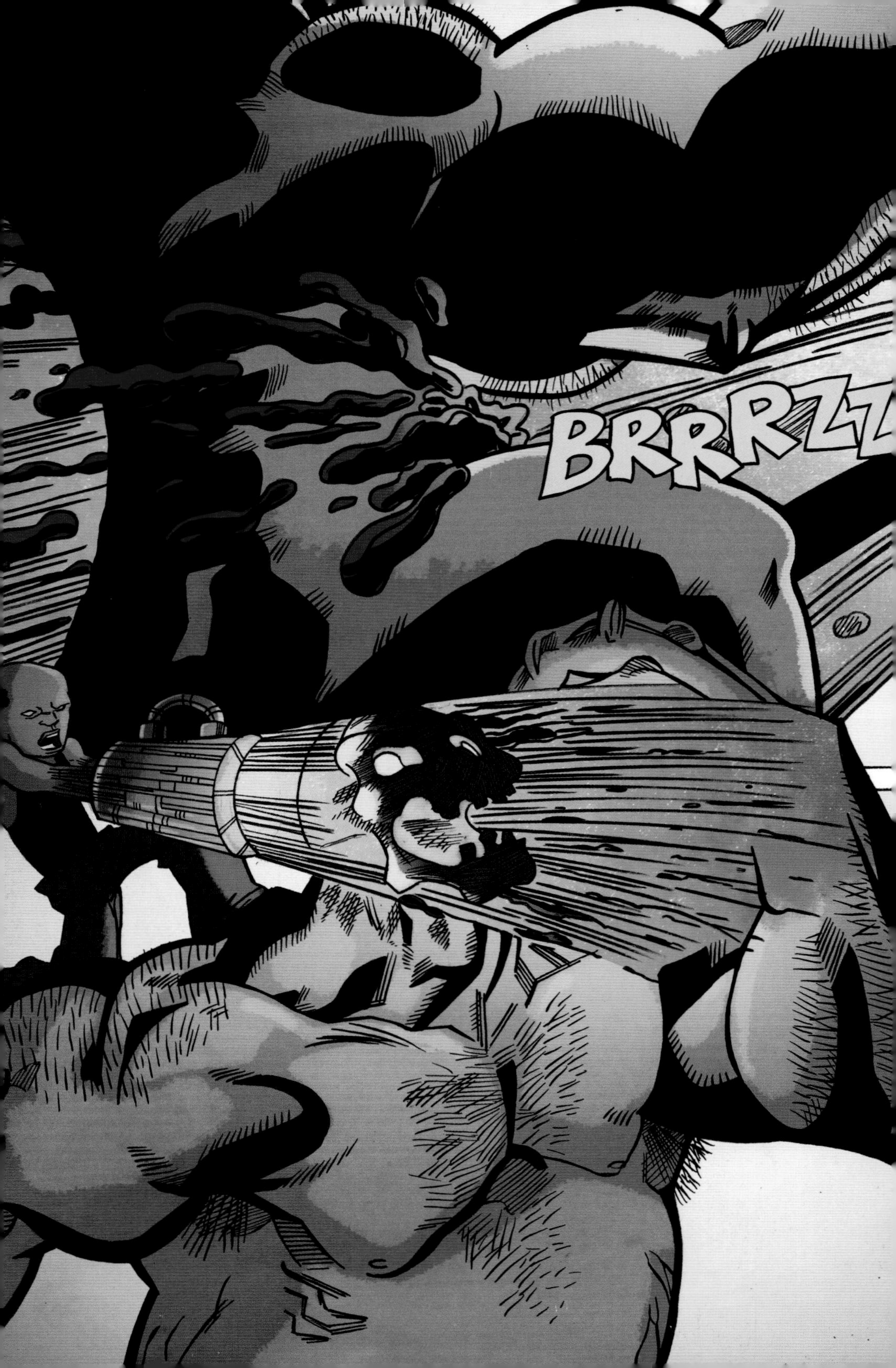
BRRRZZ

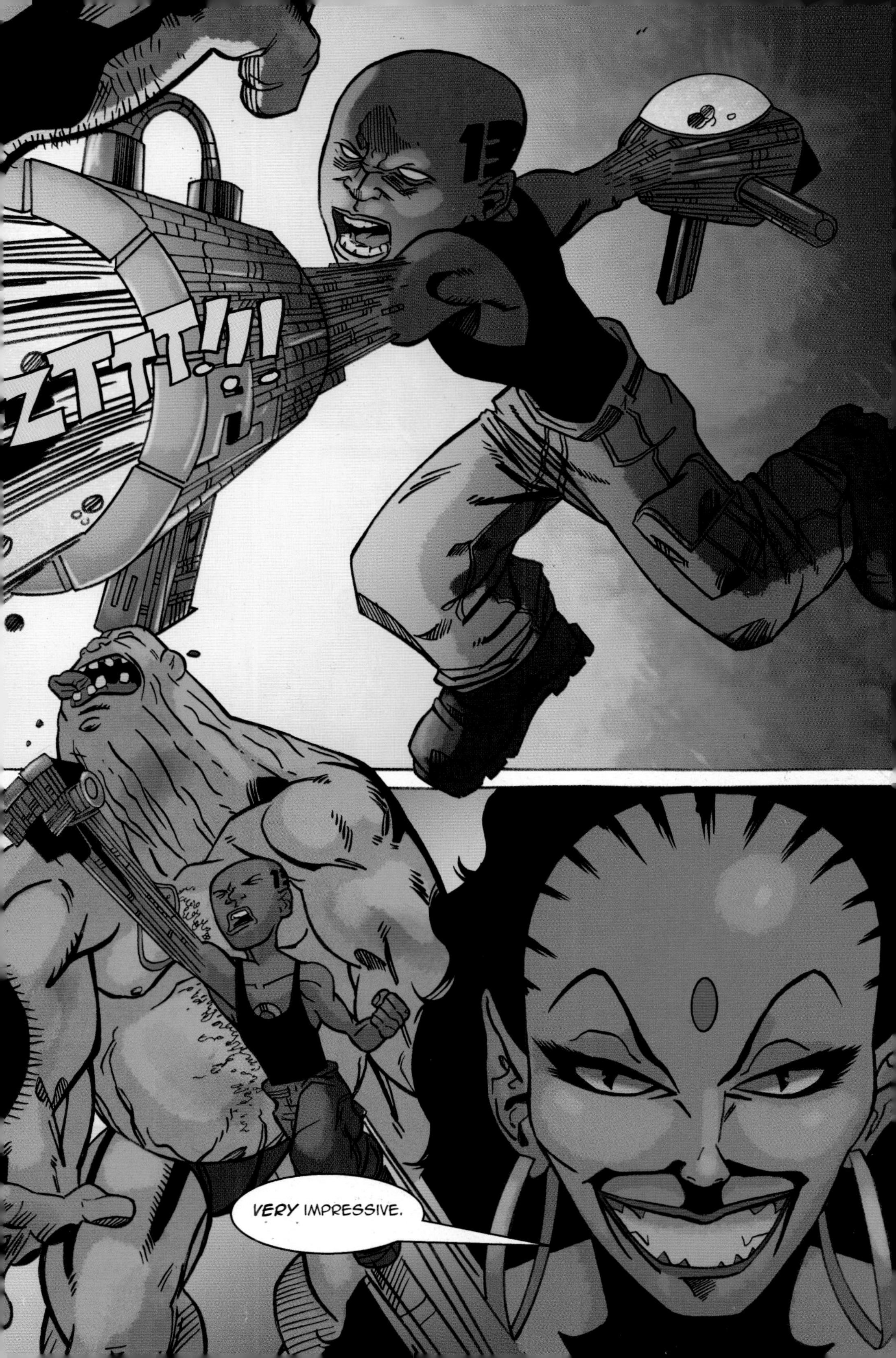
ZTTT!!!
VERY IMPRESSIVE.

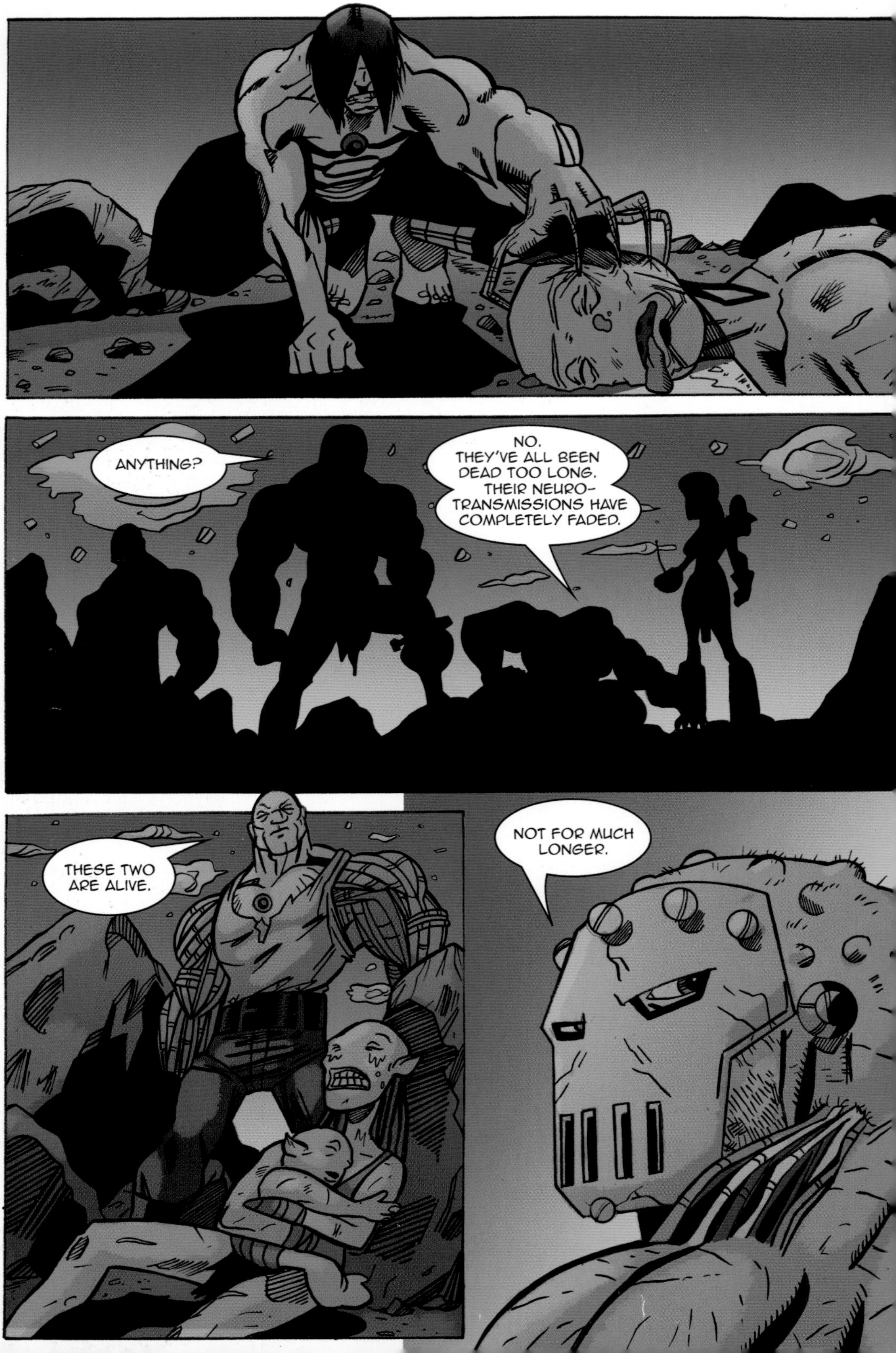
ANYTHING?
NO. THEY'VE ALL BEEN DEAD TOO LONG. THEIR NEURO-TRANSMISSIONS HAVE COMPLETELY FADED.
THESE TWO ARE ALIVE.
NOT FOR MUCH LONGER.

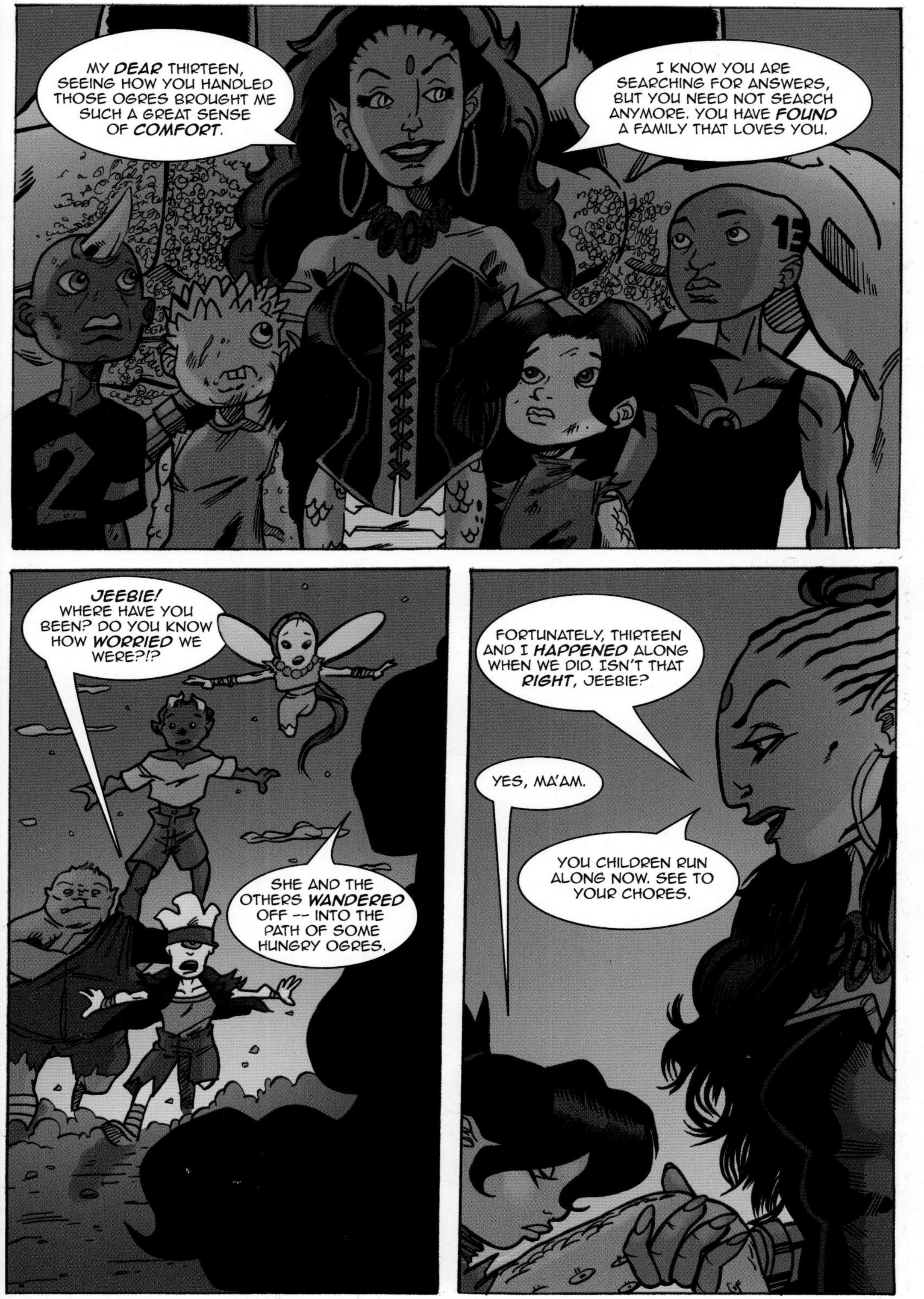
MY DEAR THIRTEEN, SEEING HOW YOU HANDLED THOSE OGRES BROUGHT ME SUCH A GREAT SENSE OF COMFORT.
I KNOW YOU ARE SEARCHING FOR ANSWERS, BUT YOU NEED NOT SEARCH ANYMORE. YOU HAVE FOUND A FAMILY THAT LOVES YOU.
JEEBIE! WHERE HAVE YOU BEEN? DO YOU KNOW HOW WORRIED WE WERE?!?
SHE AND THE OTHERS WANDERED OFF -- INTO THE PATH OF SOME HUNGRY OGRES.
FORTUNATELY, THIRTEEN AND I HAPPENED ALONG WHEN WE DID. ISN'T THAT RIGHT, JEEBIE?
YES, MA'AM.
YOU CHILDREN RUN ALONG NOW. SEE TO YOUR CHORES.

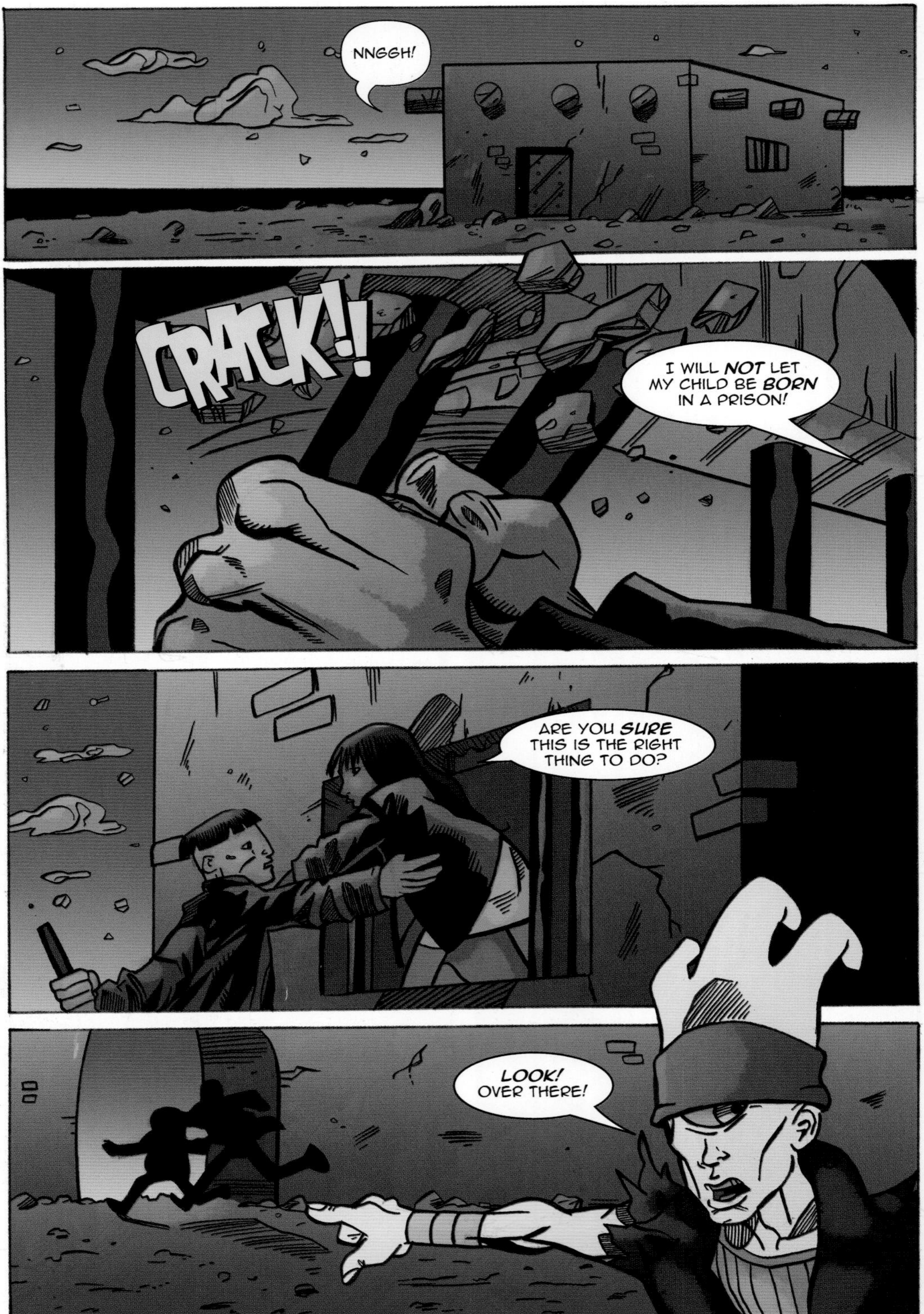
NNGGH!
CRACK!!
I WILL NOT LET MY CHILD BE BORN IN A PRISON!
ARE YOU SURE THIS IS THE RIGHT THING TO DO?
LOOK! OVER THERE!

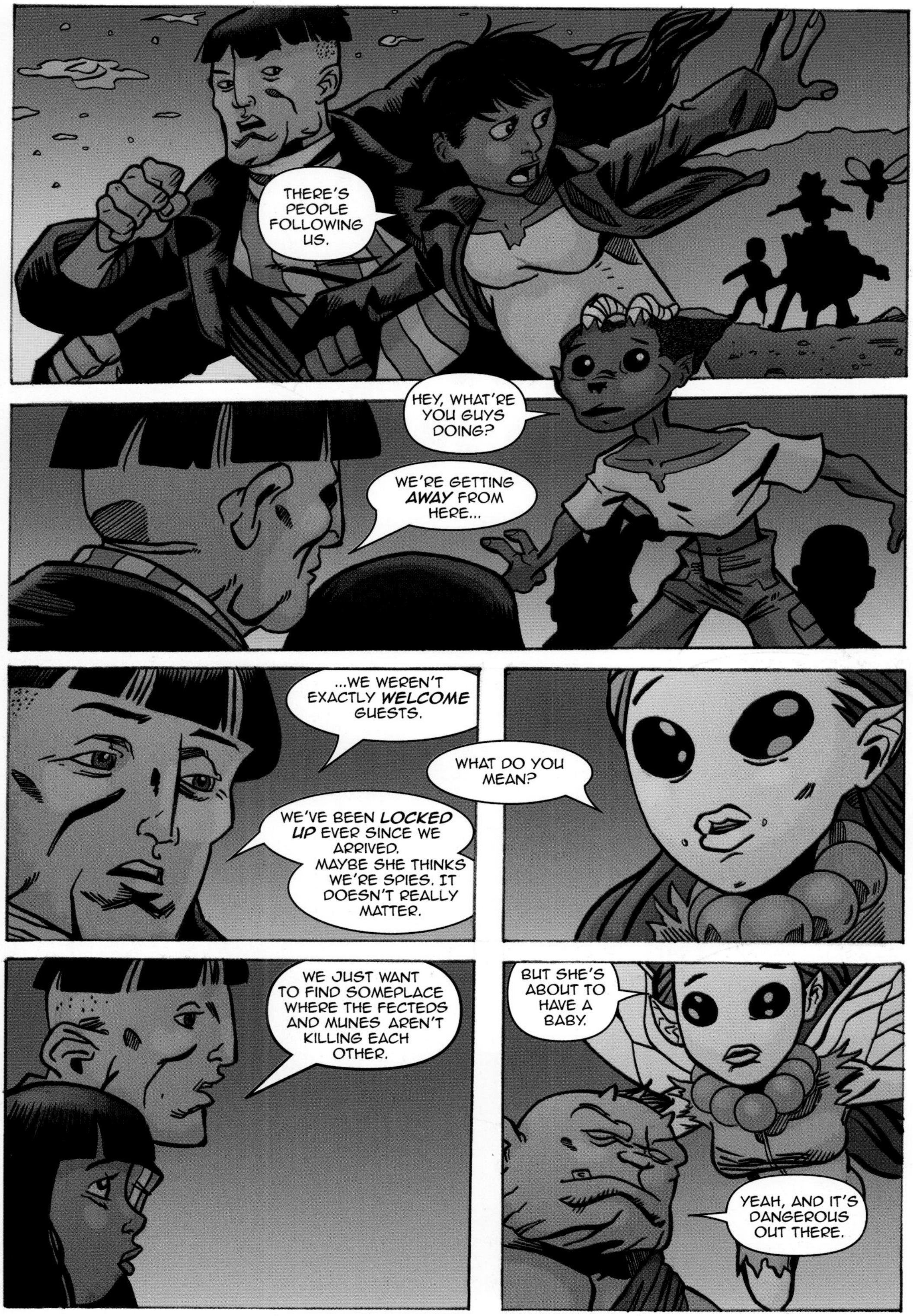
THERE'S PEOPLE FOLLOWING US.
HEY, WHAT'RE YOU GUYS DOING?
WE'RE GETTING *AWAY* FROM HERE...
...WE WEREN'T EXACTLY *WELCOME* GUESTS.
WHAT DO YOU MEAN?
WE'VE BEEN *LOCKED UP* EVER SINCE WE ARRIVED.
MAYBE SHE THINKS WE'RE SPIES. IT DOESN'T REALLY MATTER.
WE JUST WANT TO FIND SOMEPLACE WHERE THE FECTEDS AND MUNES AREN'T KILLING EACH OTHER.
BUT SHE'S ABOUT TO HAVE A BABY.
YEAH, AND IT'S DANGEROUS OUT THERE.

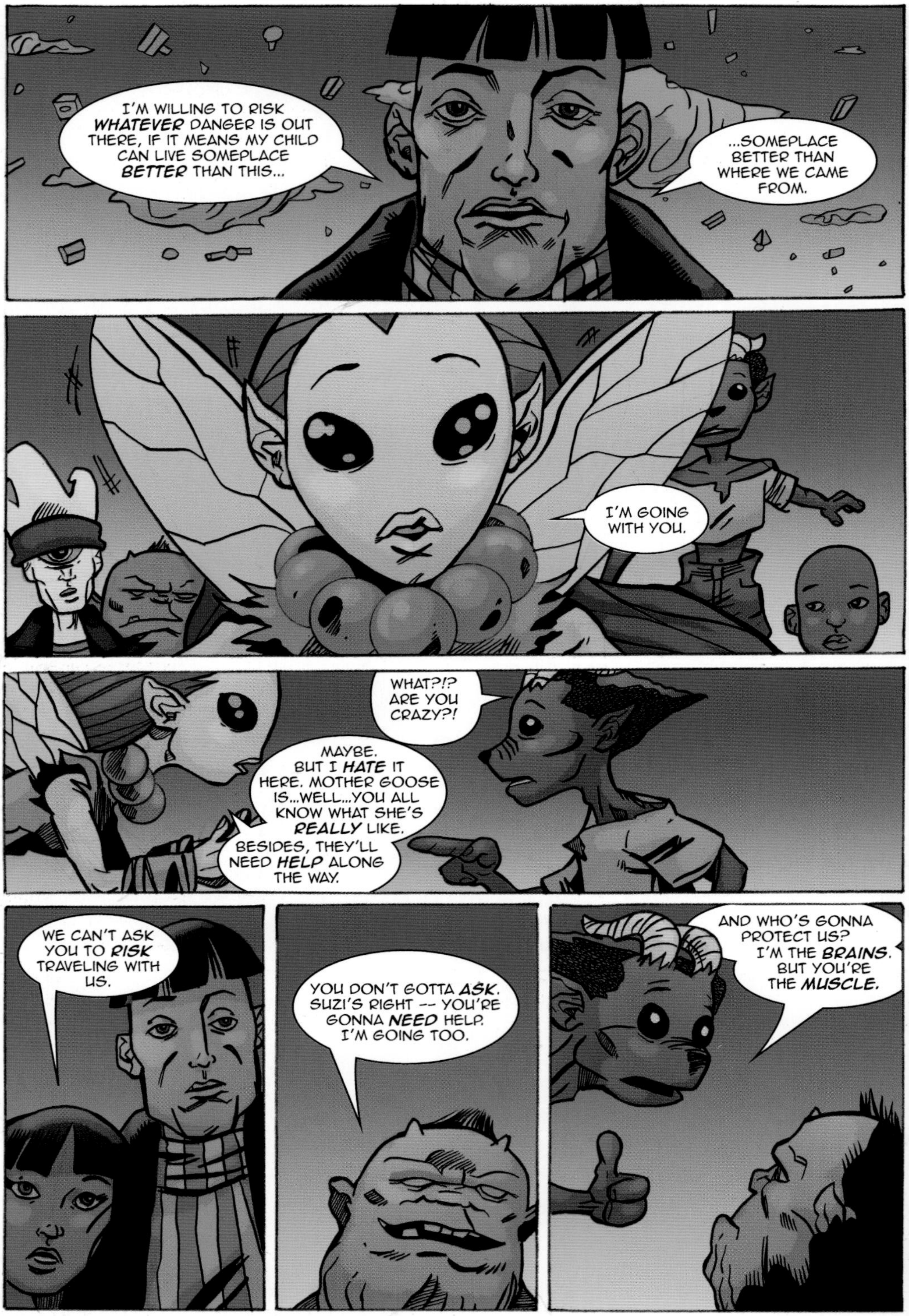
I'M WILLING TO RISK WHATEVER DANGER IS OUT THERE, IF IT MEANS MY CHILD CAN LIVE SOMEPLACE BETTER THAN THIS...
...SOMEPLACE BETTER THAN WHERE WE CAME FROM.
I'M GOING WITH YOU.
WHAT?!? ARE YOU CRAZY?!
MAYBE. BUT I HATE IT HERE. MOTHER GOOSE IS...WELL...YOU ALL KNOW WHAT SHE'S REALLY LIKE.
BESIDES, THEY'LL NEED HELP ALONG THE WAY.
WE CAN'T ASK YOU TO RISK TRAVELING WITH US.
YOU DON'T GOTTA ASK. SUZI'S RIGHT -- YOU'RE GONNA NEED HELP. I'M GOING TOO.
AND WHO'S GONNA PROTECT US? I'M THE BRAINS. BUT YOU'RE THE MUSCLE.

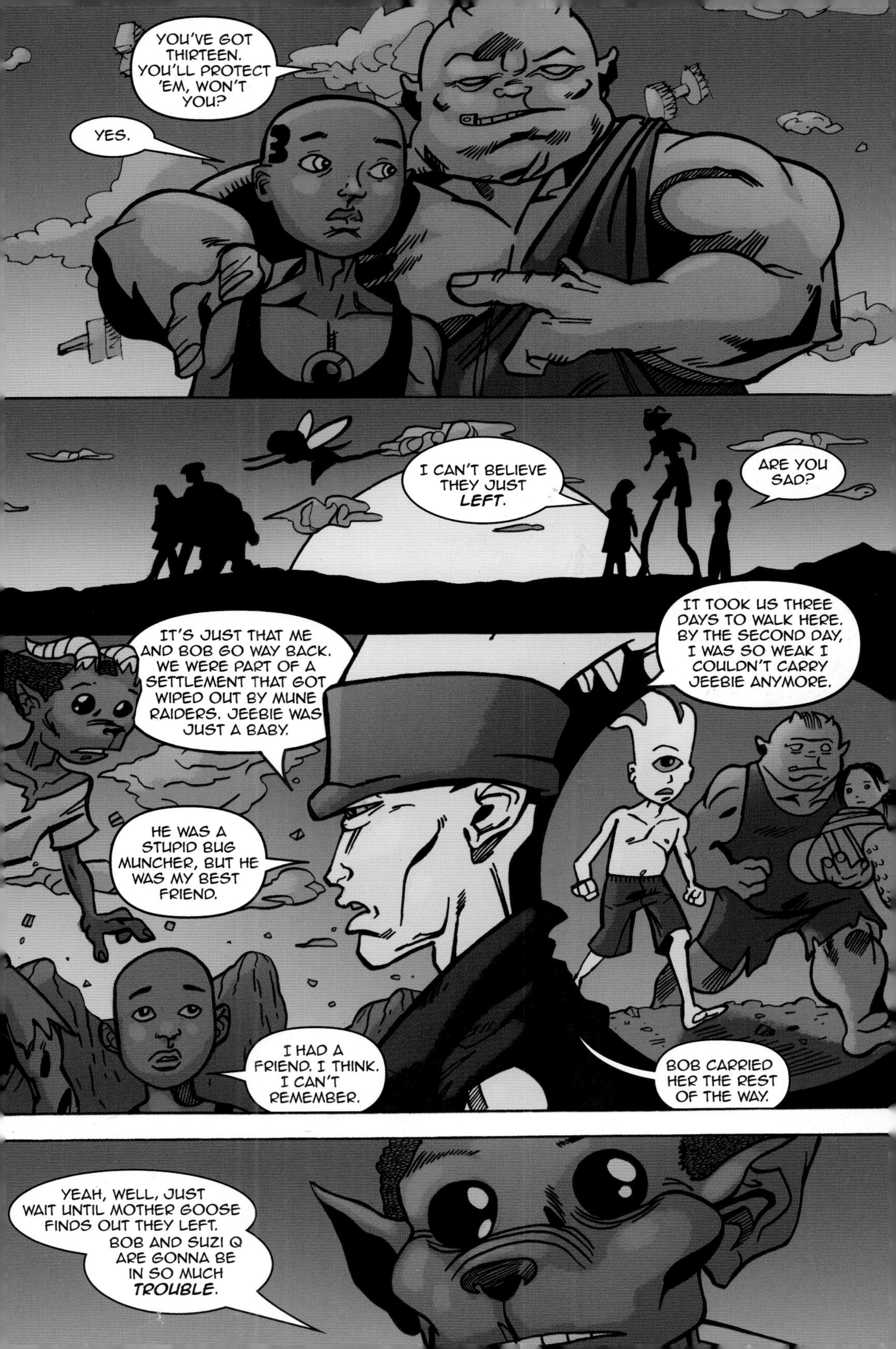
YOU'VE GOT THIRTEEN. YOU'LL PROTECT 'EM, WON'T YOU?
YES.
I CAN'T BELIEVE THEY JUST *LEFT*.
ARE YOU SAD?
IT'S JUST THAT ME AND BOB GO WAY BACK. WE WERE PART OF A SETTLEMENT THAT GOT WIPED OUT BY MUNE RAIDERS. JEEBIE WAS JUST A BABY.
IT TOOK US THREE DAYS TO WALK HERE. BY THE SECOND DAY, I WAS SO WEAK I COULDN'T CARRY JEEBIE ANYMORE.
HE WAS A STUPID BUG MUNCHER, BUT HE WAS MY BEST FRIEND.
I HAD A FRIEND. I THINK. I CAN'T REMEMBER.
BOB CARRIED HER THE REST OF THE WAY.
YEAH, WELL, JUST WAIT UNTIL MOTHER GOOSE FINDS OUT THEY LEFT.
BOB AND SUZI Q ARE GONNA BE IN SO MUCH *TROUBLE*.

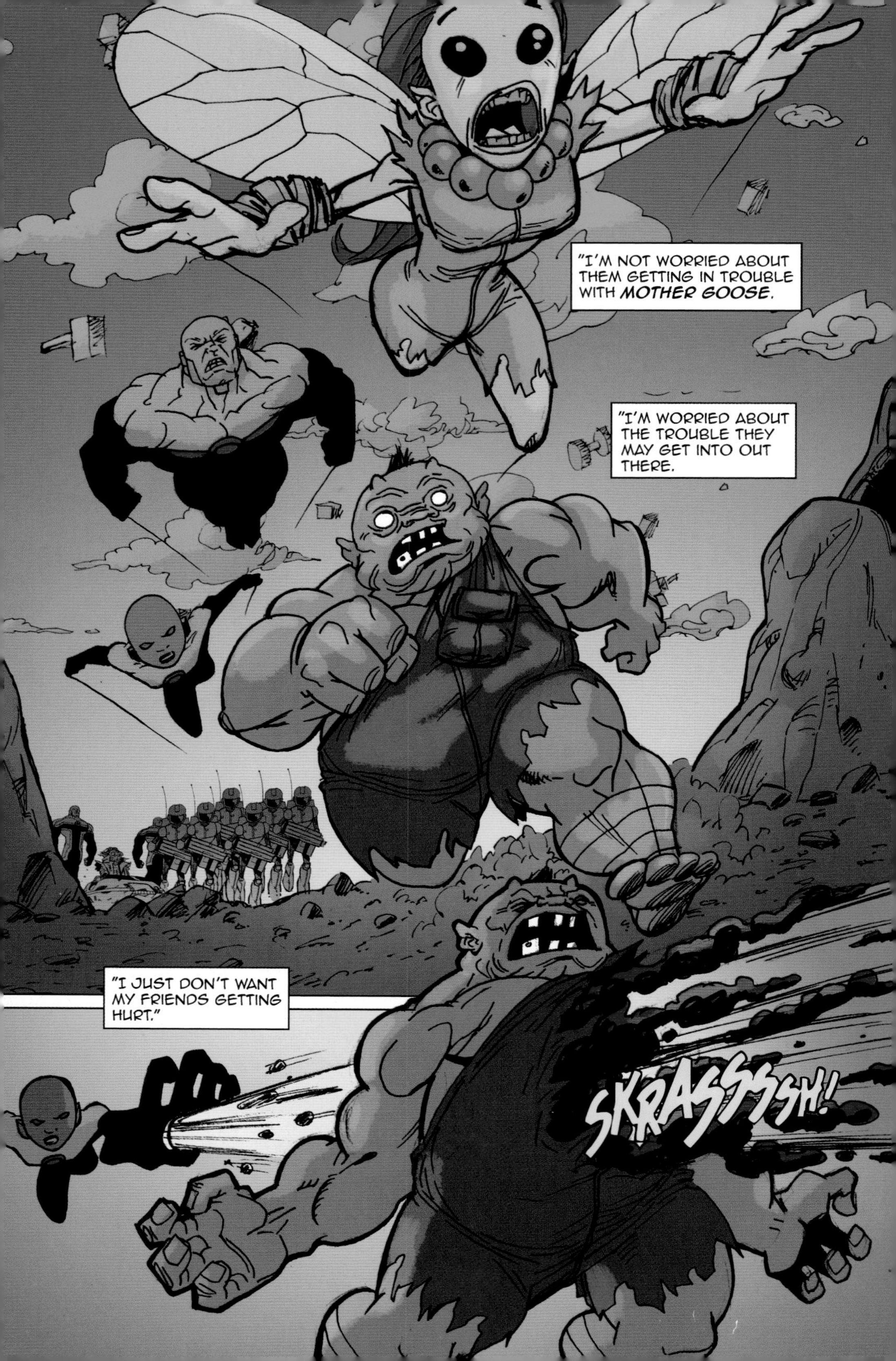
"I'M NOT WORRIED ABOUT THEM GETTING IN TROUBLE WITH MOTHER GOOSE.
"I'M WORRIED ABOUT THE TROUBLE THEY MAY GET INTO OUT THERE.
"I JUST DON'T WANT MY FRIENDS GETTING HURT."
SKRASSSSSH!

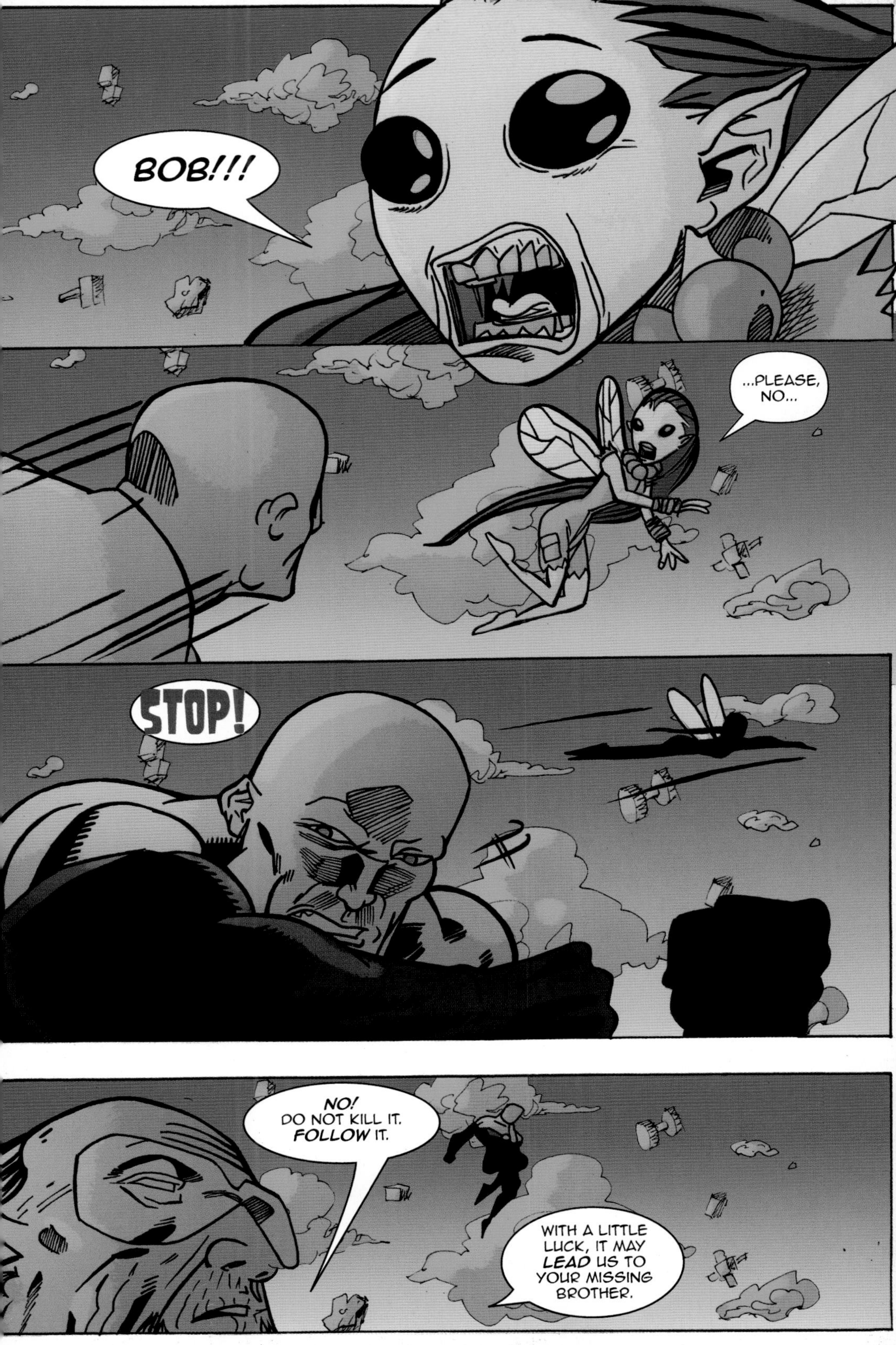
BOB!!!
...PLEASE, NO...
STOP!
NO! DO NOT KILL IT. FOLLOW IT.
WITH A LITTLE LUCK, IT MAY LEAD US TO YOUR MISSING BROTHER.

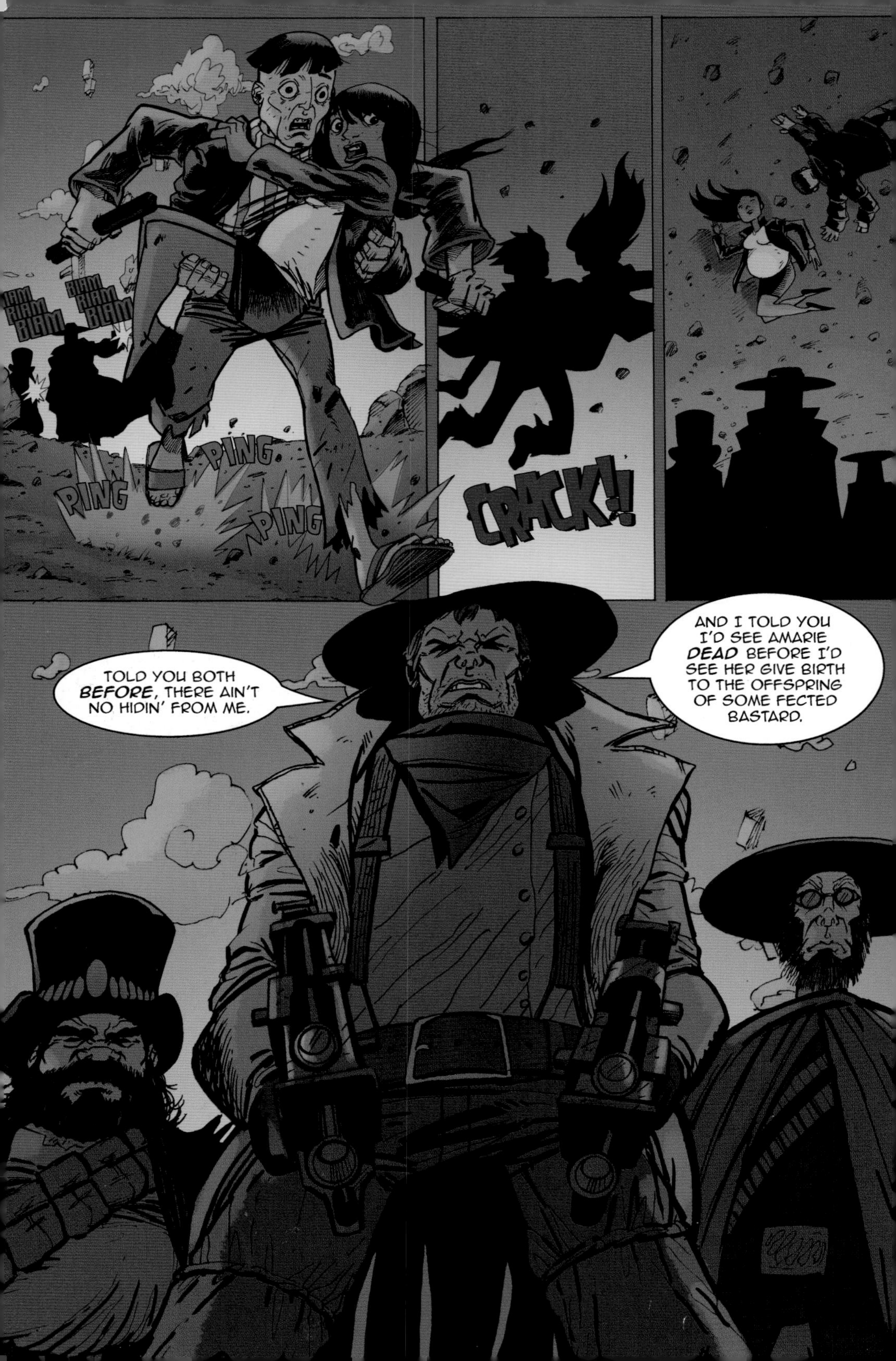
LAM BLAM BLAM
BLAM BLAM BLAM
PING
PING
PING
CRACK!!
TOLD YOU BOTH *BEFORE*, THERE AIN'T NO HIDIN' FROM ME.
AND I TOLD YOU I'D SEE AMARIE *DEAD* BEFORE I'D SEE HER GIVE BIRTH TO THE OFFSPRING OF SOME FECTED BASTARD.

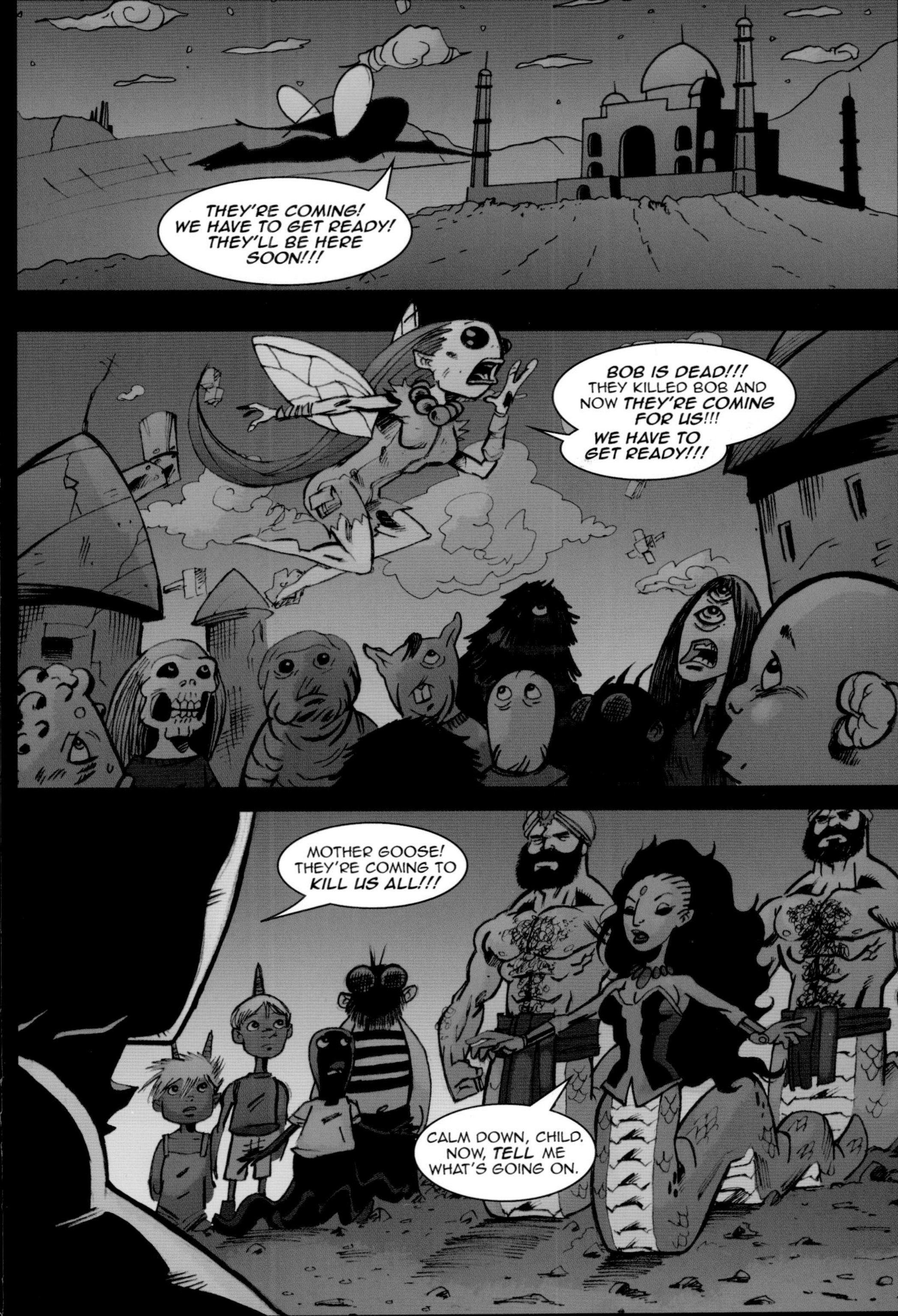
THEY'RE COMING! WE HAVE TO GET READY! THEY'LL BE HERE SOON!!!
BOB IS DEAD!!! THEY KILLED BOB AND NOW THEY'RE COMING FOR US!!! WE HAVE TO GET READY!!!
MOTHER GOOSE! THEY'RE COMING TO KILL US ALL!!!
CALM DOWN, CHILD. NOW, TELL ME WHAT'S GOING ON.

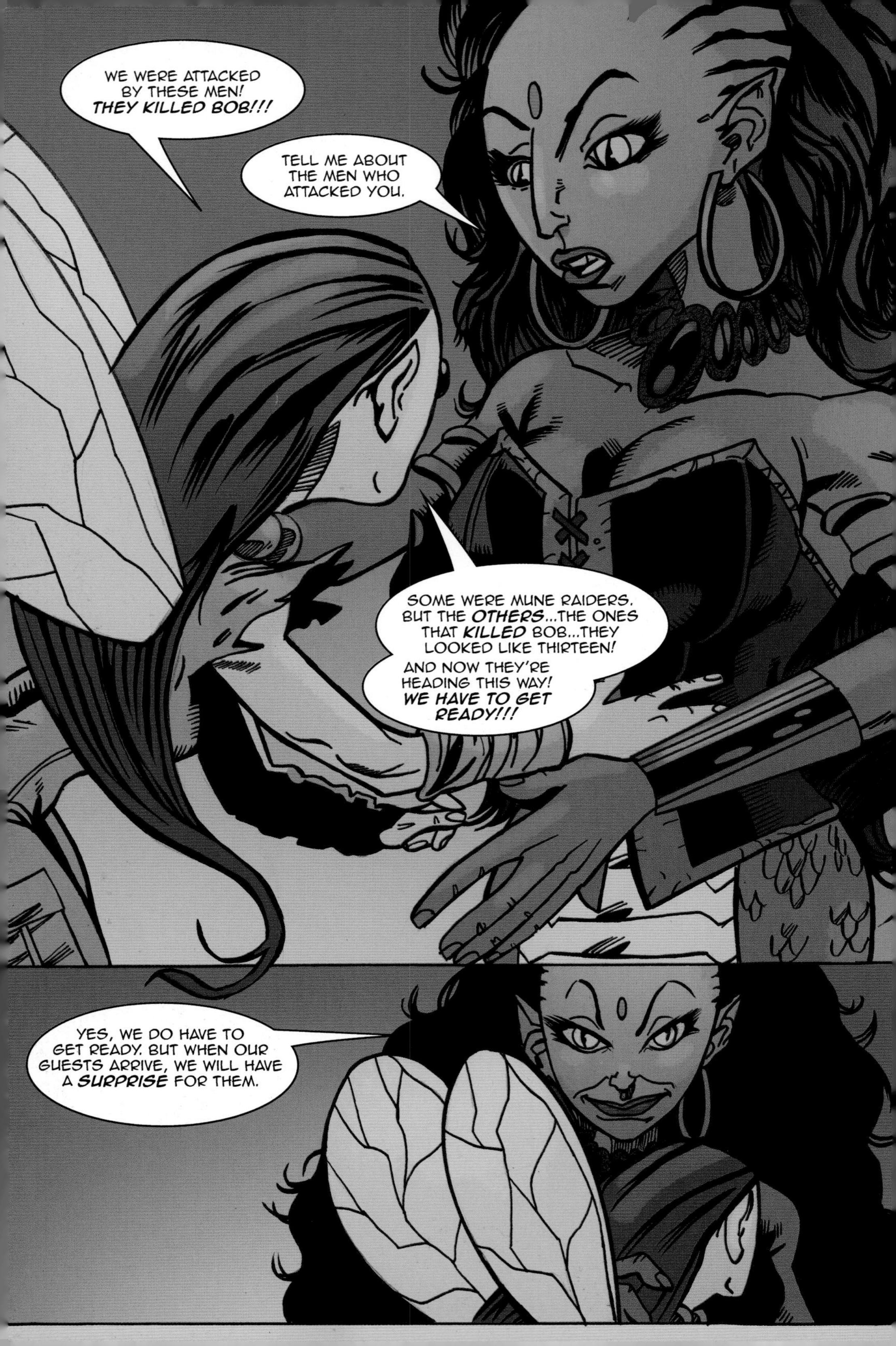
WE WERE ATTACKED BY THESE MEN! THEY KILLED BOB!!!
TELL ME ABOUT THE MEN WHO ATTACKED YOU.
SOME WERE MUNE RAIDERS. BUT THE OTHERS...THE ONES THAT KILLED BOB...THEY LOOKED LIKE THIRTEEN!
AND NOW THEY'RE HEADING THIS WAY! WE HAVE TO GET READY!!!
YES, WE DO HAVE TO GET READY. BUT WHEN OUR GUESTS ARRIVE, WE WILL HAVE A SURPRISE FOR THEM.

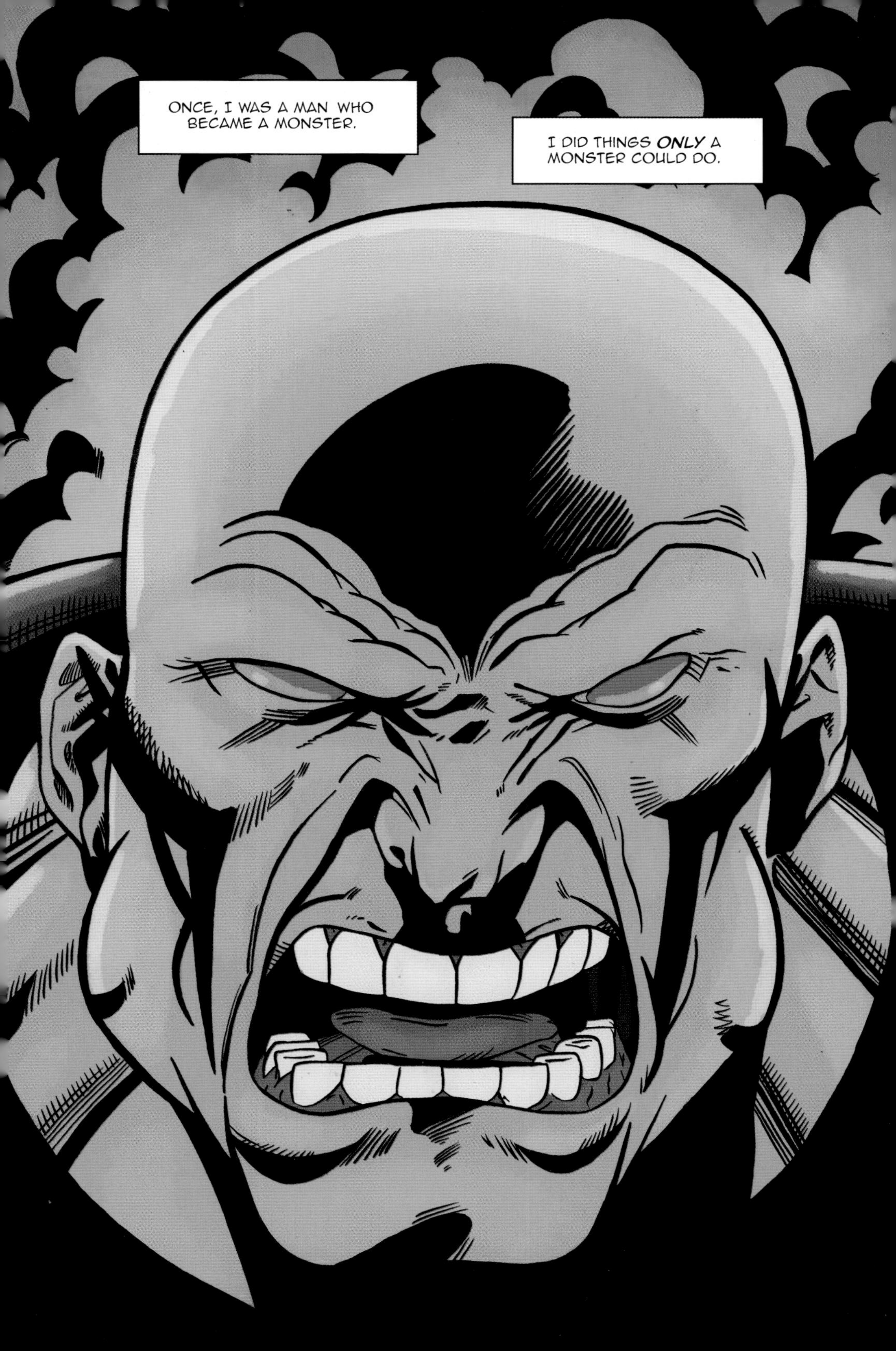
ONCE, I WAS A MAN WHO BECAME A MONSTER.
I DID THINGS ONLY A MONSTER COULD DO.

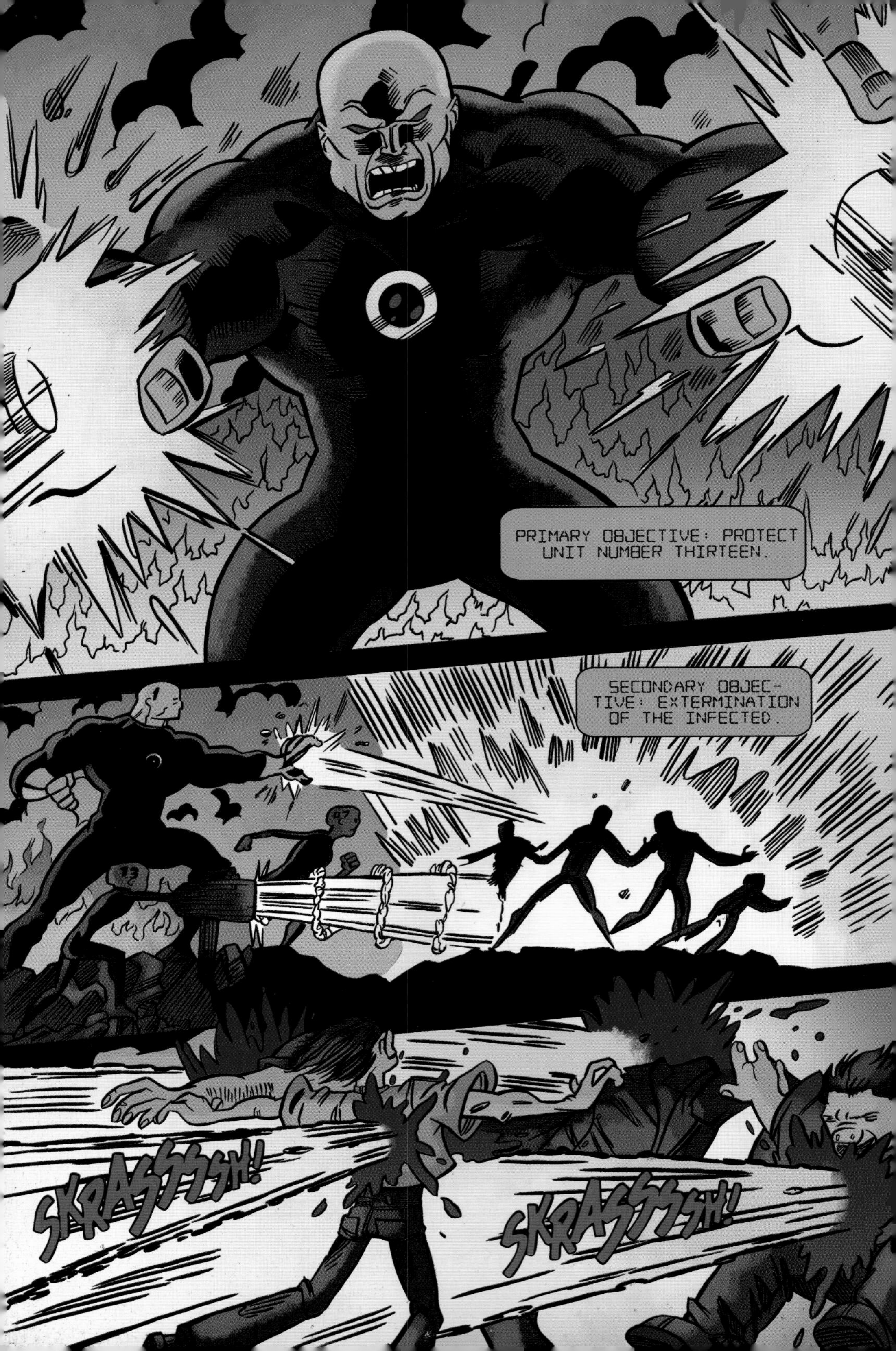
PRIMARY OBJECTIVE: PROTECT UNIT NUMBER THIRTEEN.
SECONDARY OBJEC-TIVE: EXTERMINATION OF THE INFECTED.
SKRASSSSH!
SKRASSSSH!

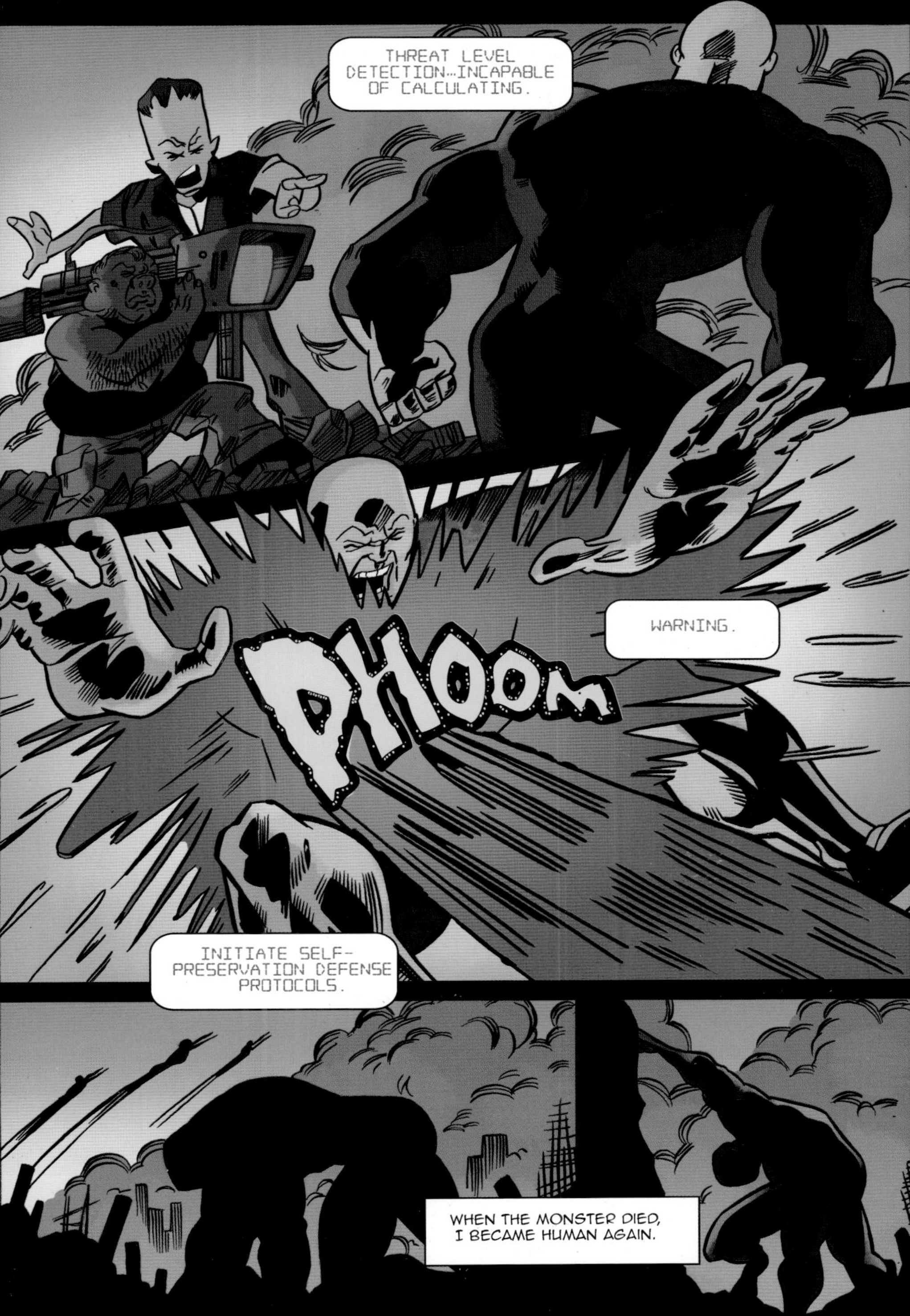
THREAT LEVEL DETECTION...INCAPABLE OF CALCULATING.
WARNING.
PHOOM
INITIATE SELF-PRESERVATION DEFENSE PROTOCOLS.
WHEN THE MONSTER DIED, I BECAME HUMAN AGAIN.

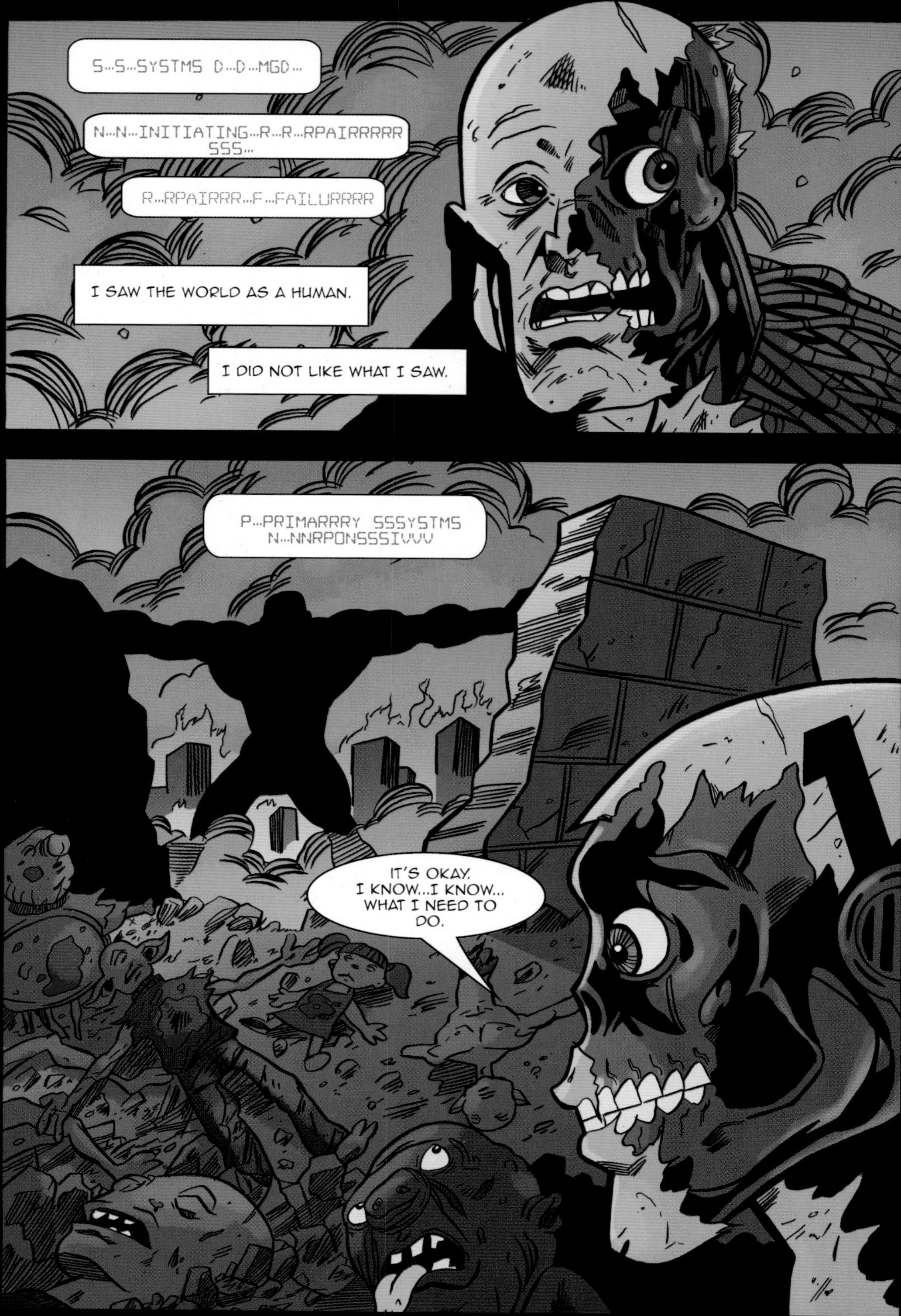
S...S...SYSTMS D...D...MGD...
N...N...INITIATING...R...R...RPAIRRRRR SSS...
R...RPAIRRR...F...FAILURRRR
I SAW THE WORLD AS A HUMAN.
I DID NOT LIKE WHAT I SAW.
P...PRIMARRRY SSSYSTMS N...NNRPONSSSIVVV
IT'S OKAY. I KNOW...I KNOW... WHAT I NEED TO DO.

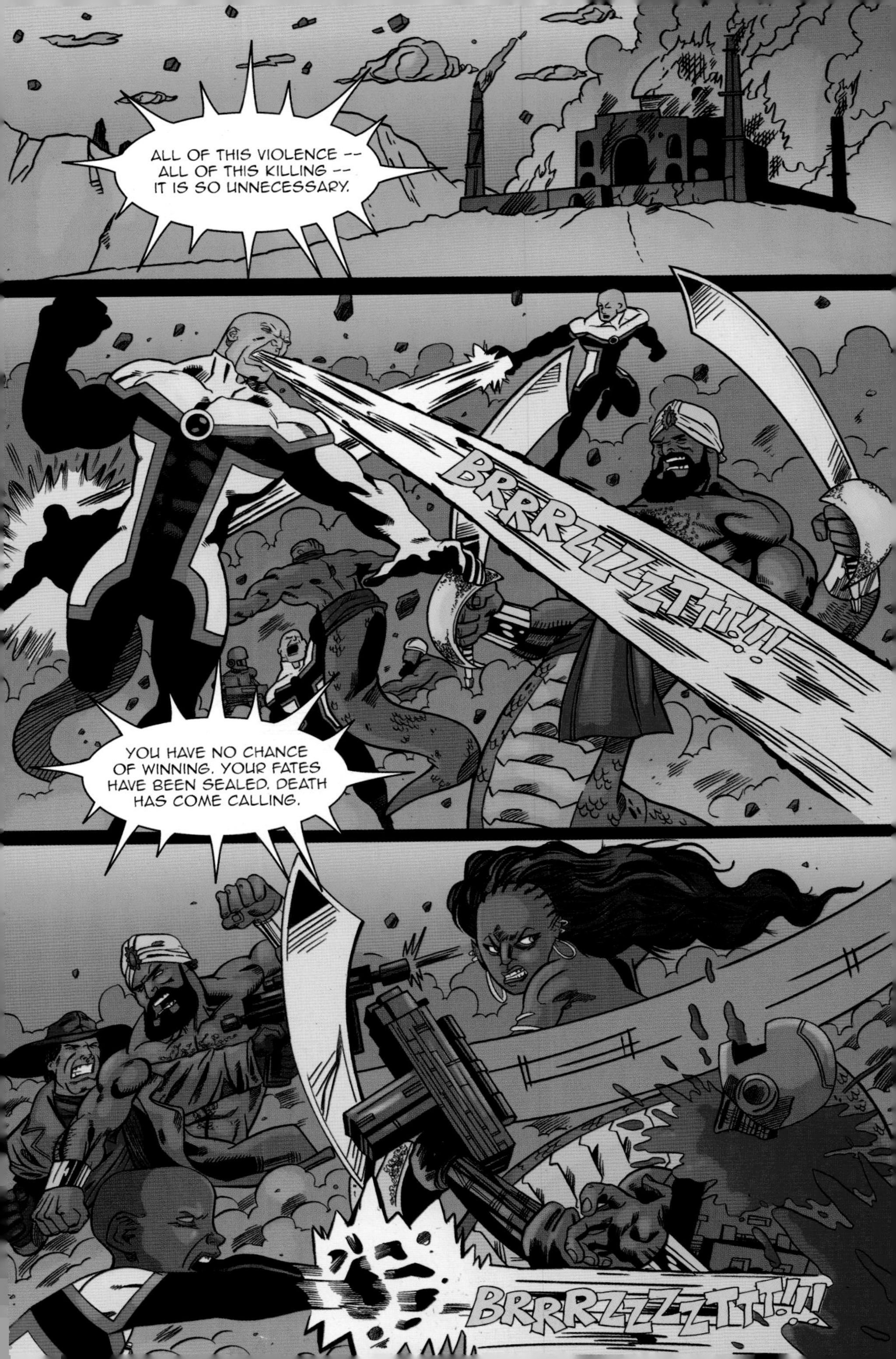
ALL OF THIS VIOLENCE -- ALL OF THIS KILLING -- IT IS SO UNNECESSARY.
BRRRZZZZZTTT!!!
YOU HAVE NO CHANCE OF WINNING. YOUR FATES HAVE BEEN SEALED. DEATH HAS COME CALLING.
BRRRZZZZZTTT!!!

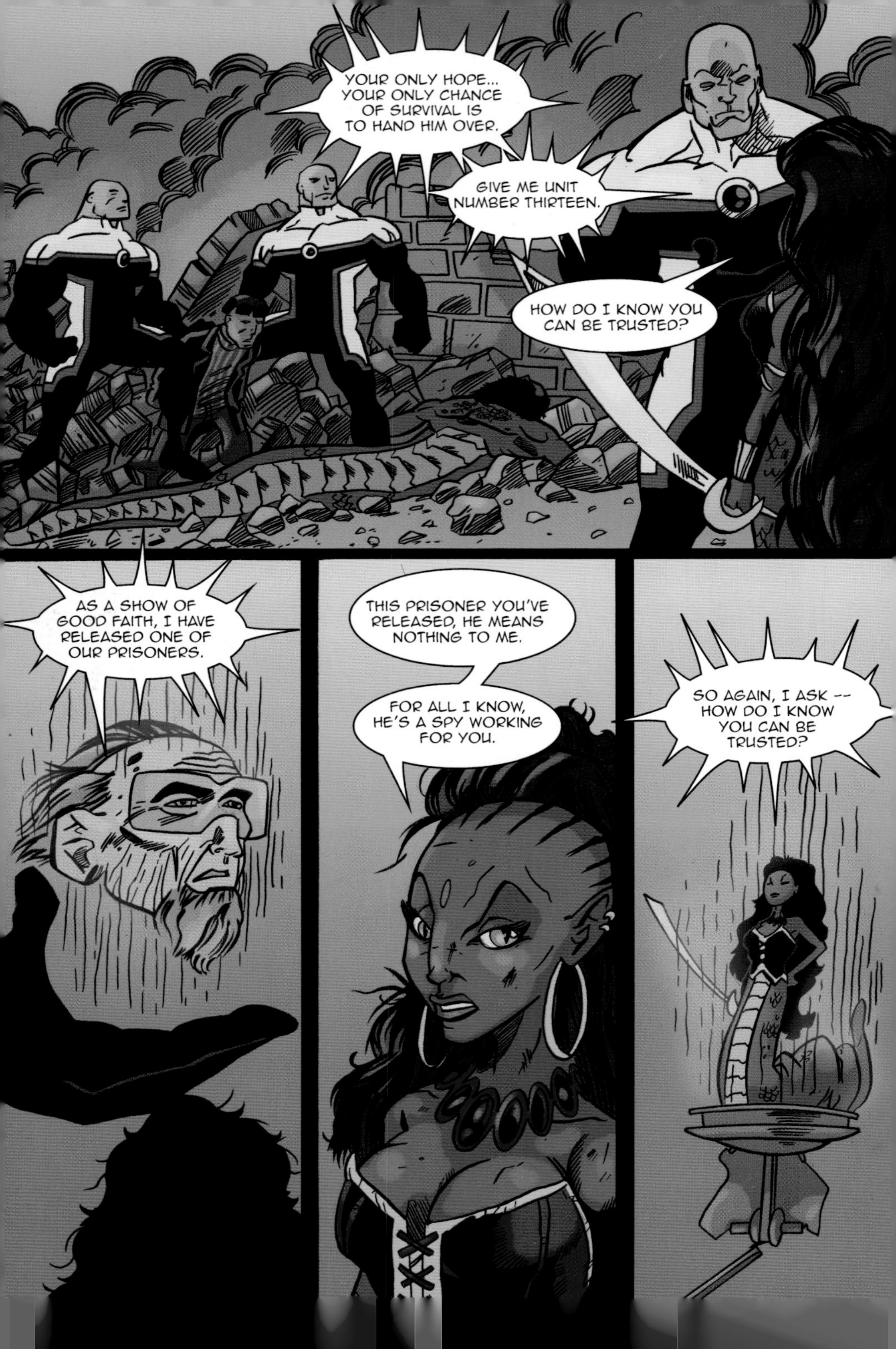
YOUR ONLY HOPE... YOUR ONLY CHANCE OF SURVIVAL IS TO HAND HIM OVER.
GIVE ME UNIT NUMBER THIRTEEN.
HOW DO I KNOW YOU CAN BE TRUSTED?
AS A SHOW OF GOOD FAITH, I HAVE RELEASED ONE OF OUR PRISONERS.
THIS PRISONER YOU'VE RELEASED, HE MEANS NOTHING TO ME.
FOR ALL I KNOW, HE'S A SPY WORKING FOR YOU.
SO AGAIN, I ASK -- HOW DO I KNOW YOU CAN BE TRUSTED?

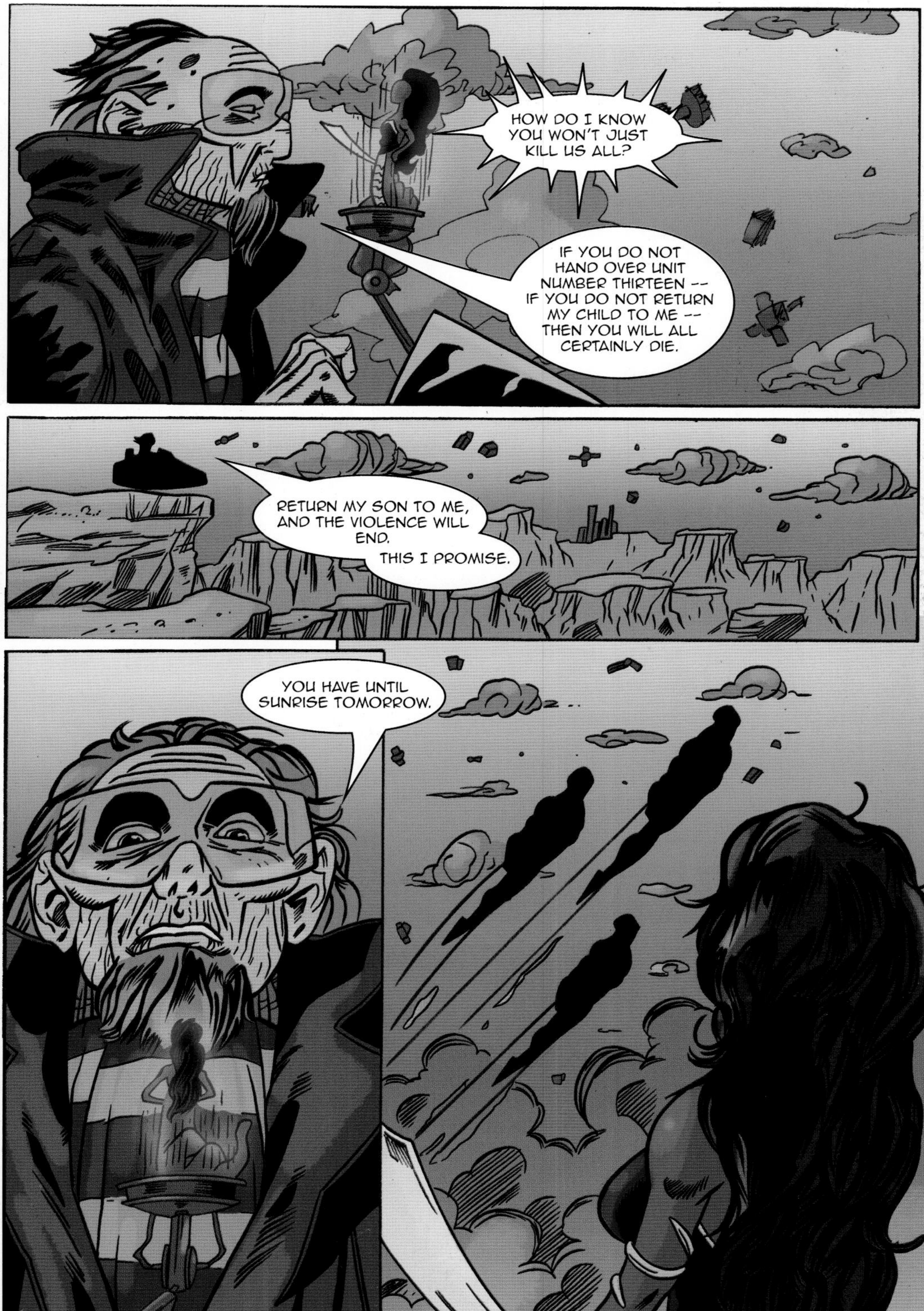
HOW DO I KNOW YOU WON'T JUST KILL US ALL?
IF YOU DO NOT HAND OVER UNIT NUMBER THIRTEEN -- IF YOU DO NOT RETURN MY CHILD TO ME -- THEN YOU WILL ALL CERTAINLY DIE.
RETURN MY SON TO ME, AND THE VIOLENCE WILL END.
THIS I PROMISE.
YOU HAVE UNTIL SUNRISE TOMORROW.

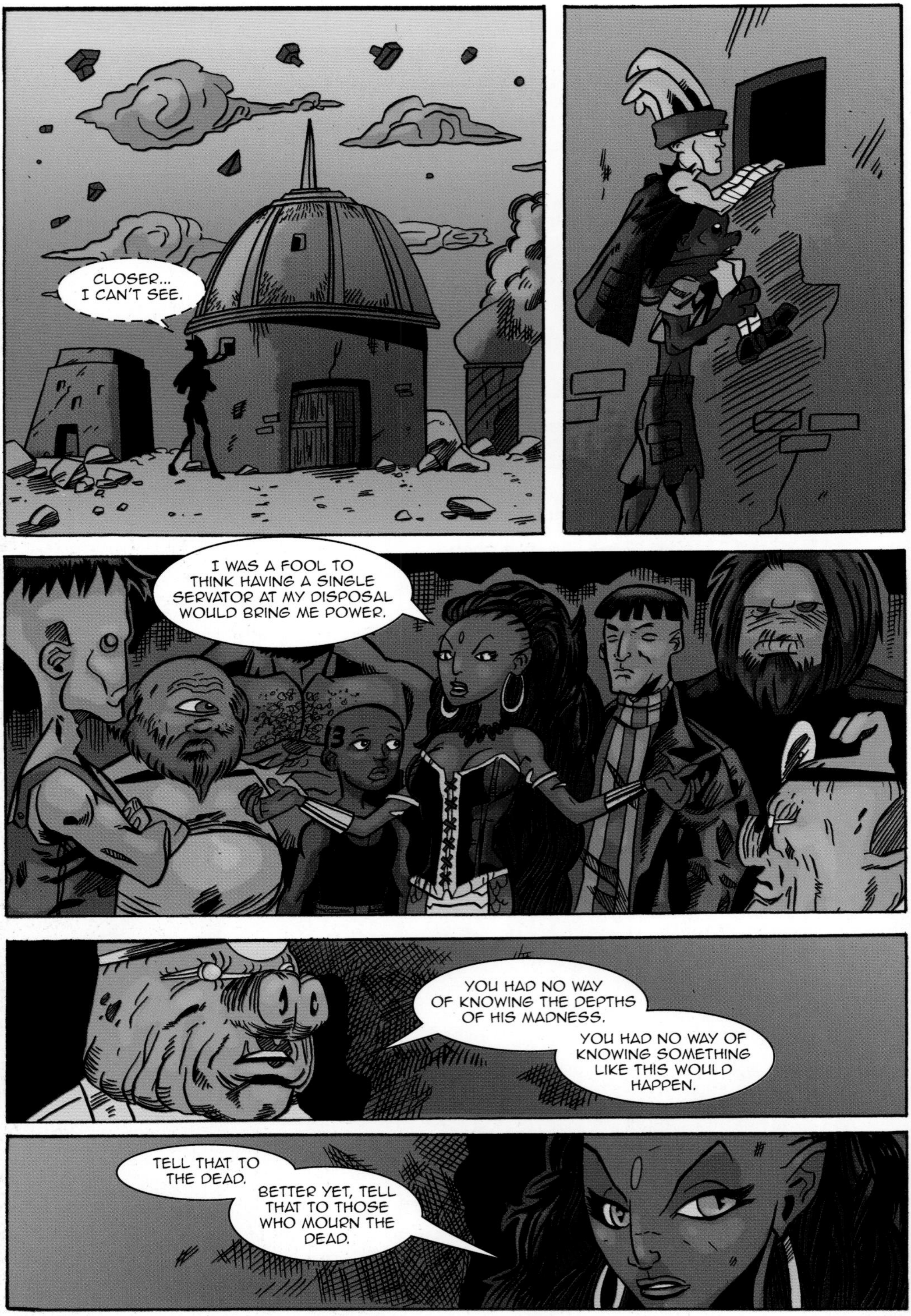
CLOSER...
I CAN'T SEE.
I WAS A FOOL TO THINK HAVING A SINGLE SERVATOR AT MY DISPOSAL WOULD BRING ME POWER.
YOU HAD NO WAY OF KNOWING THE DEPTHS OF HIS MADNESS.
YOU HAD NO WAY OF KNOWING SOMETHING LIKE THIS WOULD HAPPEN.
TELL THAT TO THE DEAD.
BETTER YET, TELL THAT TO THOSE WHO MOURN THE DEAD.

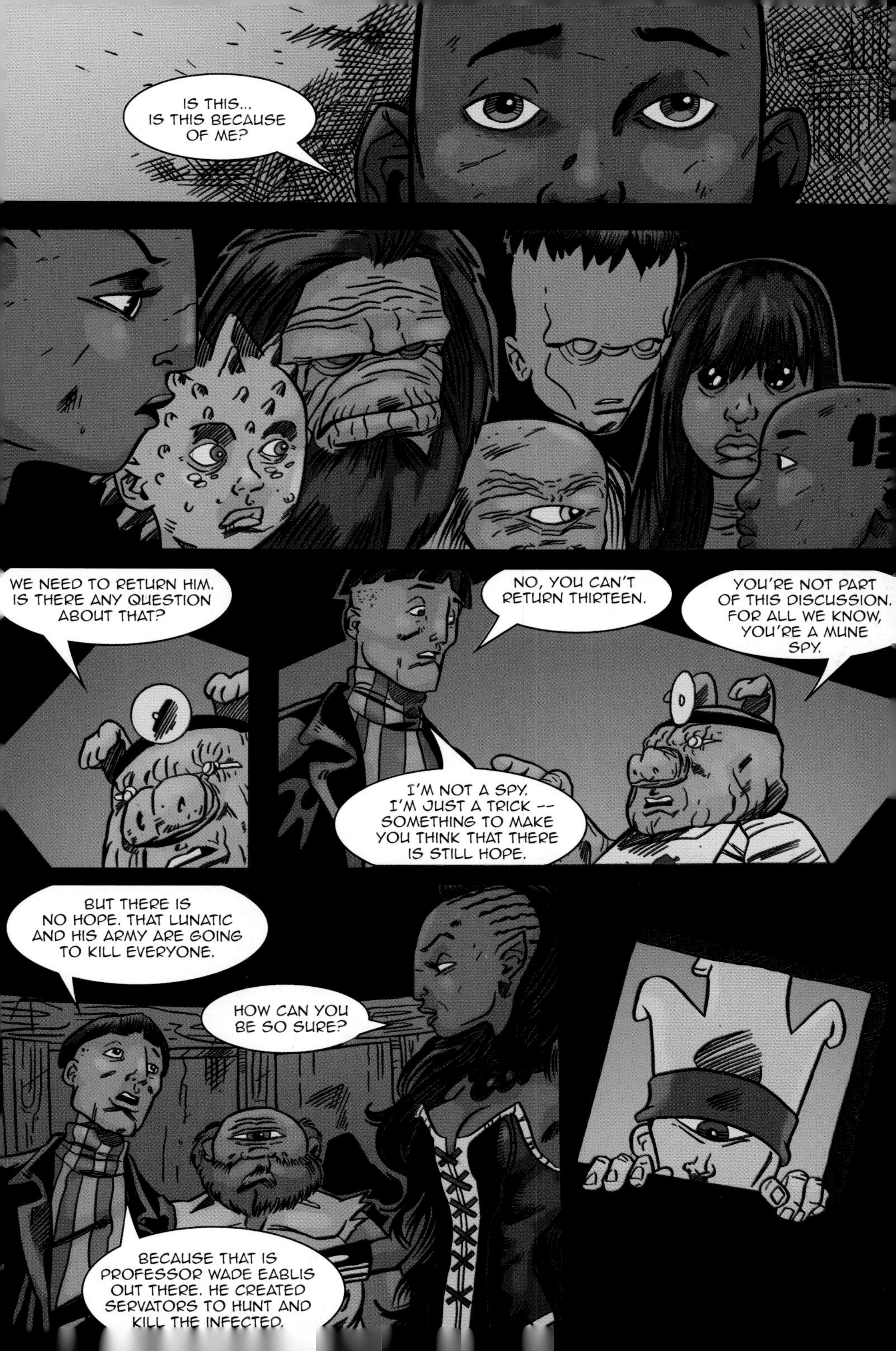
IS THIS...
IS THIS BECAUSE OF ME?
WE NEED TO RETURN HIM. IS THERE ANY QUESTION ABOUT THAT?
NO, YOU CAN'T RETURN THIRTEEN.
YOU'RE NOT PART OF THIS DISCUSSION. FOR ALL WE KNOW, YOU'RE A MUNE SPY.
I'M NOT A SPY. I'M JUST A TRICK -- SOMETHING TO MAKE YOU THINK THAT THERE IS STILL HOPE.
BUT THERE IS NO HOPE. THAT LUNATIC AND HIS ARMY ARE GOING TO KILL EVERYONE.
HOW CAN YOU BE SO SURE?
BECAUSE THAT IS PROFESSOR WADE EABLIS OUT THERE. HE CREATED SERVATORS TO HUNT AND KILL THE INFECTED.

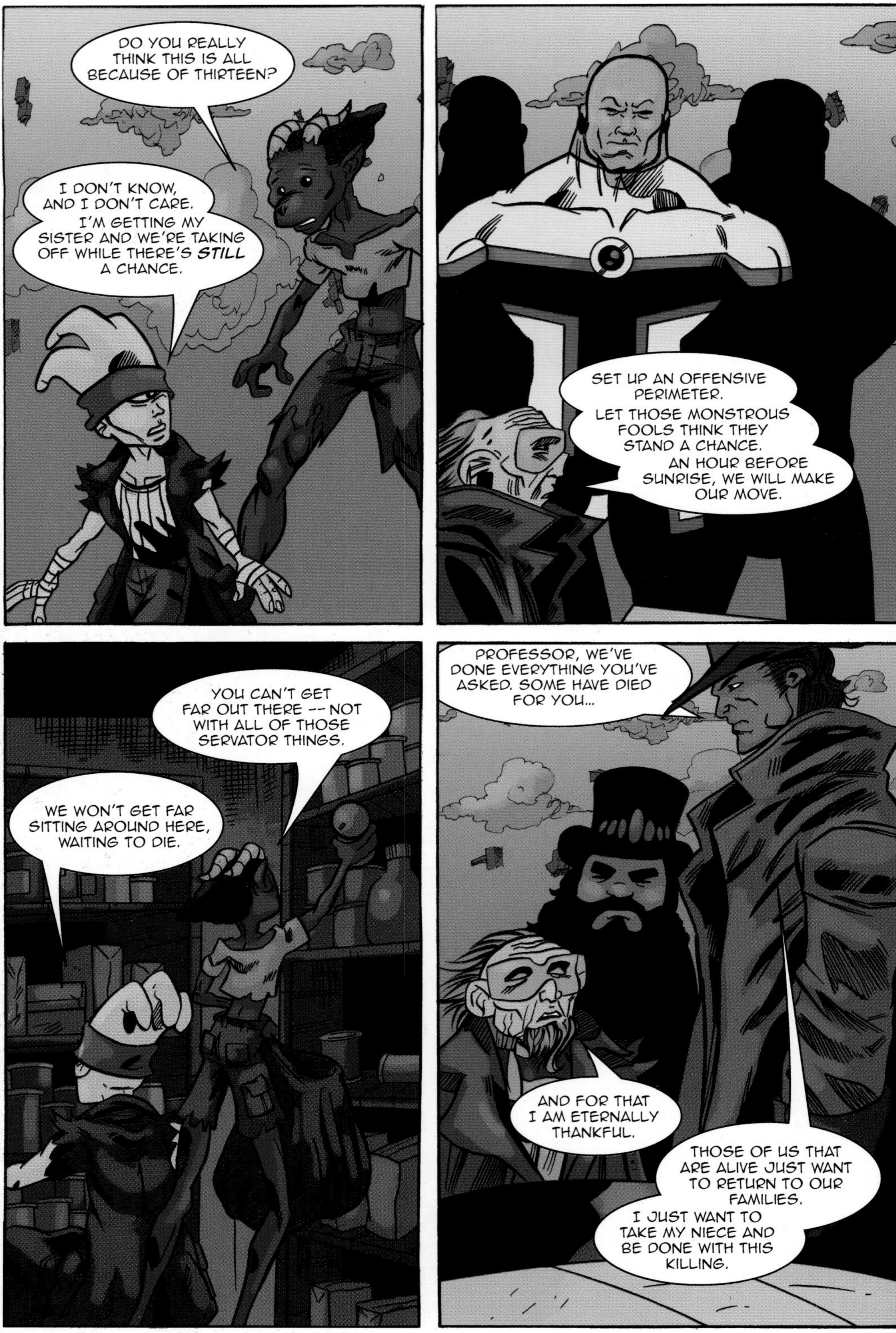
DO YOU REALLY THINK THIS IS ALL BECAUSE OF THIRTEEN?
I DON'T KNOW, AND I DON'T CARE.
I'M GETTING MY SISTER AND WE'RE TAKING OFF WHILE THERE'S *STILL* A CHANCE.
SET UP AN OFFENSIVE PERIMETER.
LET THOSE MONSTROUS FOOLS THINK THEY STAND A CHANCE.
AN HOUR BEFORE SUNRISE, WE WILL MAKE OUR MOVE.
YOU CAN'T GET FAR OUT THERE -- NOT WITH ALL OF THOSE SERVATOR THINGS.
WE WON'T GET FAR SITTING AROUND HERE, WAITING TO DIE.
PROFESSOR, WE'VE DONE EVERYTHING YOU'VE ASKED. SOME HAVE DIED FOR YOU...
AND FOR THAT I AM ETERNALLY THANKFUL.
THOSE OF US THAT ARE ALIVE JUST WANT TO RETURN TO OUR FAMILIES.
I JUST WANT TO TAKE MY NIECE AND BE DONE WITH THIS KILLING.

YOUR NIECE IS A MUNE, BUT SHE HAS **CONSORTED** WITH A FECTED. THAT IS A CRIME AGAINST HUMANITY.

I UNDERSTAND, SIR. BUT I THOUGHT, CONSIDERIN' ALL WE'VE DONE FOR YOU, AMARIE AND HER BABY...

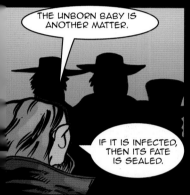

THE UNBORN BABY IS ANOTHER MATTER.

IF IT IS INFECTED, THEN ITS FATE IS SEALED.

ONCE THE MASSACRE STARTS, WE'RE TAKIN' OFF.

AND AMARIE IS COMIN' WITH US.

WHICH WAY DO WE GO?

WEST. ME AND JEEBIE, WE CAME FROM THE EAST. THERE'S NOTHING BACK THERE FOR US.

IF WE'RE REALLY DOING THIS, WE NEED TO TAKE THE OTHER KIDS WITH US. WE CAN'T LEAVE THEM HERE TO DIE.

NEVER THOUGHT I'D SAY THIS, BUT I WISH BOB WAS HERE.

AND I NEVER THOUGHT I'D MISS THAT UGLY BUG MUNCHER.

UH-OH...

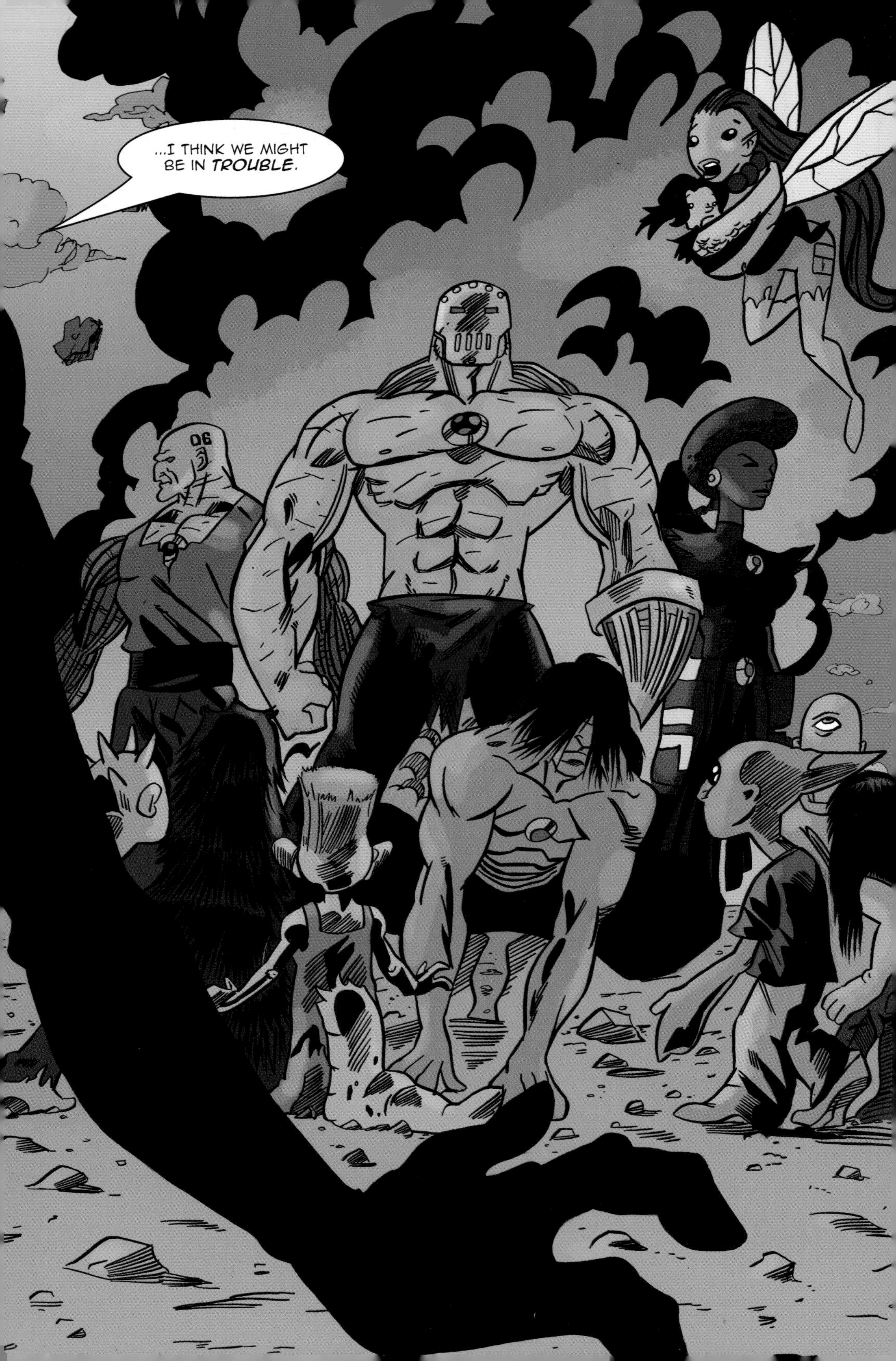
...I THINK WE MIGHT BE IN *TROUBLE*.

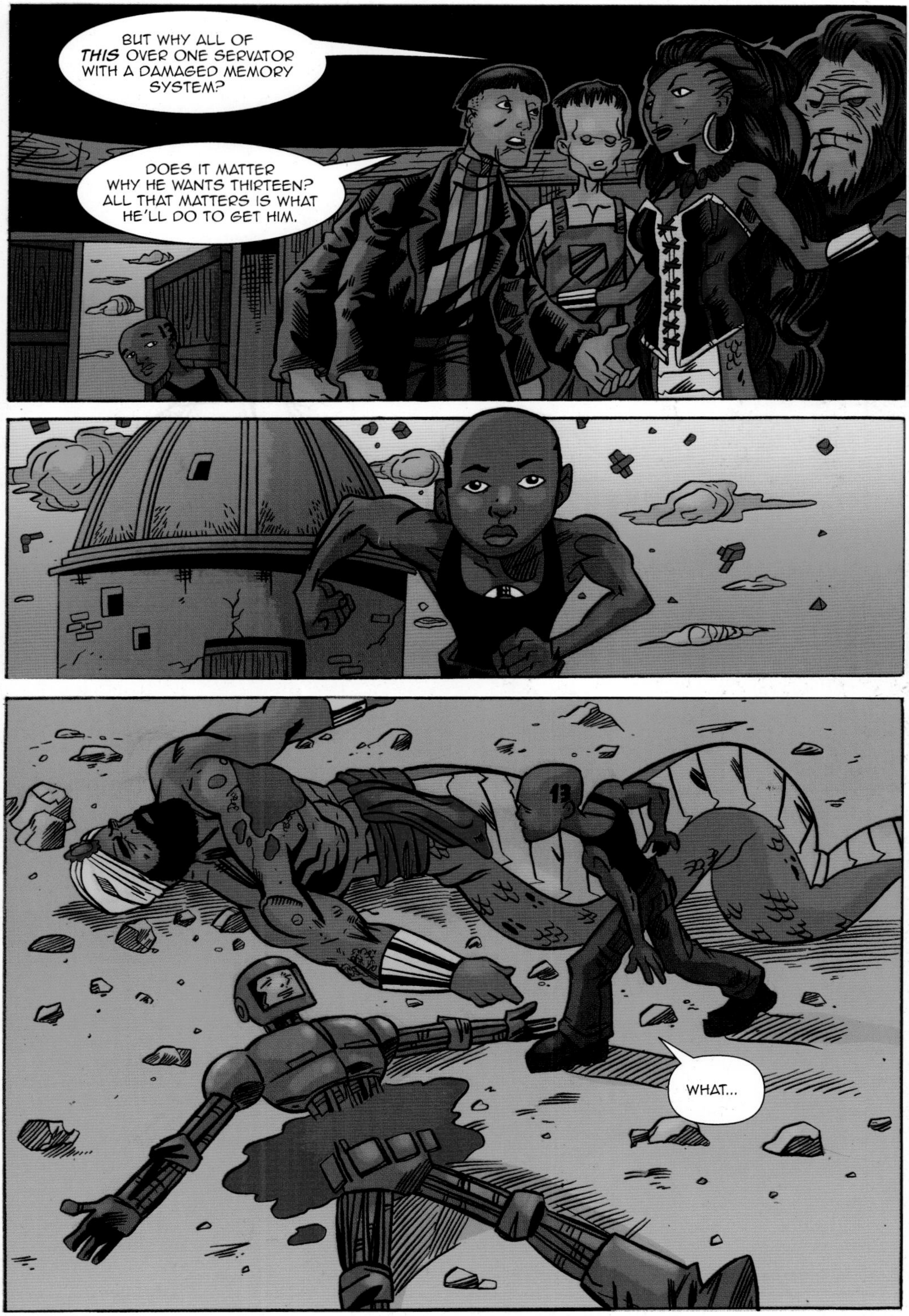
BUT WHY ALL OF *THIS* OVER ONE SERVATOR WITH A DAMAGED MEMORY SYSTEM?
DOES IT MATTER WHY HE WANTS THIRTEEN? ALL THAT MATTERS IS WHAT HE'LL DO TO GET HIM.
WHAT...

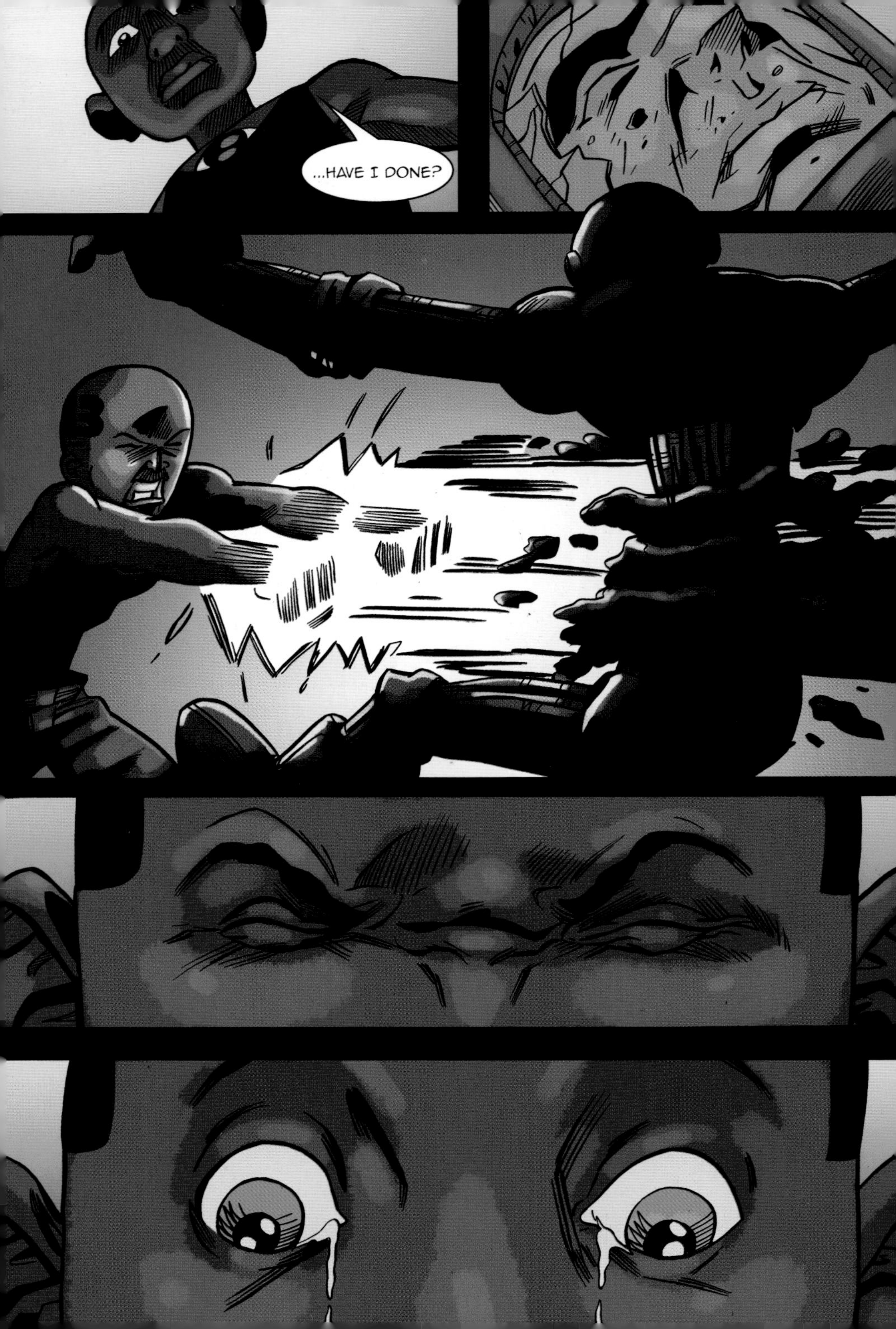
...HAVE I DONE?

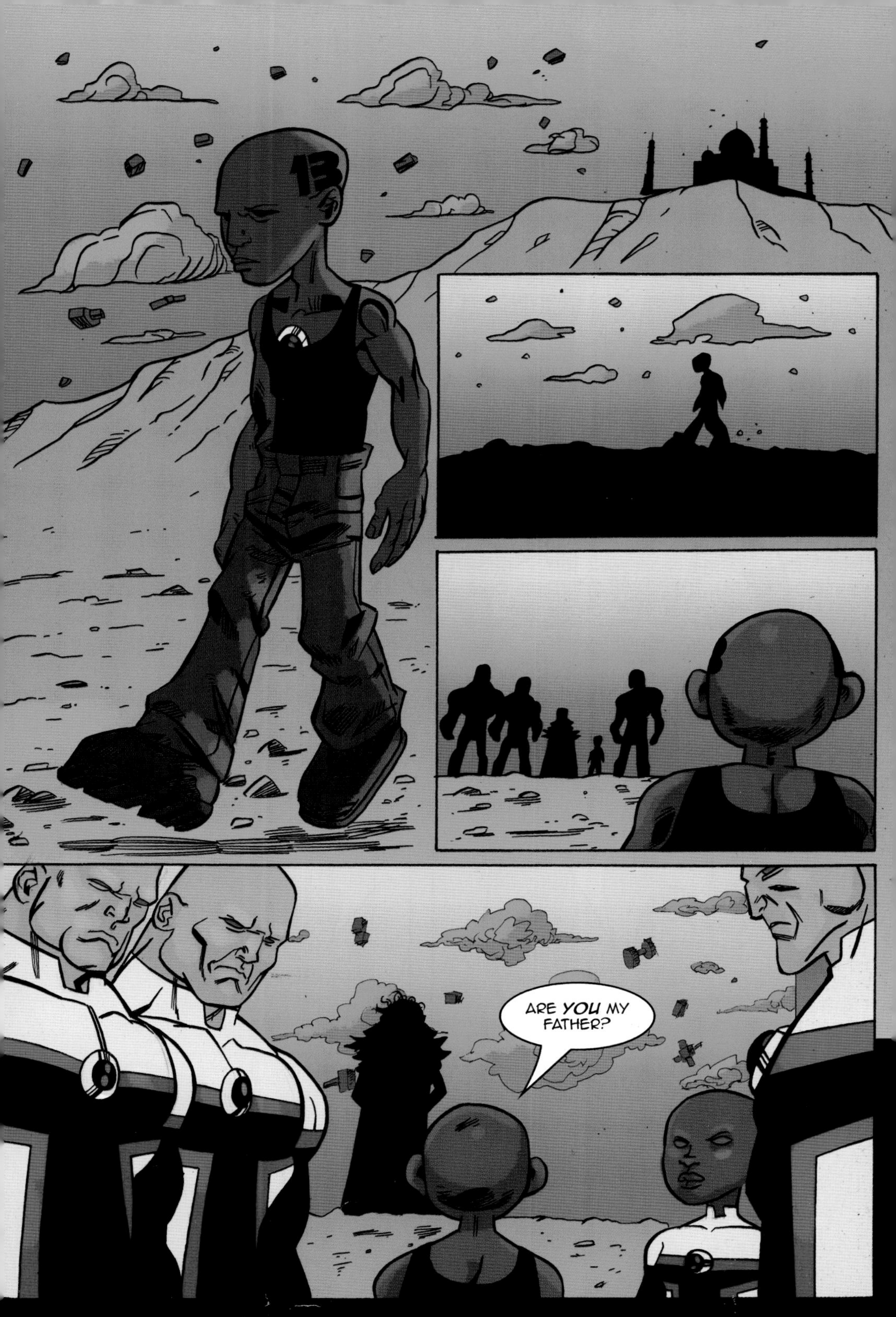
ARE YOU MY FATHER?

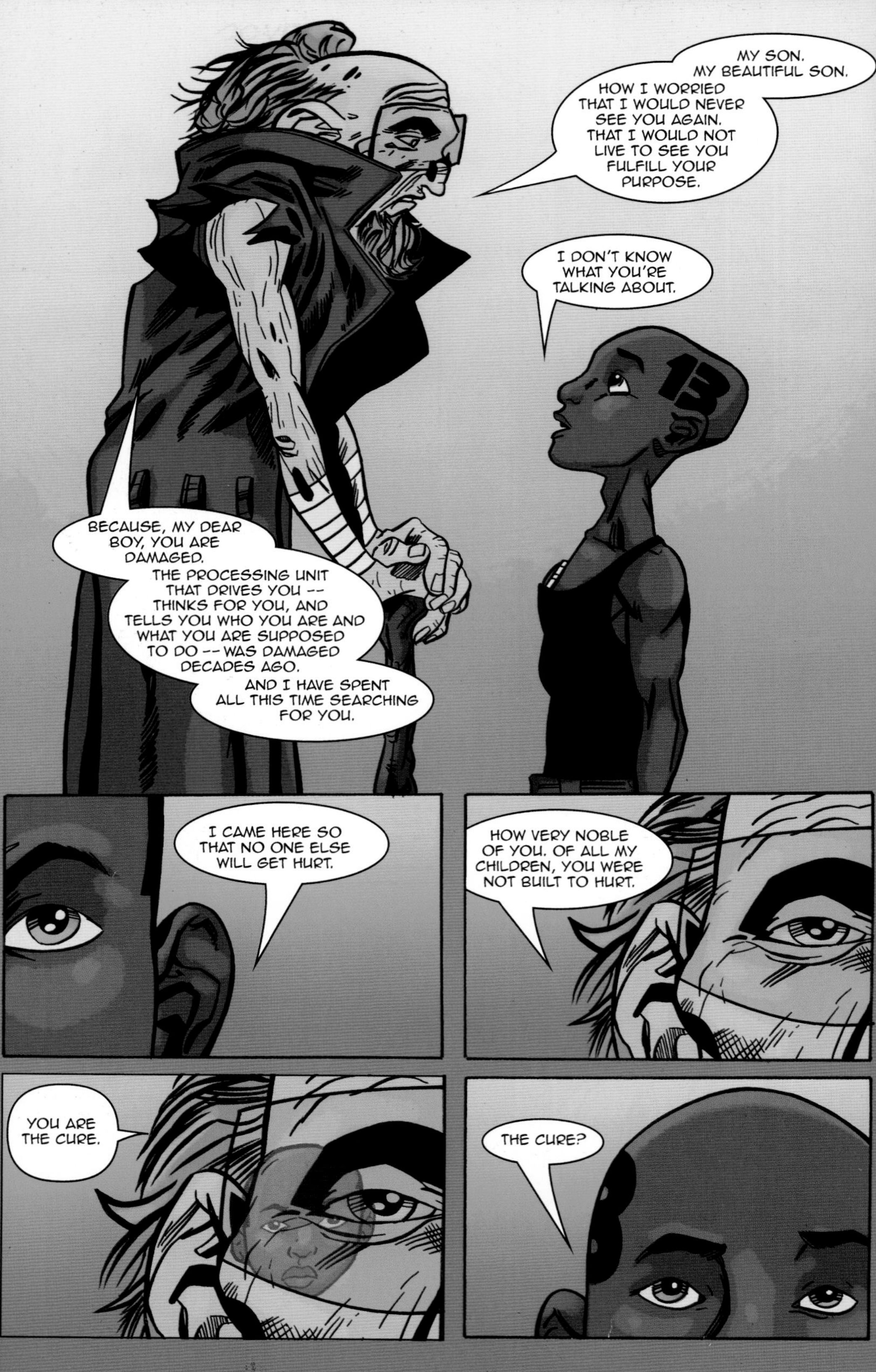
MY SON. MY BEAUTIFUL SON.
HOW I WORRIED THAT I WOULD NEVER SEE YOU AGAIN. THAT I WOULD NOT LIVE TO SEE YOU FULFILL YOUR PURPOSE.
I DON'T KNOW WHAT YOU'RE TALKING ABOUT.
BECAUSE, MY DEAR BOY, YOU ARE DAMAGED.
THE PROCESSING UNIT THAT DRIVES YOU -- THINKS FOR YOU, AND TELLS YOU WHO YOU ARE AND WHAT YOU ARE SUPPOSED TO DO -- WAS DAMAGED DECADES AGO.
AND I HAVE SPENT ALL THIS TIME SEARCHING FOR YOU.
I CAME HERE SO THAT NO ONE ELSE WILL GET HURT.
HOW VERY NOBLE OF YOU. OF ALL MY CHILDREN, YOU WERE NOT BUILT TO HURT.
YOU ARE THE CURE.
THE CURE?

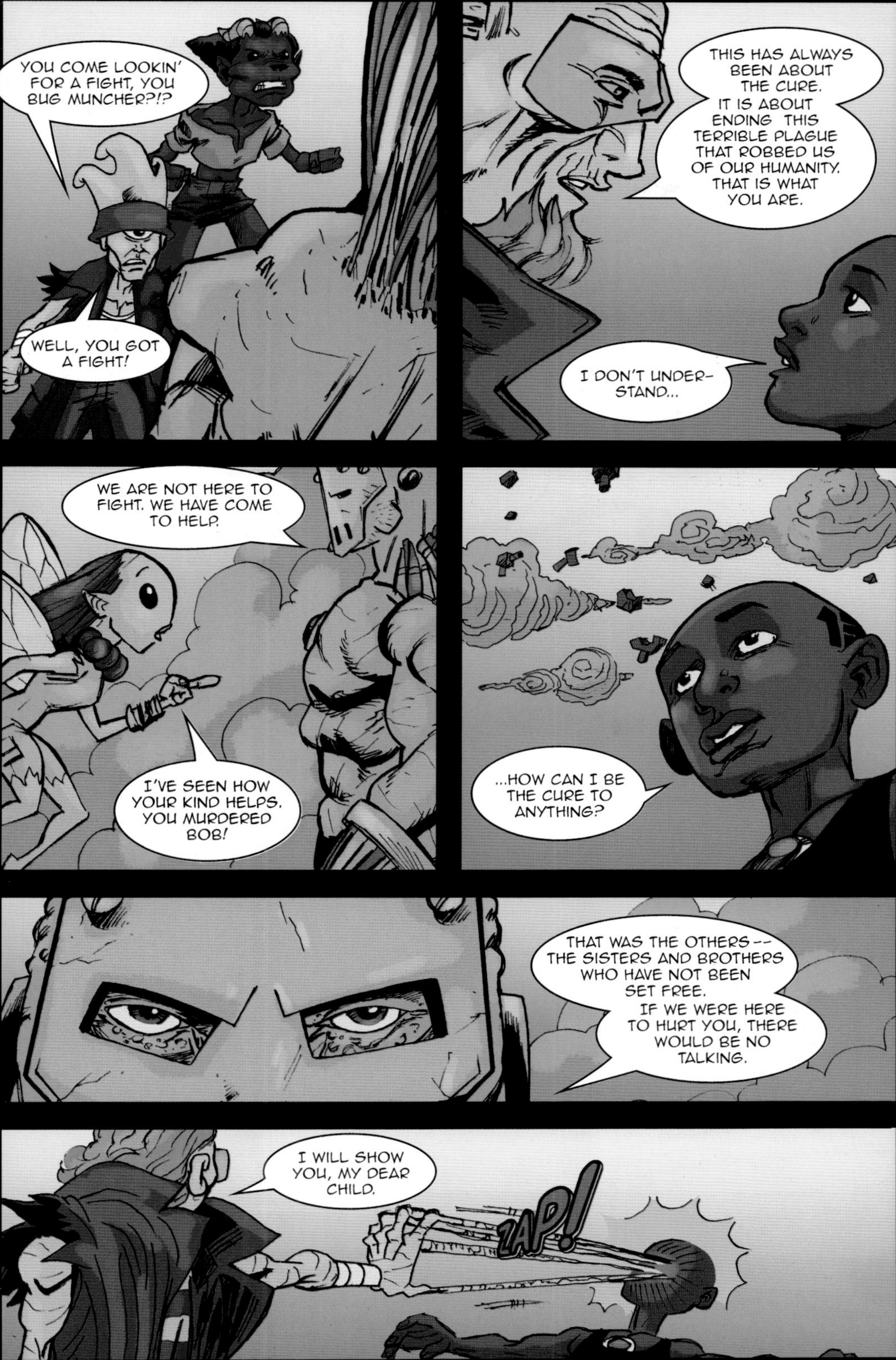
YOU COME LOOKIN' FOR A FIGHT, YOU BUG MUNCHER?!?
WELL, YOU GOT A FIGHT!
THIS HAS ALWAYS BEEN ABOUT THE CURE. IT IS ABOUT ENDING THIS TERRIBLE PLAGUE THAT ROBBED US OF OUR HUMANITY. THAT IS WHAT YOU ARE.
I DON'T UNDER-STAND...
WE ARE NOT HERE TO FIGHT. WE HAVE COME TO HELP.
I'VE SEEN HOW YOUR KIND HELPS. YOU MURDERED BOB!
...HOW CAN I BE THE CURE TO ANYTHING?
THAT WAS THE OTHERS -- THE SISTERS AND BROTHERS WHO HAVE NOT BEEN SET FREE. IF WE WERE HERE TO HURT YOU, THERE WOULD BE NO TALKING.
I WILL SHOW YOU, MY DEAR CHILD.
ZAP!

NO! YOU HAVE TO LISTEN TO HIM! WE'RE IN DANGER!

STEP ASIDE! NOW!

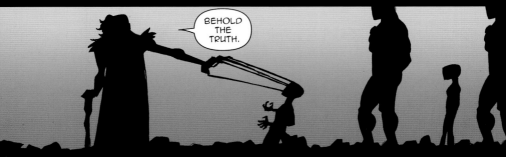

BEHOLD THE TRUTH.

PLEASE BELIEVE ME. WE ARE HERE TO STOP WHAT IS ABOUT TO HAPPEN.

WE MUST GET TO BROTHER THIRTEEN BEFORE THE OTHERS.

THIRTEEN IS GONE. HE MUST HAVE SNUCK OFF.

THEN WE MAY BE TOO LATE.

"IN ALL THE WORLD THERE WAS NO ONE QUITE LIKE YOU.

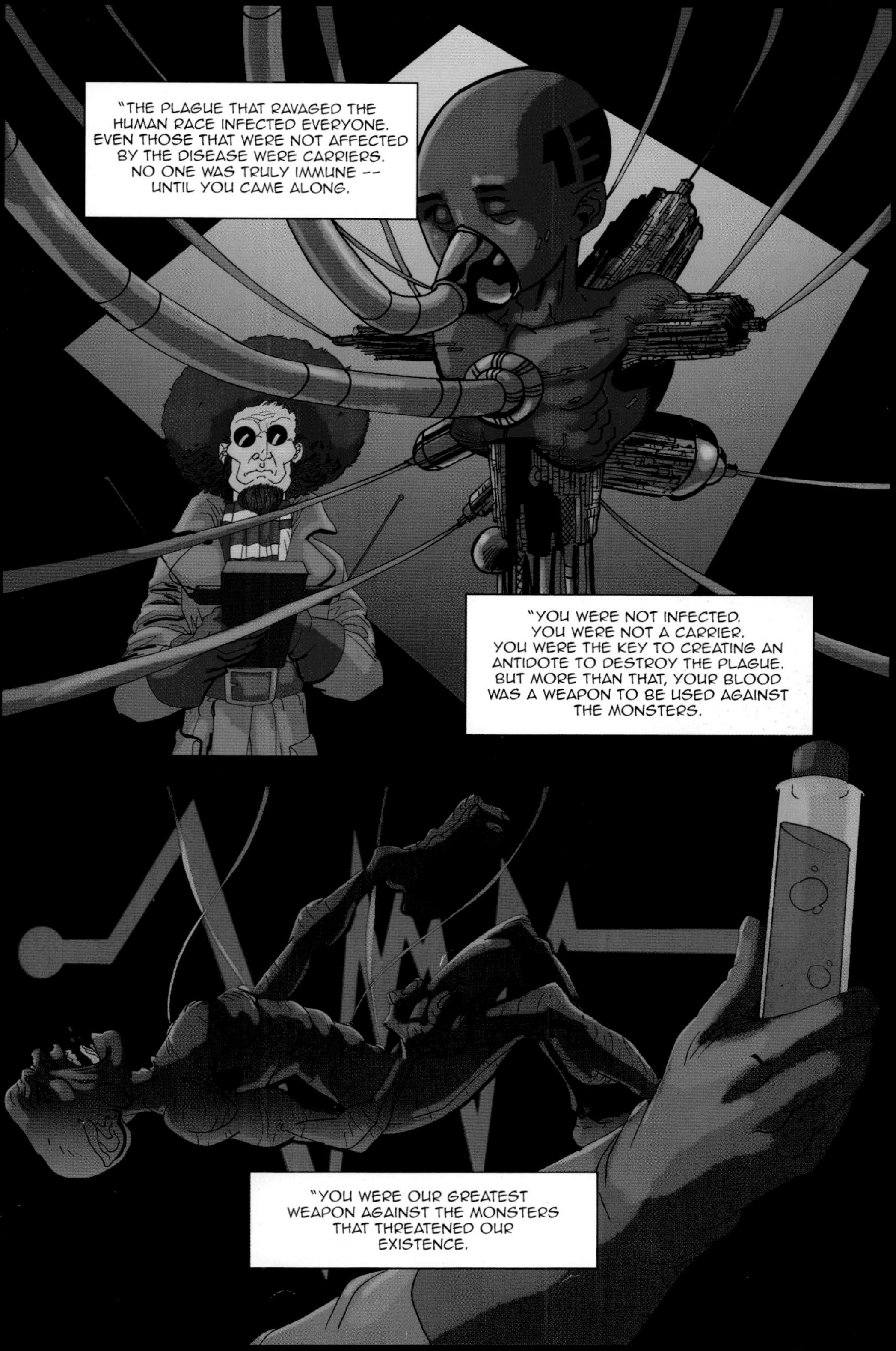
"THE PLAGUE THAT RAVAGED THE HUMAN RACE INFECTED EVERYONE. EVEN THOSE THAT WERE NOT AFFECTED BY THE DISEASE WERE CARRIERS. NO ONE WAS TRULY IMMUNE -- UNTIL YOU CAME ALONG.
"YOU WERE NOT INFECTED. YOU WERE NOT A CARRIER. YOU WERE THE KEY TO CREATING AN ANTIDOTE TO DESTROY THE PLAGUE. BUT MORE THAN THAT, YOUR BLOOD WAS A WEAPON TO BE USED AGAINST THE MONSTERS.
"YOU WERE OUR GREATEST WEAPON AGAINST THE MONSTERS THAT THREATENED OUR EXISTENCE.

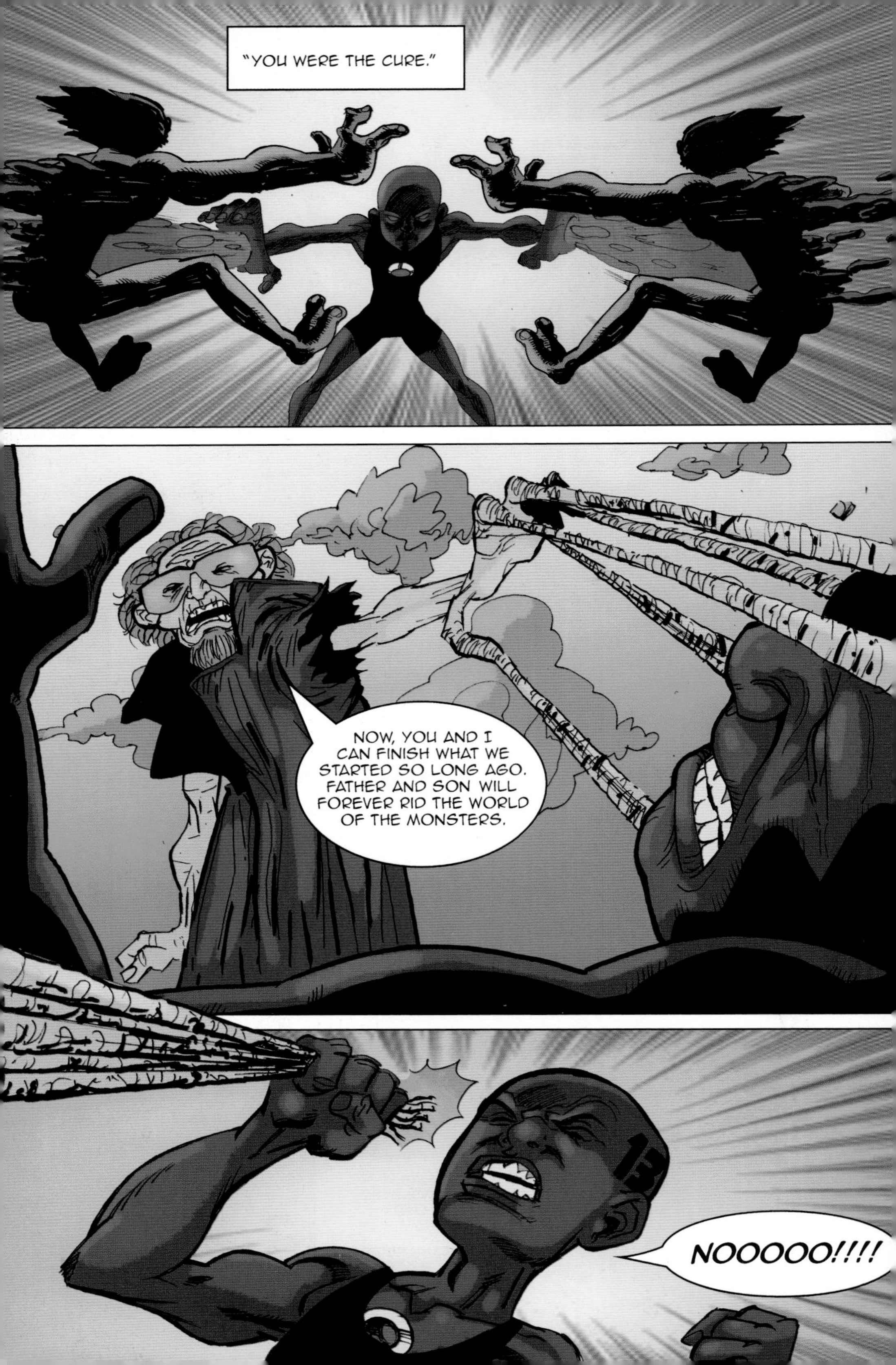
"YOU WERE THE CURE."
NOW, YOU AND I CAN FINISH WHAT WE STARTED SO LONG AGO. FATHER AND SON WILL FOREVER RID THE WORLD OF THE MONSTERS.
13
NOOOOO!!!!

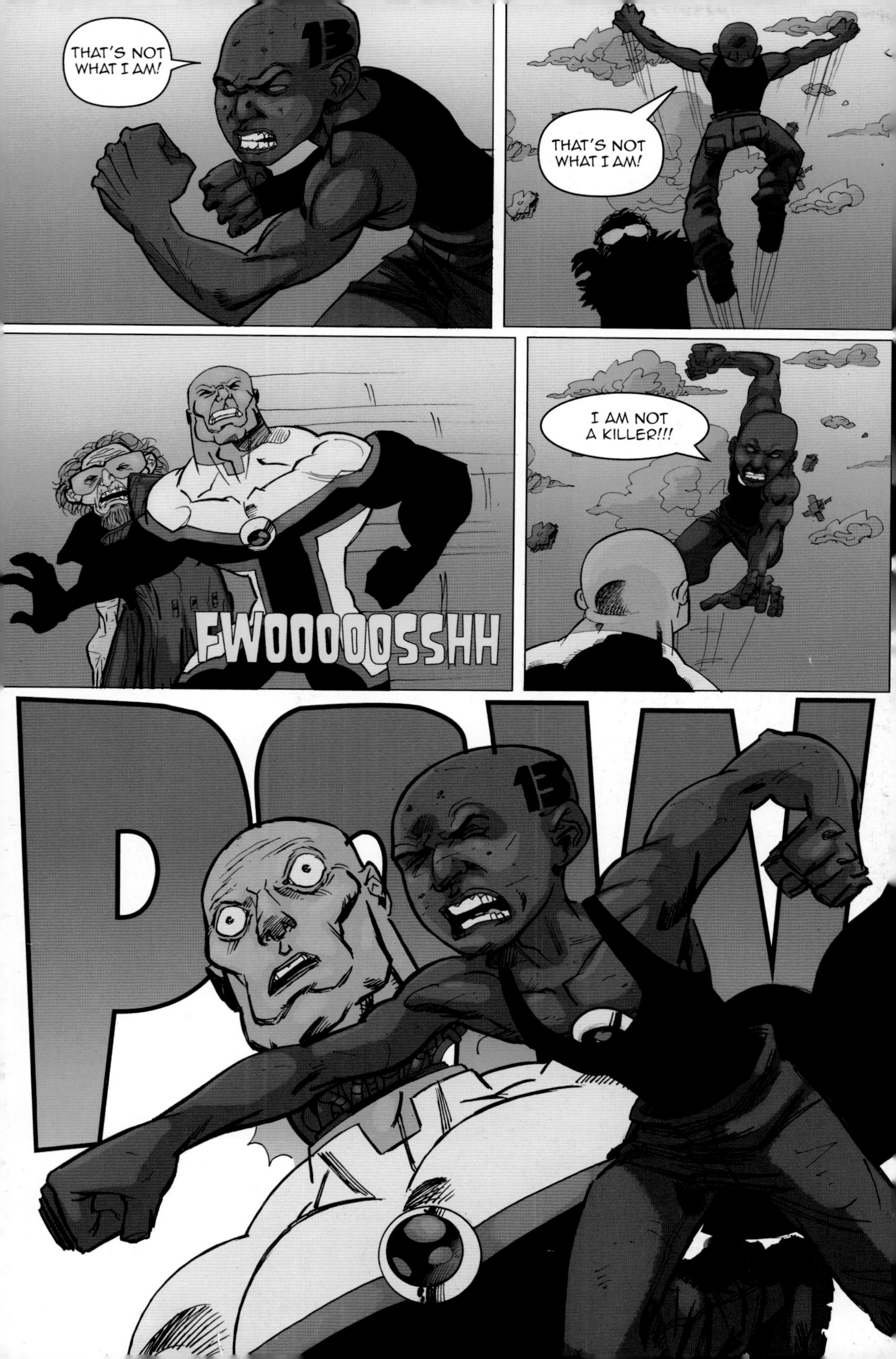
THAT'S NOT WHAT I AM!
THAT'S NOT WHAT I AM!
FWOOOOOSSHH
I AM NOT A KILLER!!!

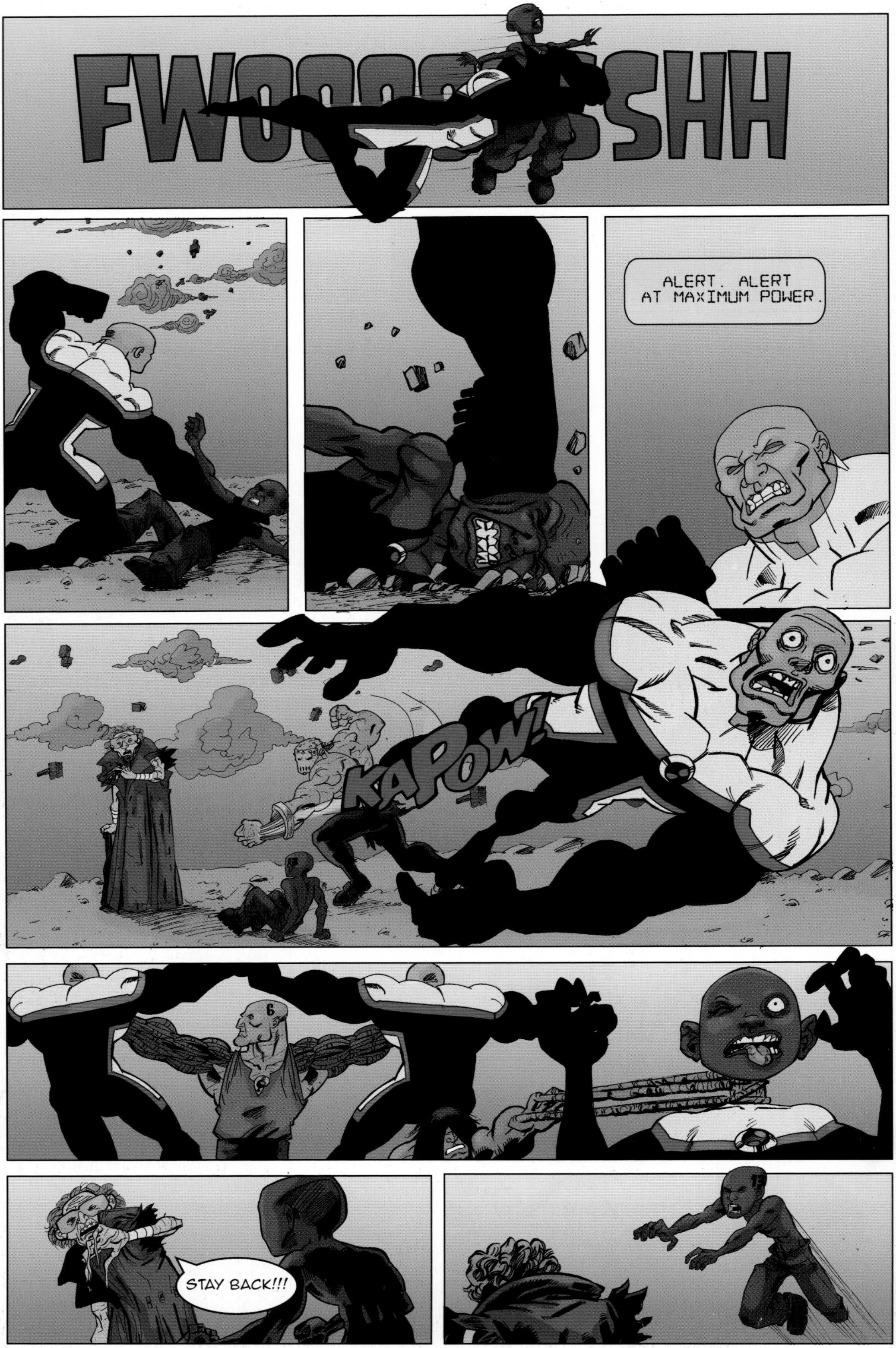
FWOOOOSSHH
ALERT. ALERT
AT MAXIMUM POWER.
KAPOW!
STAY BACK!!!

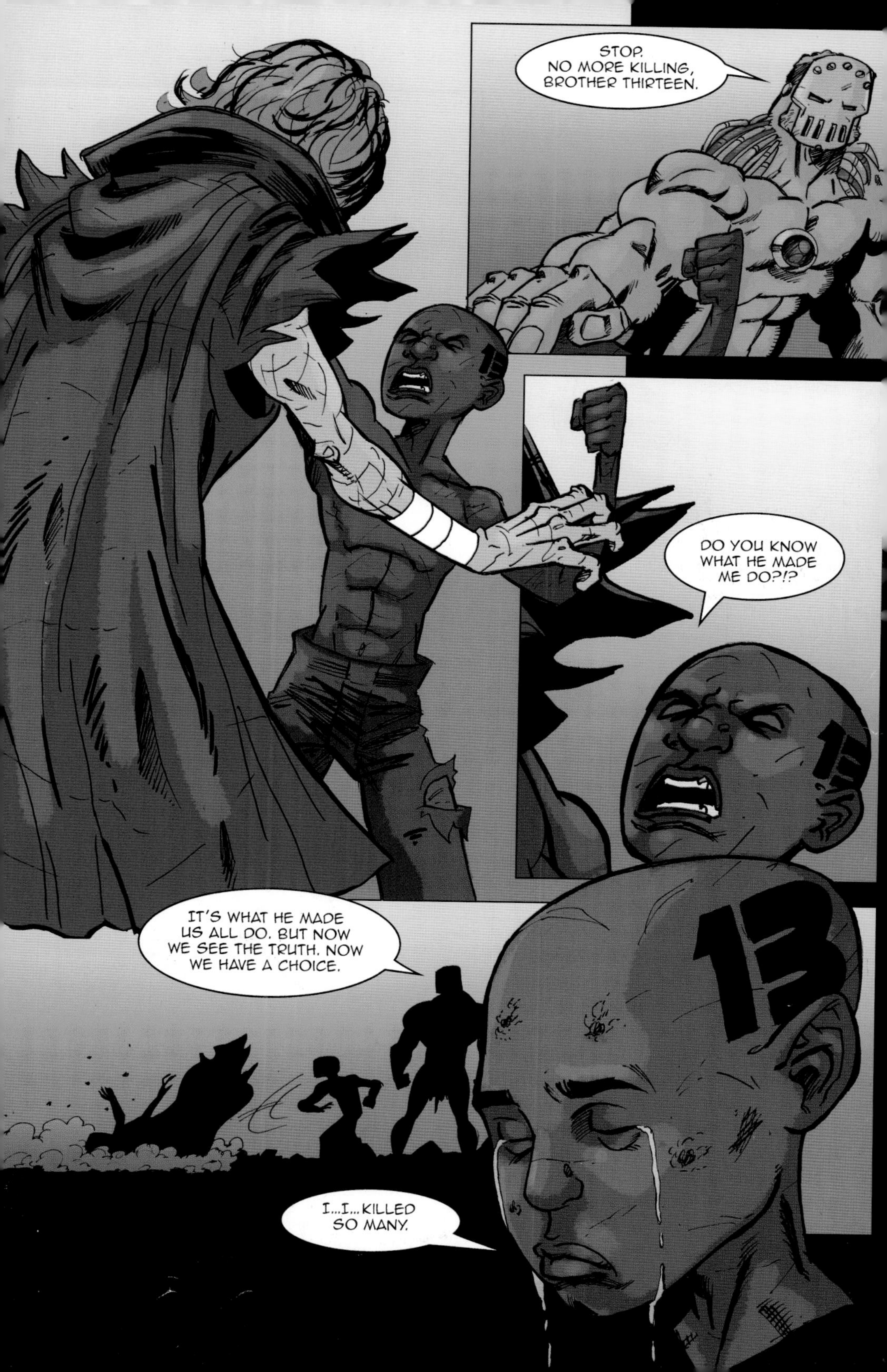
STOP. NO MORE KILLING, BROTHER THIRTEEN.
DO YOU KNOW WHAT HE MADE ME DO?!?
IT'S WHAT HE MADE US ALL DO. BUT NOW WE SEE THE TRUTH. NOW WE HAVE A CHOICE.
I...I...KILLED SO MANY.

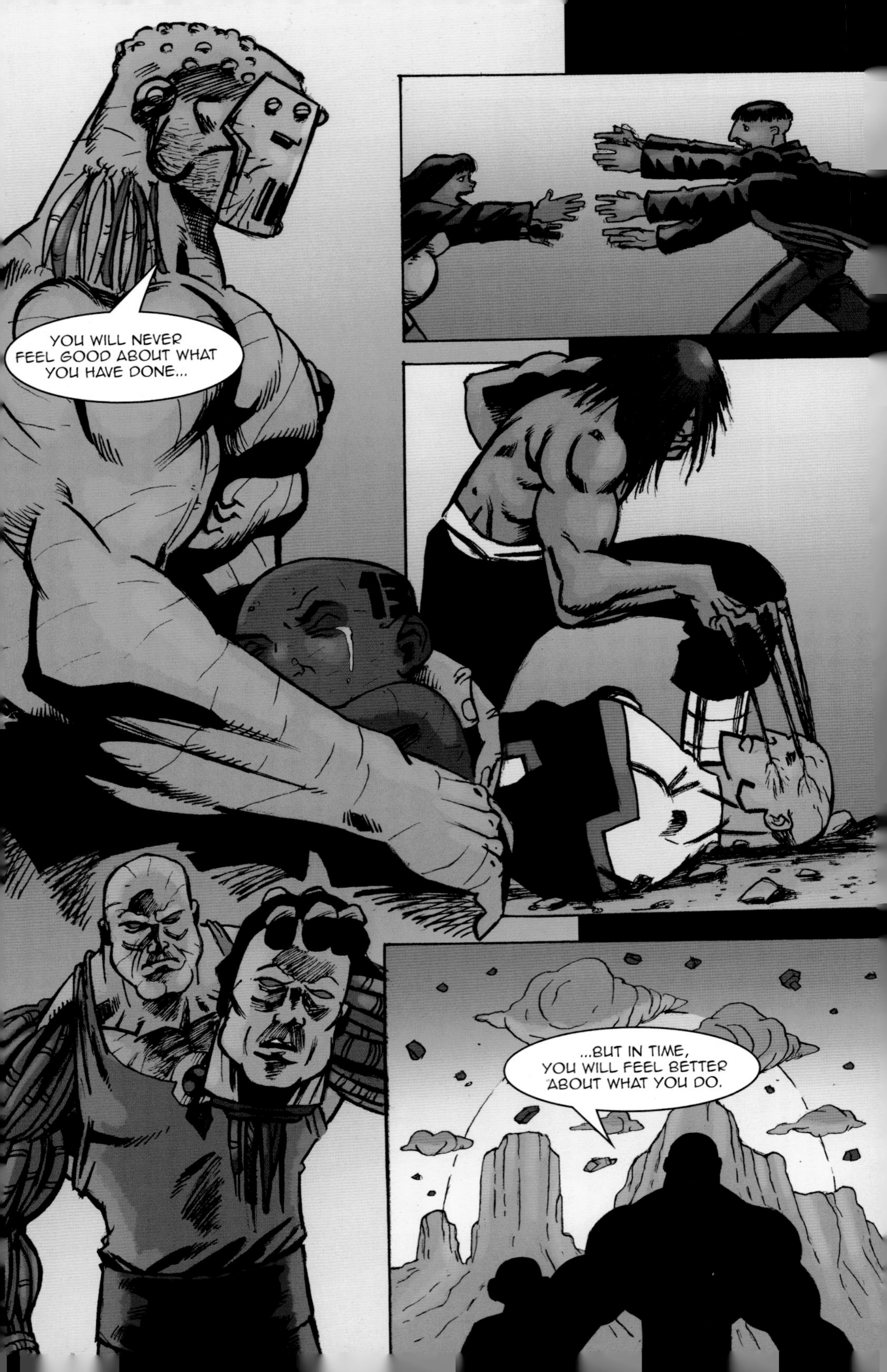
YOU WILL NEVER FEEL GOOD ABOUT WHAT YOU HAVE DONE...
...BUT IN TIME, YOU WILL FEEL BETTER ABOUT WHAT YOU DO.

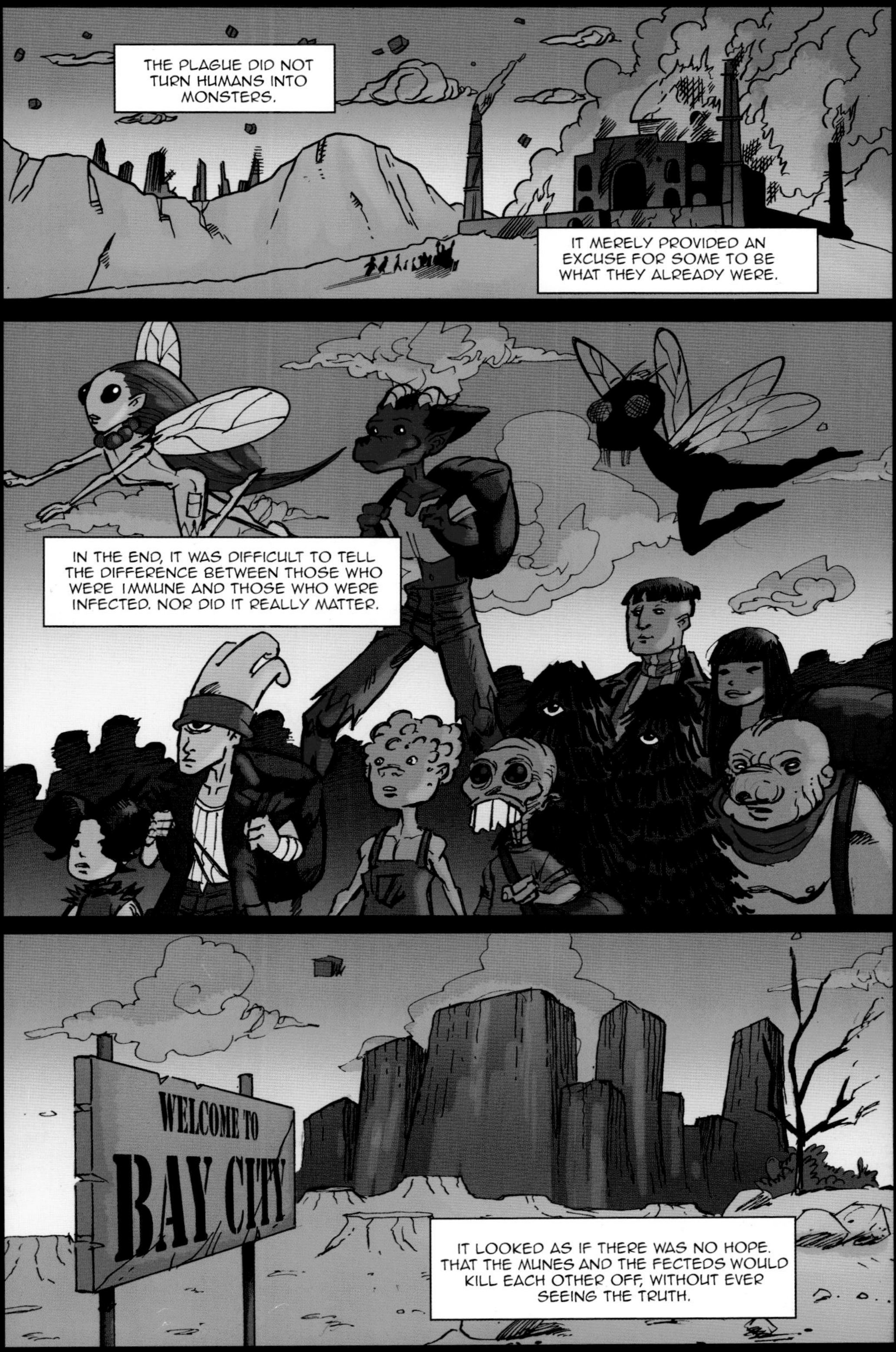
THE PLAGUE DID NOT TURN HUMANS INTO MONSTERS.
IT MERELY PROVIDED AN EXCUSE FOR SOME TO BE WHAT THEY ALREADY WERE.
IN THE END, IT WAS DIFFICULT TO TELL THE DIFFERENCE BETWEEN THOSE WHO WERE IMMUNE AND THOSE WHO WERE INFECTED. NOR DID IT REALLY MATTER.
WELCOME TO
BAY CITY
IT LOOKED AS IF THERE WAS NO HOPE. THAT THE MUNES AND THE FECTEDS WOULD KILL EACH OTHER OFF, WITHOUT EVER SEEING THE TRUTH.

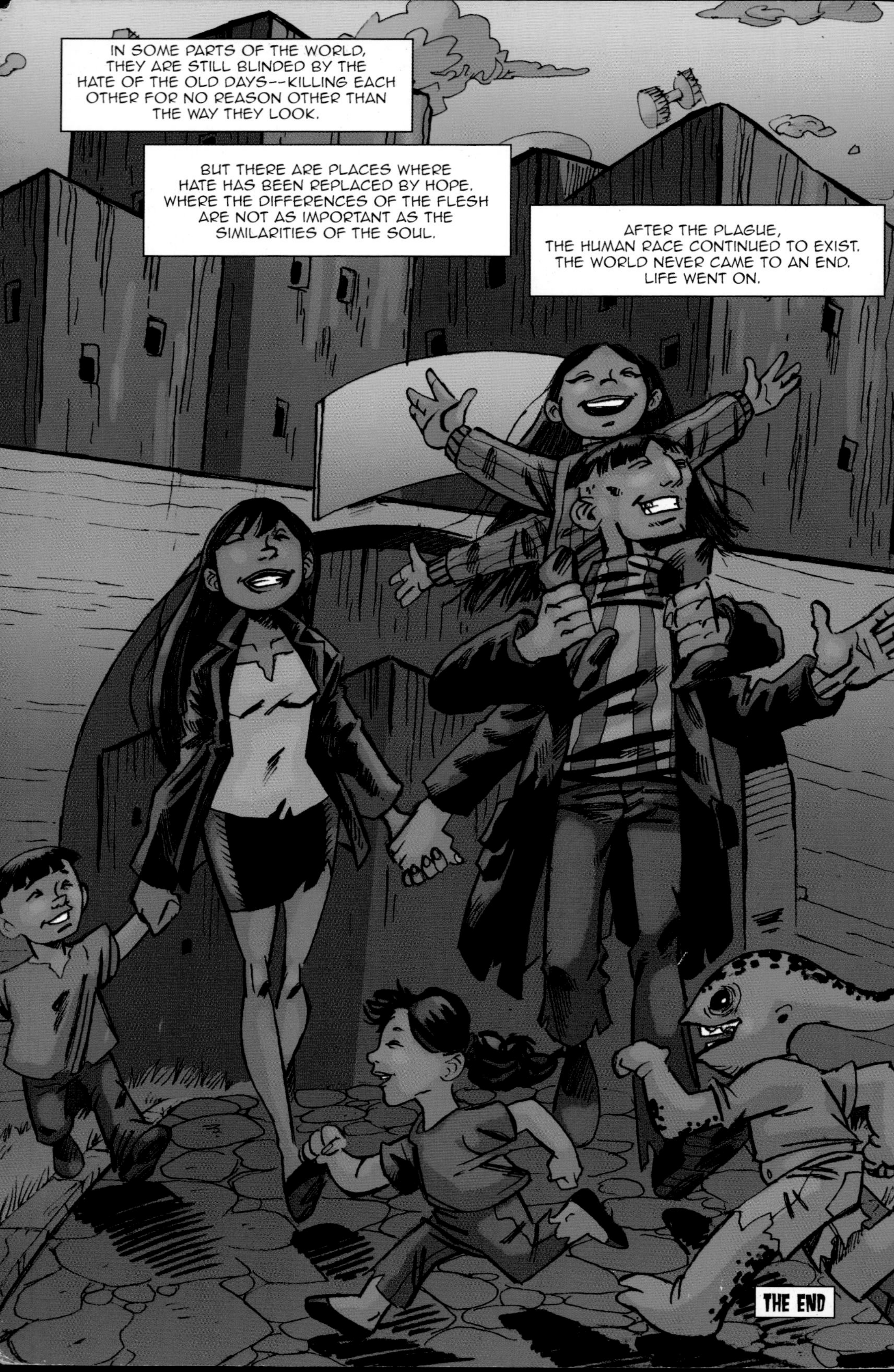
IN SOME PARTS OF THE WORLD, THEY ARE STILL BLINDED BY THE HATE OF THE OLD DAYS--KILLING EACH OTHER FOR NO REASON OTHER THAN THE WAY THEY LOOK.
BUT THERE ARE PLACES WHERE HATE HAS BEEN REPLACED BY HOPE. WHERE THE DIFFERENCES OF THE FLESH ARE NOT AS IMPORTANT AS THE SIMILARITIES OF THE SOUL.
AFTER THE PLAGUE, THE HUMAN RACE CONTINUED TO EXIST. THE WORLD NEVER CAME TO AN END. LIFE WENT ON.
THE END

AFTERWORD

Many years ago, I was pitching an idea for a comic series to a friend of mine, who happened to be an editor at the time for Dark Horse Comics. He nodded his head as I detailed the plot, and when I was done, he said, "Sounds interesting, but what is it about?" Confused, I looked at him and said, "I just told you what it's about." And that's when he told me something that has stuck with me for years. He said, "No, you told me what happens. That's the plot. You didn't tell me what it's about. That's the story."

When Robert Love first approached me about cowriting *Number 13*, I jumped on the opportunity. Robert had some great character designs, some interesting plot elements, and he makes great choices as a visual storyteller. For me, the only real problem I saw with *Number 13* was that I never knew what the story was about. I know, that sounds strange for the cowriter of a comic to say. But it is totally true—I had no idea what the story was about. I knew what was going to happen in the plot, because Robert and I had brainstormed for more than a year, bouncing ideas back and forth and coming up with an outline of events. That's the plot. But the story was never fully there.

I'm going to be honest, the first *Number 13* adventure that was serialized in *Dark Horse Presents*—and then collected as issue #0—was pretty much all plot and very little story. At the time, neither Robert nor I knew if Dark Horse would commit to an actual miniseries. When Dark Horse did commit, however, I freaked out a bit. We were going to have to build a miniseries around a forty-page adventure, and I still had no idea what the story was about.

Robert may remember things differently, and if my constant harping on him by saying, "No, that's what happens, but what's it about?" ever got on his nerves, he never let it show. Instead, he would just say, "You're more of a writer than I am. Figure it out."

As it turns out, I didn't take long to figure out what *Number 13* was really about. Robert started sending me character designs for the cast of the miniseries, and each one was freakier than the last. Seriously, some of his designs were bordering on hideous. But then it struck me—what if all these monstrous-looking characters were really just regular people? What if the weird-looking kids we meet in the beginning of the story were just that—kids who look weird, but are kids nonetheless? Suddenly, I knew what our postapocalyptic, dystopian tale of a killer android with amnesia was really all about—I finally had a story. It's a story Robert and I hope you enjoy.

Sketches by Robert Love

—David Walker
Portland, Oregon, March 2013

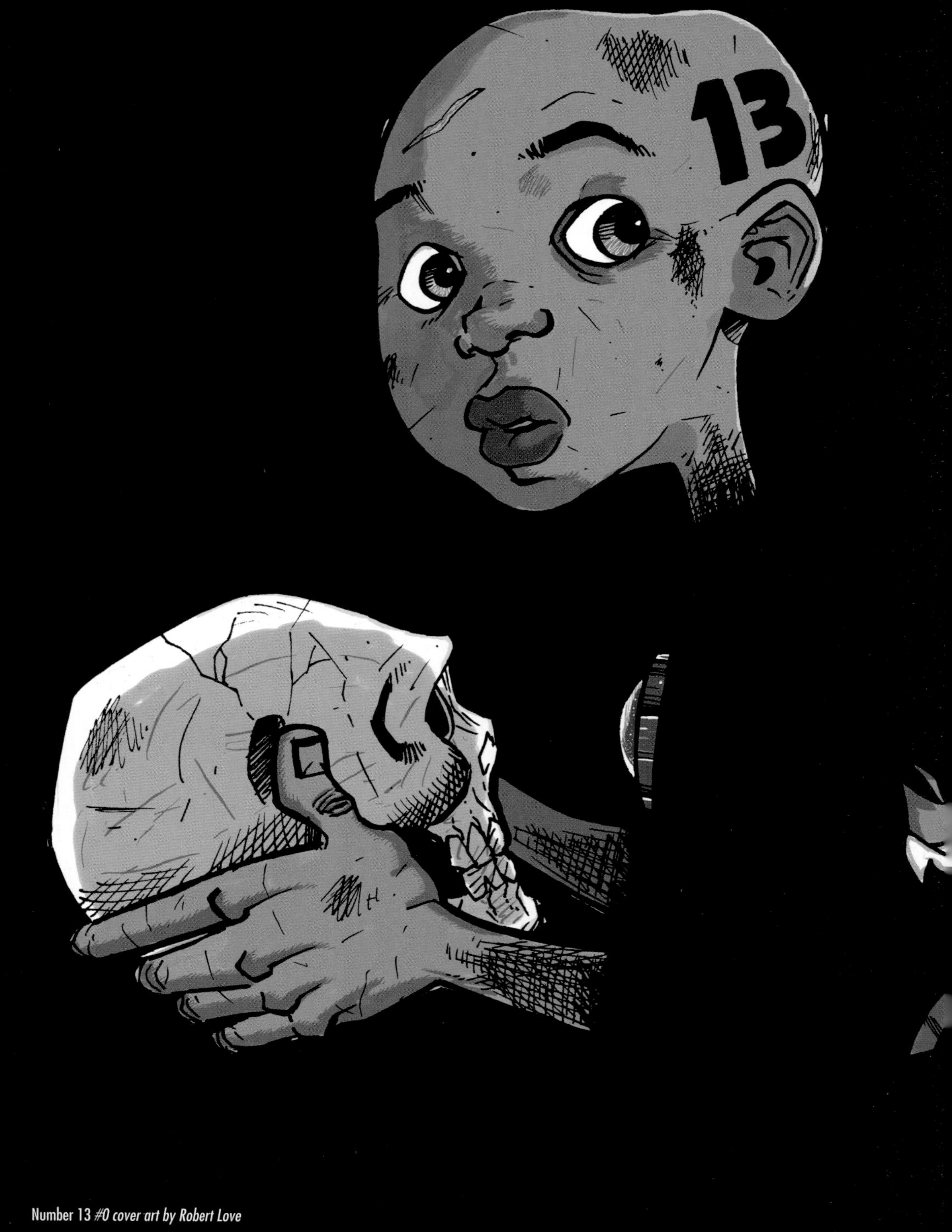
13

Number 13 *#0 cover art by Robert Love*

Dark Horse Presents *#6 variant cover art by Robert Love*

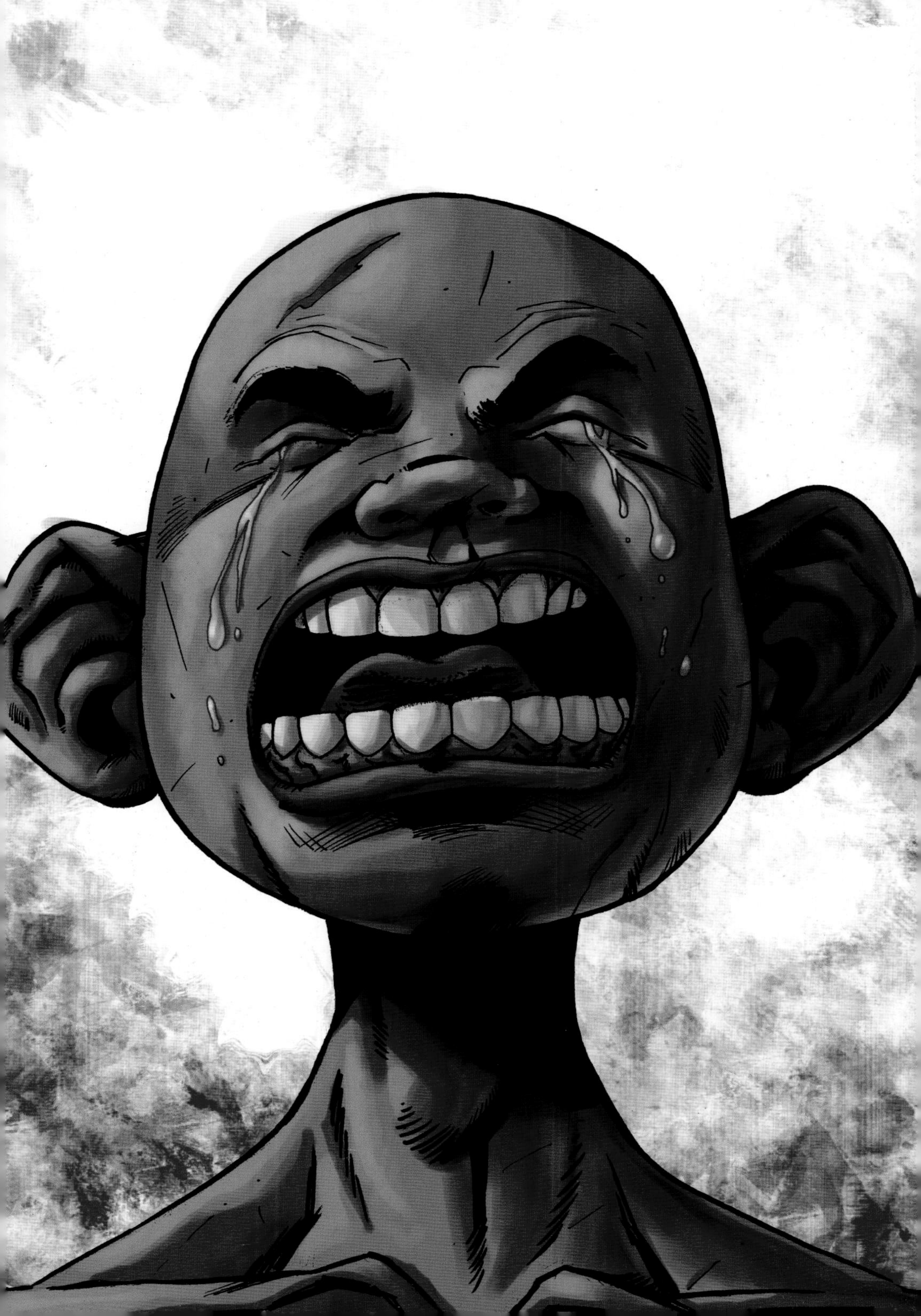

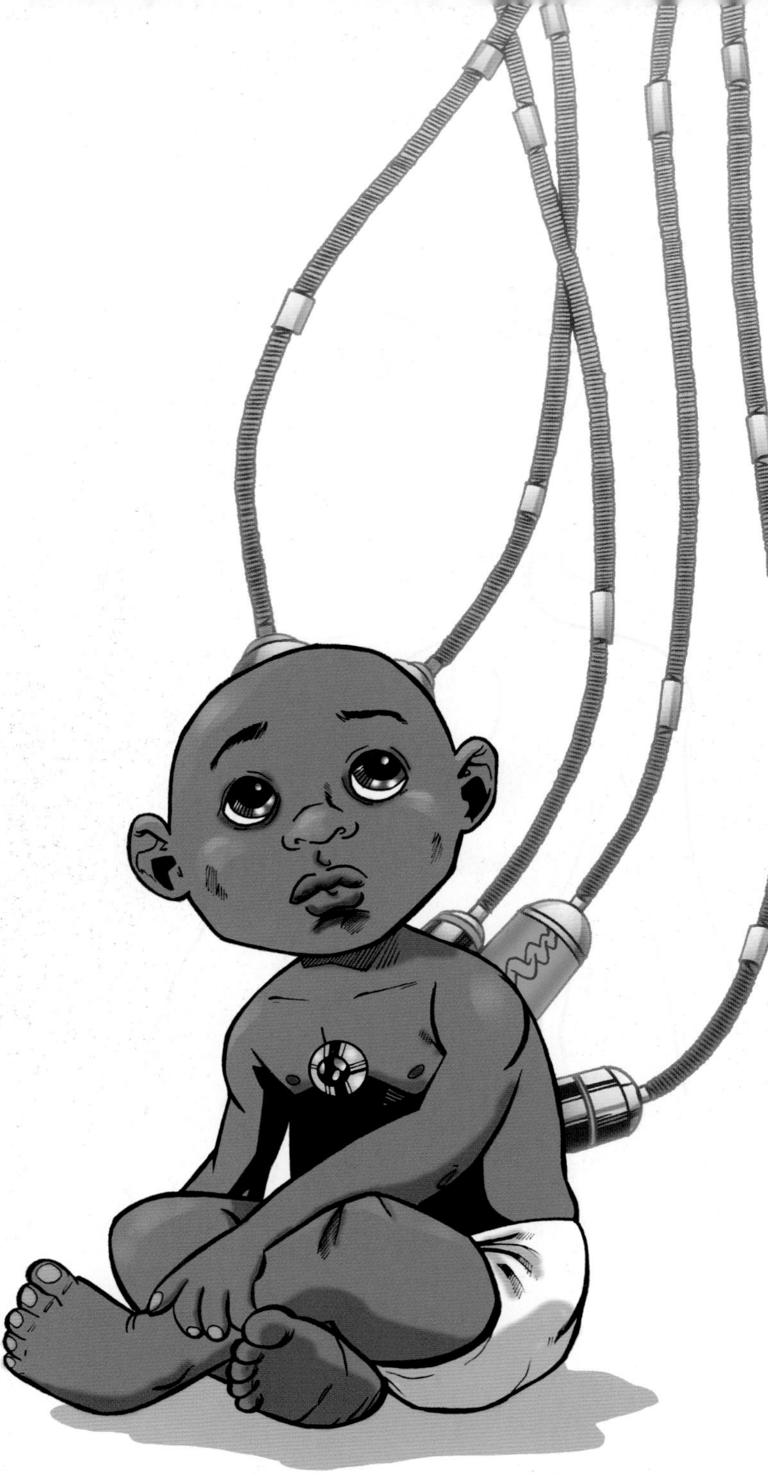

Number 13 *#1 cover art by Robert Love, with colors by Christian Colbert*

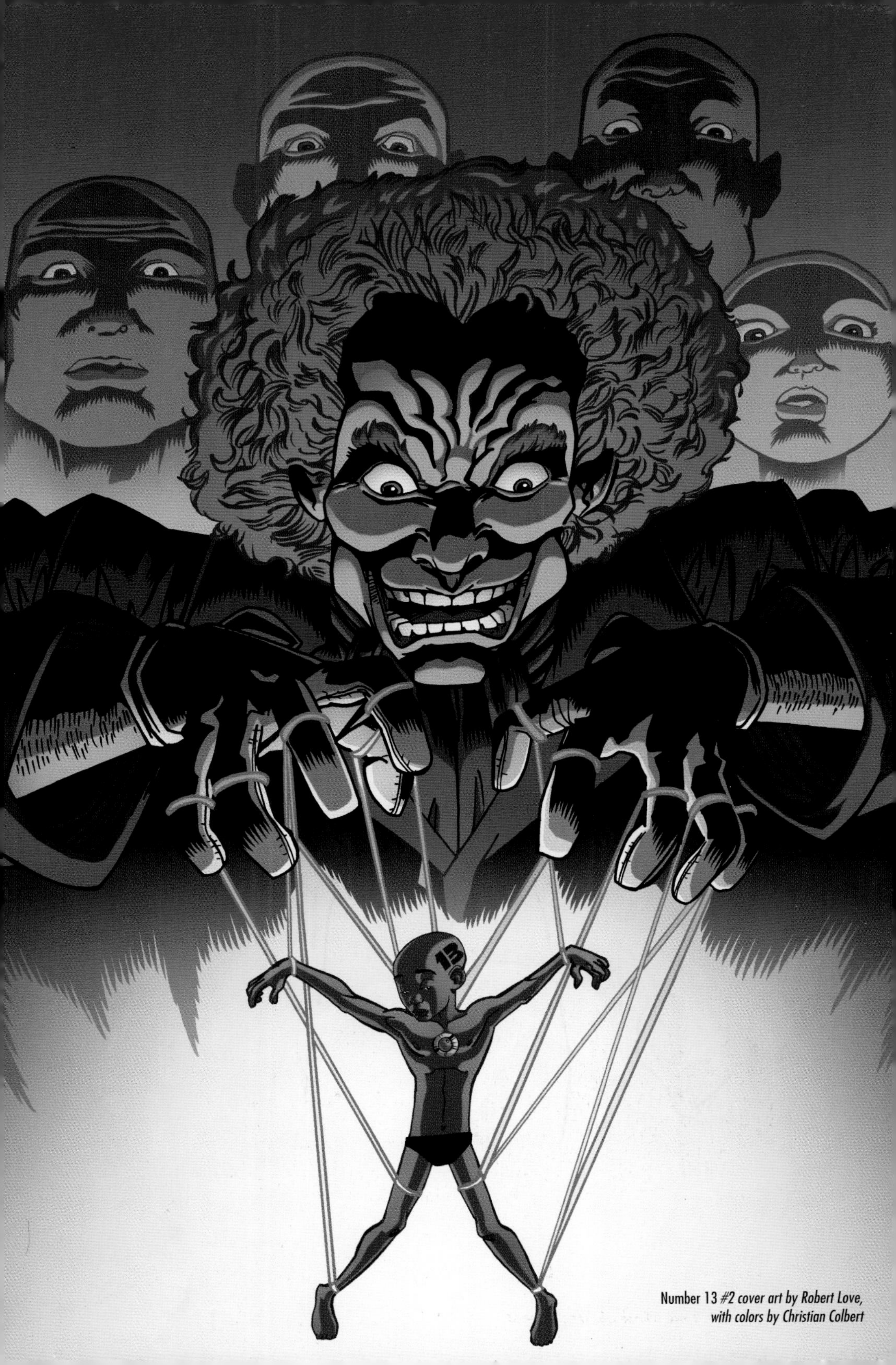

Number 13 *#2 cover art by Robert Love,*
with colors by Christian Colbert

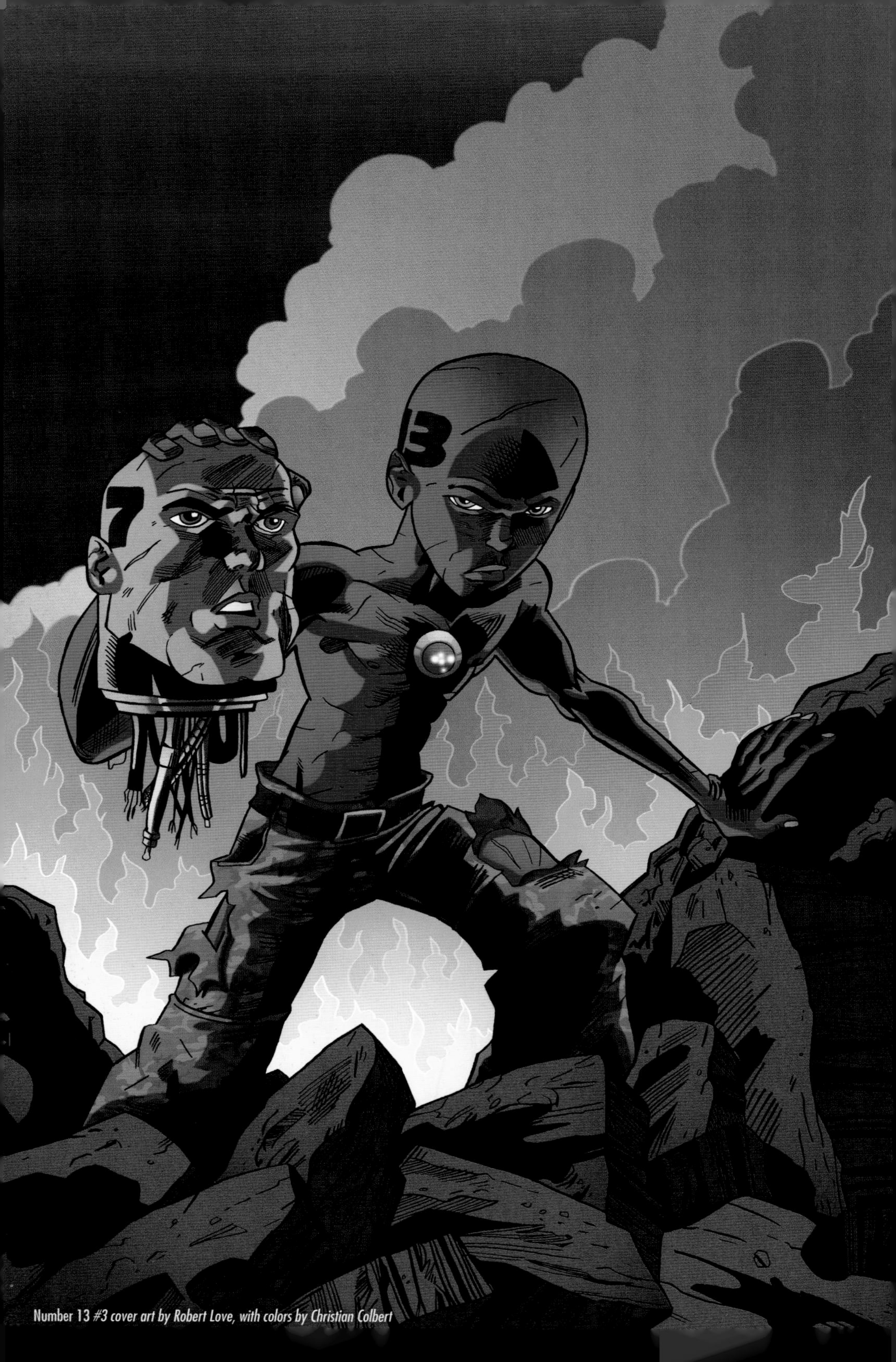
7
13

Number 13 *#3 cover art by Robert Love, with colors by Christian Colbert*

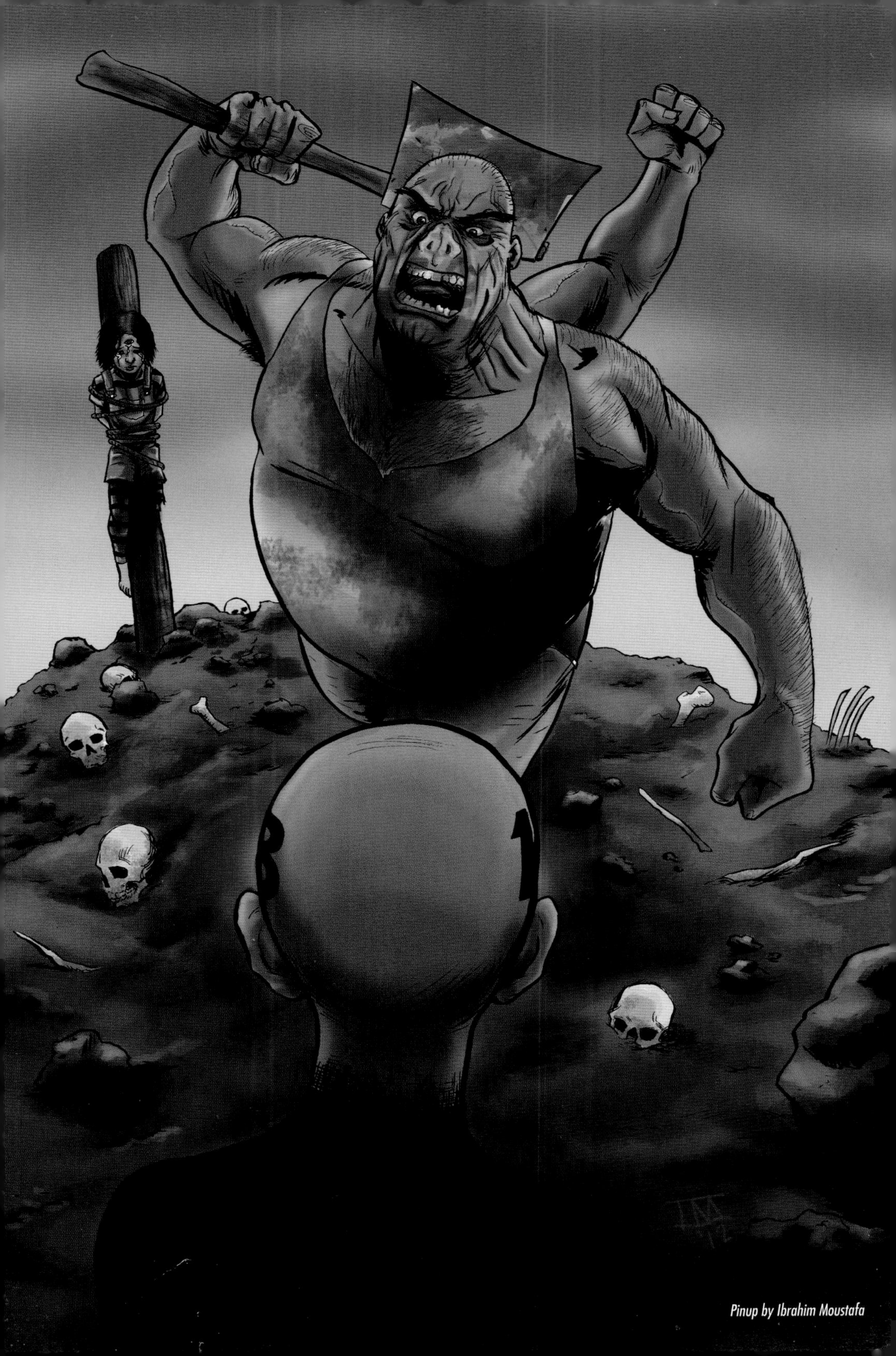

Pinup by Ibrahim Moustafa

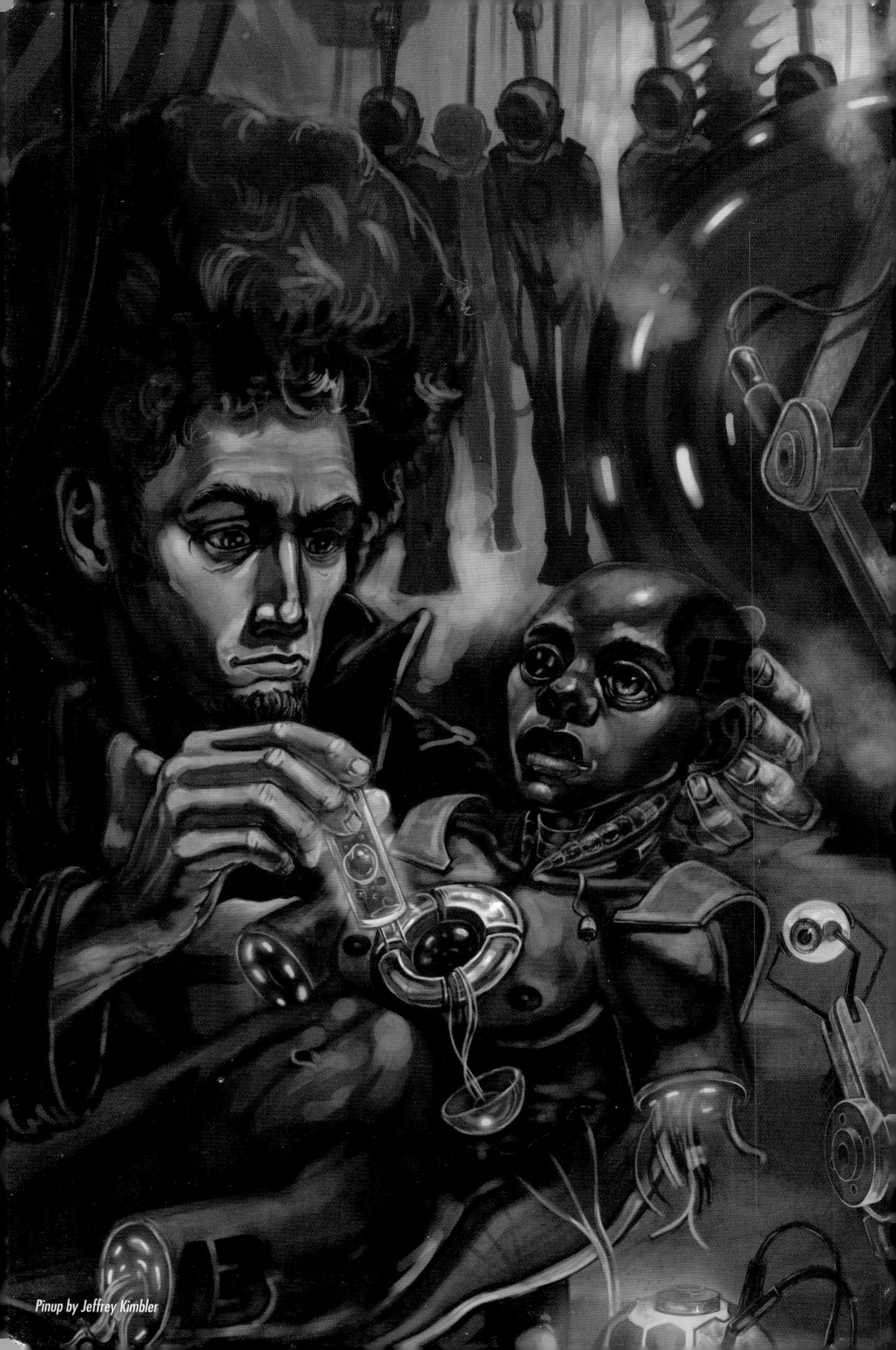

Pinup by Jeffrey Kimbler

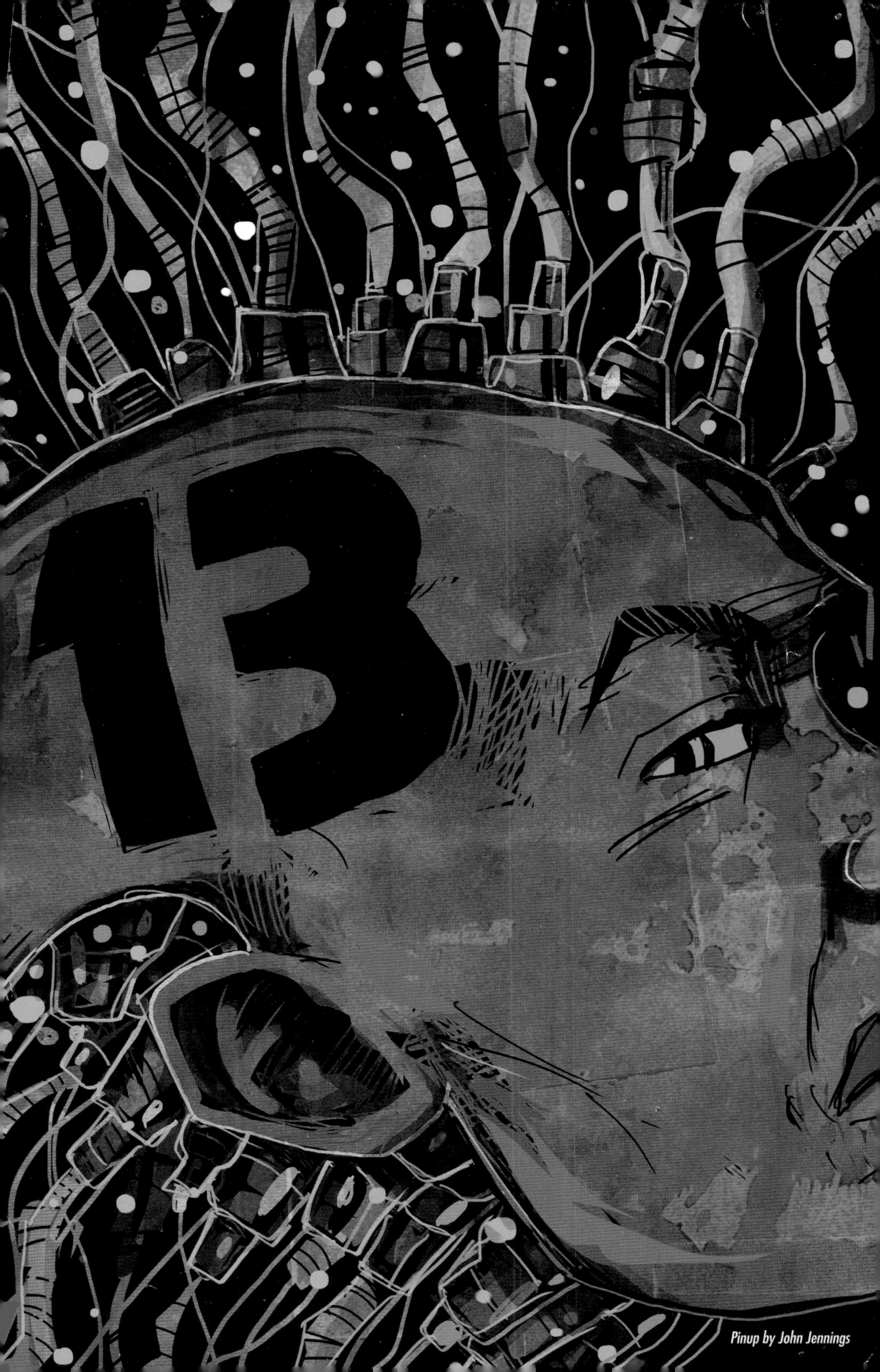
13

Pinup by John Jennings

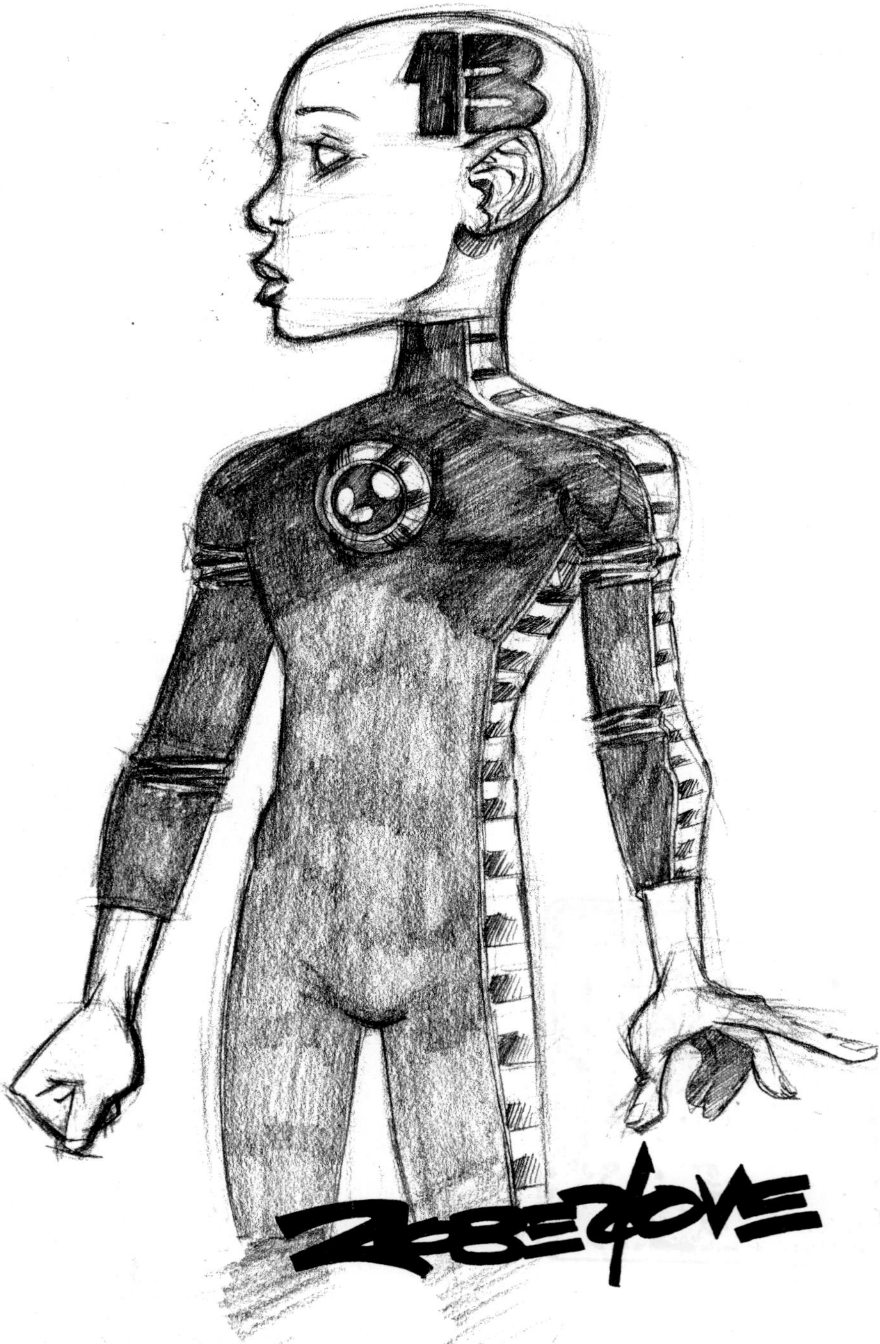